Discipleship by Grace
walking in the transforming power of the gospel

by Derek Joseph Levendusky

To the One who sits on the throne,
and to the Lamb.

Special thanks to my wife, Heidi Jo, and my children, for your patience and love as I worked on this book for what seemed like endless hours and days.

Special thanks to Sharon Ryan and Mary Pratt for your labor of love in helping to edit this book and make it better.

Special thanks to James, Preston, Lois, and Dara for handling the lion's share of office work while I finished the book.

Discipleship by Grace, by Derek Joseph Levendusky

© *2009 Derek Joseph Levendusky*

Distributed by Isaiah Six Ministries, Inc.
P.O. Box 10A
Lima, NY 14485
www.isaiahsix.com

Published and further distribution by 5 Stone Publishing,
493 Republic Street
Potter, Kansas 66002
Email: Randy2905@gmail.com

5 Stone Publishing is a division of The International Localization Network
© 2009 All Rights Reserved

ISBN 978-1-935018-17-9

Scripture quotations marked (NASB) are taken from the Holy Bible, New
American Standard Bible, © 1971 The Lockman Foundation. UBP. ARR.

Scripture quotations marked (NIV) are taken from the
Holy Bible, New International Version®, NIV®.
Copyright © 1973, 1978, 1984 by Biblica, Inc.™
Used by permission of Zondervan. All rights reserved worldwide.

Scripture quotations marked (KJV) are taken from the Holy Bible, King James
Version, public domain.

Scripture quotations marked (NKJV) are taken from the Holy Bible, New King
James Version. Copyright © 1982 by Thomas Nelson,
Inc. Used by permission. All rights reserved.

Cover photography by Morris Image. Cover design by Ryan Morris.

Table of Contents

8

Foreword

by Michael P. Cavanaugh

"So you see, our love for Him comes as a result of His loving us first."
(1 John 4:19 TLB)

No biblical truth has affected me more then the simple reality that our love for God originates in our realizing that He loved us first. It is impossible for us to love God with out first receiving His love. If I try to love God with out first accepting the fact that He loves me completely just as I am and will never love me more then he does at this very moment, I become like a loveless child trying to win the favor of preoccupied parents through good behavior. Is there anything sadder then a child that has no confidence that it is loved? A child who sees its whole existence as an effort to win approval, to find a place of complete acceptance, a child who lives with the constant anxiety that there is no one in this whole world who loves them completely and with out reservation no matter how they compare to others.

I remember as a seven-year-old sitting in my second grade class as the teacher promised a gold star to the child who sat up the straightest. I tried to be the quietest and the straightest in my class as the teacher walked up and down the aisles of the classroom judging us. The teacher did this many times in class but I never received the star. I was never approved, I never won the competition, and my sincerest efforts were not enough.

Many Christians feel exactly like this with God. They are trying to win His approval, to be good enough, to bring a smile to His face through their best efforts at worship, evangelism or giving but some how they are never really sure the have done enough. They never feel like they have received the gold star, or the smile of His approval and as a result they live their life in a perpetual state of anxiety because even if they are acceptable to Him today what if they slip up tomorrow? There is no confidence, no peace, no assurance that they are loved completely and forever. The best that they can ever hope for is a temporary performance based peace like the actor who receives a standing ovation at the end of a performance only to realize that the next show is coming and no one cares how good he acted yesterday. They only value him for what he does today.

This kind of life is not the Good News that Christ died to bring us. The Good News is that God loves you completely and that at this very moment His interest in you is passionate and personal. That even though He is aware of every weakness, frailty and even future failure in your life that He cherishes His relationship with you. That the greatest love of any parent for a child is only a pale shadow of the love God has for you. That the fire of the most intense romance ever found on earth is only a dying spark next to the passion God has for you. That the kindness of the most merciful king on the planet fades before the depth of compassion God has for you. That the deepest sense of camaraderie that two soldiers ever shared on a battlefield doesn't even compare to God's loyalty to you. You are free to love God because He has first loved you.

"And I pray that Christ will be more and more at home in your hearts, living within you as you trust in him. May your roots go down deep into the soil of God's marvelous love; and may you be able to feel and understand, as all God's children should, how long, how wide, how deep, and how high his love really is; and to experience this love for yourselves, though it is so great that you will never see the end of it or fully know or understand it. And so at last you will be filled up with God himself" (Eph 3:17-19 TLB).

In *Discipleship by Grace*, Derek J. Levendusky will freshly introduce you to this incredible love of God and help you to build a Christian life on the only foundation that produces genuine internal change. Grace!

Introduction

"And of his fullness have all we received, and grace for grace."
(John 1:16, KJV)

A few years ago I was praying for revival, and I sensed the Holy Spirit speak to me, "If you're going to see revival in your generation where the lost are coming to Christ, first you need to see a revival of laborers. You won't see many coming to Jesus until there are many preaching Jesus."

So my prayer changed. "Lord," I cried, "send out laborers into your harvest! Revive your Church!" Then the Holy Spirit spoke to me again. "If you're going to see a revival of laborers, first you need to see a revival of worshipers. If my children will love Me with all their hearts, they'll love the lost with all their hearts."

So my prayer changed again! "Lord," I pleaded, "raise up a generation of worshipers who will love You and love what You love!" Then the Holy Spirit changed my prayer one more time. "My son," He said, "if you're going to see a revival of worshipers, first you need to see a revival of people who understand grace."

"Why, Lord?" I asked.

"Because no one will love Me if they'll not see that I first loved them, nor will they understand the message of the gospel if they don't have a revelation of grace."

I've followed the river back to the source, and what I found there may the surprise you: the doctrines of grace. Since God revealed Himself to Moses as "The Lord, the Lord God, merciful and gracious" (Exodus, 34:6a), we see that understanding grace is priority in the heart of our Father.

This is why proclaiming God's grace has become the passion of my life. I am convinced that understanding grace is the doorway to changing the world and is the springhead of every good thing we have, are, and do in Christ.

The simple premise of this book is that we cannot become or make a Christlike disciple by simply introducing and enforcing Christian behavior. We must learn what to *believe* before we learn what to *do*. The *doing* will flow from the *believing*. The gospel does not say, "Try harder!" or "Behave and pray!" The gospel says, "Lazarus, come forth!" It teaches us that a man is dead (Ephesians 2:1) without Christ and must be resurrected, not that a man is bad and must reform himself to become good. Before we can work for God, God must work in us. For this to happen, we must first understand, believe, and then experience the transforming love and grace of God given at the cross. We must also understand who we are and what we have in Christ. Only then can we become true disciples, and only then can we make authentic followers of Jesus.

The true essence of living by faith is living according to what we believe and not what we feel. That's why the major focus of this book is about what we believe, and I've dedicated my efforts to exposing lies and teaching truth. Truth stands alone, unaffected by the whims of the soul or the best arguments of the day. My hope is to show that when we live according to truth and not our feelings, we begin to experience the great promise Jesus gave us: "You shall know the truth and the truth shall make you free" (John 8:32, NKJV).

We've all heard the phrase "salvation by grace" (Ephesians 2:8). This phrase speaks of our coming to Christ; that we offer nothing to God but filthy rags, and that He rescues us by His mercy and power. This book is an attempt to encourage the believer that after we are *saved* by grace, the rest of the Christian life is *discipleship* by grace—that we still offer nothing but trust, have no power to change our nature, and still must depend upon God throughout the process of our sanctification. I want the reader to see how grace permeates every facet of Christian life, how it affects our whole journey, from salvation to sanctification, from evangelism to discipleship. I also want to encourage anyone involved in disciple-making in what I believe are the fruit-bearing teachings and methods of the Bible.

By the curious title of *Discipleship by Grace*, I also mean to imply that grace is an instructor, as we will clearly see (Titus 2:11), and that those who sit at the feet of God's grace sit at the feet of an amazing teacher that will lead us into the vista of God's love, and the joy of God's will.

Author C.J. Mahaney wrote, "Very small errors in a person's understanding of the gospel seemed to result in very big problems in that person's life." [1] It is crucial that the believer in Christ truly grasp grace, for we will ultimately stand or fall to the degree that we do.

In discussing grace with some friends in ministry, we realized that we have often thought of grace as a "sissy" word. We use it when someone needs to be hugged, whispering gently, "Just think of God's grace." To further this idea, I know of no men named "Grace." It's only used for a girl's name (one of my daughters is named Grace!). But now I see that grace is the most powerful force in the universe.

The ideas within did not come from a book, but were "taught to me from the Holy Spirit" (Galatians 1:12). The revelation of the gospel that I received came from the red-hot burning of the Refiner's Fire; from the painful wounds of the Pruner; from the frightening scourge of the Father's discipline. I was a lost soul indeed (even though I walked among the saints), but by God's grace, He used a fiery trial to bring me home, and I will never leave again. No man, devil, church, teacher, or denomination will ever again take my freedom in Christ from me.

These ideas are not new (God help me if they are), but have been believed and taught by God's servants since the days of Christ's ascension. Then why write this book? As a great preacher and my personal friend Michael Cavanaugh once told me, our duty is not to say something *new*, but to *say something true in a new way*. If you look closely at my words, you will find them to be in harmony with the likes of Martin Luther, Charles Spurgeon, Matthew Henry, and Andrew Murray, although I do not count myself among their ranks. I do quote authors like these often.

---

[1] C.J. Mahaney, *Christ Our Mediator*, (Sisters, Oregon: Multnomah Publishers, Inc.) © 2004 Sovereign Grace Ministries, p.40. This statement actually came from one of Mahaney's friends in ministry, who made the statement in a letter describing a situation he had encountered with a young woman in his church.

It is the duty of those who teach the Word in every generation to "make the Word flesh," so that the hearer can see it, believe, and be saved. It is our duty and privilege to bring fresh bread to beggars, so that the gospel is indeed preached to the poor, just as our Master taught us to do.

I use a lot of Scripture in my writing, as it is my aim to show the reader that what I teach is not merely advice, but truth. And as I've said, I quote many other authors, dead and living. I have discovered nothing new, and wish to show that all I am doing in this book is reminding the saints of the tried and true doctrines that have brought righteousness, peace, and joy to so many others throughout the generations. I also quote some of those who have mentored me. I am indebted to those God has used to disciple me and sharpen my faith, and I've learned much from sitting at their feet.

I do not consider myself a theologian or scholar. Those who know me know that I don't take myself that seriously. Some have asked if I count myself a prophet. I do not know what I am for "I do not judge myself."[2] But if I am a prophet, I pray that I be a loving prophet, for the world has seen enough angry ones. May the words in this book encourage and inspire, bother and provoke, enlighten and equip. And please remember with every page, that if God chooses to accomplish anything I just said, the author is well aware that dust did not make eternal things. God simply used dust.

The very fact that this book exists, and that God used me to write it, is because of grace. May God strengthen you to receive all that He has for you as you read it.

---

[2] 1 Corinthians 4:3

Section 1

DISCOVERING GRACE

CHAPTER 1
The Tale of Two Men

"[Martin] Luther was like a man climbing in the darkness of a winding staircase in the steeple of an ancient cathedral. In the blackness he reached out to steady himself, and his hand laid hold of a rope. He was startled to hear the clanging of a bell." [3] — Roland Bainton

Most people that have changed the world never set out to change it. The beginning of their journey is usually marked by a conflict of soul that drove them to find their own freedom. In finding it, they unwittingly became trailblazers for all those who would follow them. Like Luther, they reach out to steady themselves in the darkness and clang the bell, and the news goes far and wide.

For years I asked God to make me a useful vessel for Him, and when He finally began to answer my prayer, the crucible was red hot and the agents employed in the transformation unexpected. The change was far beyond the surface and was painfully thorough, as a master surgeon carefully taking away all that threatens life.

When I lived in northern New York, there was a small church congregation in the nearby town of Canton that decided to move its location. This is not abnormal, as churches often move into new buildings. The only unique part of this move was that *they were not going to change buildings*. They decided to take their church with them. They poured a new foundation about a mile down the road on a new piece of property, and literally picked up the old building, drove it down the road, and put it on the new foundation!

This is a picture of what happened in my life over the last ten years. I've experienced a grace conversion that literally shifted my whole life from one foundation of dead works and performance to

---

[3] Roland Bainton, *Here I Stand* (NAL, 1978).

a new foundation of grace and the finished work of Christ. I will never be the same. *I can never be the same.*

Grace conversions are not a new experience for followers of Jesus as we'll see in this book. "The Tale of Two Men" might be the title given to the story of anyone that has experienced a grace conversion, but let's start by taking a look at Paul the Apostle.

> *"Although I myself might have confidence even in the flesh. If anyone else has a mind to put confidence in the flesh, I far more: circumcised the eighth day, of the nation of Israel, of the tribe of Benjamin, a Hebrew of Hebrews; as to the Law, a Pharisee; as to zeal, a persecutor of the church; as to the righteousness which is in the Law, found blameless. But whatever things were gain to me, those things I have counted as loss for the sake of Christ.*

> *"More than that, I count all things to be loss in view of the surpassing value of knowing Christ Jesus my Lord, for whom I have suffered the loss of all things, and count them but rubbish so that I may gain Christ, and may be found in Him, not having a righteousness of my own derived from the Law, but that which is through faith in Christ, the righteousness which comes from God on the basis of faith, that I may know Him and the power of His resurrection and the fellowship of His sufferings, being conformed to His death." (Philippians 3:4-10, NASB)*

Paul was once a self-sufficient man, driven by his performance. He sought to attain righteousness through his works, as if God's holiness is something to be achieved through the works of the Law. But the man who once gloried in his own strength would soon be brought low by a merciful God who had a plan to make him something entirely different.

> *"As he was traveling, it happened that he was approaching Damascus, and suddenly a light from heaven flashed around him; and he fell to the ground and heard a voice saying to him, 'Saul, Saul, why are you persecuting Me?' And he said, 'Who are You, Lord?' And He said, 'I am Jesus whom you are persecuting.'" (Acts 9:3-5, NASB)*

18

Paul, reaping a murderous heart, the only possible outcome for a man who trusts in his flesh, was en route to do more killing. He was sure he was doing God's service. That was when God murdered Paul's self-righteous heart. Soon Paul would go away to Arabia for several years. Could that be the place, hidden from humanity and even any Scriptural record, that the next passage I cite took place?

> *"For we know that the Law is spiritual, but I am carnal, sold under sin. For what I am doing, I do not understand. For what I will to do, that I do not practice; but what I hate, that I do. If, then, I do what I will not to do, I agree with the Law that it is good. But now, it is no longer I who do it, but sin that dwells in me. For I know that in me (that is, in my flesh) nothing good dwells; for to will is present with me, but how to perform what is good I do not find." (Romans 7:14-18, NKJV)*

> *"O wretched man that I am! Who will deliver me from this body of death? I thank God — through Jesus Christ our Lord! So then, with the mind I myself serve the Law of God, but with the flesh the law of sin. There is therefore now no condemnation to those who are in Christ Jesus, who do not walk according to the flesh, but according to the Spirit. For the law of the Spirit of life in Christ Jesus has made me free from the law of sin and death." (Romans 7:24-8:2, NKJV)*

What is happening to Paul? The old man is passing away. The new man in Christ is being formed. Like many of us, I'm sure Paul wondered why he must endure the suffering of bondage he faced in Romans 7. Why wouldn't God just *fix it?* It was because God had a deeper purpose that went beyond answering the 911 call of a man wanting healing. Paul was in a classroom. The class was "Grace 101." Paul was about to have a *grace conversion.*

Romans 7 is a passage full of bondage. *The good I want to do I do not do.* It is a passage full of failure and inner death. *That which I hate, I do.* Paul could not escape his inability to keep the Law. He *wanted* to keep the Law, but found himself absolutely depraved and bankrupt of any faculty to actually do it. Paul calls himself a "wretched man." One of my dear friends, pastor and author Mike Chorey, says that "every man must have a 'wretched man moment' before he can see the power of the cross."[4]

The word *wretched* literally means "exhausted from hard labor." Paul was spiritually tired from attempts to keep the Law, his inability to attain holiness, and his bent toward habitual sin in the inner man. Looking up from the bottom of the valley of bondage, there he discovers grace. Note that he does not say "*what* will rescue me" but "*who* will rescue me". His salvation is a person. The same person who brought Him low on the road to Damascus—Jesus Christ our Lord!

Romans 8 is a passage full of freedom and life. No longer a slave to sin, Paul is a new man empowered by grace and God-sized life that does not originate with him. From the pit of what he was experiencing in Romans 7, now looking up for an answer, Paul fixes his eyes on the only One who can save him—the Lamb of God who takes away the sin of the world!

There are fifteen "I's" in Romans 7, and there are none in Romans 8. The man of bondage was focused on himself; on his willpower. The man of freedom was focused on grace. On the Spirit. On Jesus Christ.

When the new man emerged from Arabia, he would look nothing like the man that went in. The first Paul was self-righteous. The second depended on Christ and Him crucified for his righteousness. The first was a slave to the Law. The second was a son of God. The first was in bondage. The second was set free. The first taught Law. The second preached grace. He would never be the same.

MY STORY

Often times in Scripture, people are known by their afflictions. The Blind Man Bartimaeus. Doubting Thomas. If I were known by my affliction, I would be Derek the Afraid or Derek the Weak.

"Romans 7 comes before Romans 8," my pastor told me, reminding me that God's ways are often that suffering and

---

[4] Mike Chorey spoke this at Niagara '08, an annual event hosted by the ministry he founded and directs, *Joshua Revolution*. (www.joshuarevolution.org)

striving precede a greater understanding grace and freedom. I sat before him in the cold northern New York winter of 2001, absolutely confused, broken and tormented, descending into a deep dark valley of depression, and not seeing the way out.

This was not where I expected to be. I had moved from Texas to New York along with my wife and baby daughter back in 1999. Having visited the Pensacola revival at the Brownsville Assembly of God, I was smitten with the visitation of God in that place, where over 400,000 people eventually committed or recommitted their lives to Christ. Longing to see revival come, I moved Isaiah Six Ministries back to New York, where I'd grown up, hoping to bring revival to the northeast.

To be an agent of revival, I concluded, I must become a champion of spiritual disciplines. So I worked hard to attain the life of spiritual so-called success: I prayed an hour every day, I read my Bible religiously, I fasted once a week, I witnessed to at least one person every day, I attended morning prayers at the church, I tithed, I worshiped, I was in church every time the doors were open. I traveled the world over, teaching and preaching what I understood of the Scriptures. Yet, by late 2000, I was physically and spiritually exhausted.

I was reading a book called *Spiritual Authority*[5] by an author named Watchman Nee during that time, when he cited John 4:34, "Jesus said, 'My food is to do the will of Him who sent me and to accomplish His work.'"[6] Nee made the point that since the will of God is like food, doing the will of God should cause us to feel full and not empty. As I read, I realized that this did not describe me at all. Instead, I was getting burned out.

Then one day, I had a spiritual car crash. It was as if my world caved in as irrational fears that had plagued me from childhood returned with unbearable intensity. "I feel like I'm losing my mind," I told my wife. I tried to function, but found my condition too debilitating.

I reasoned that if I could just get through the holidays, get some rest, and press into 2001, I would improve. I reasoned that

---

[5] Watchman Nee, *Spiritual Authority*. © 1972 by Christian Fellowship Publishers.
[6] NASB

I'd been tired before, and always found endurance to be the antidote. It wouldn't work that way this time. By February 2001, I feared I was going insane. I had all but given up trying to function in my ministry office work, where I would sit at my desk, frozen in fear, too debilitated to function with any productivity. Most days I spent at home, reduced to survival. I was losing weight, struggling through sleepless nights, fighting off daily headaches and nausea, and struggling to do even the most basic of functions, as my energy seemed to be drained from my body. I lost all desire to do anything that I once found pleasurable, from food, to sports, to entertainment, to making love to my wife. But worst of all, I lost hope. That was when I decided to meet with my pastor and friend, Rick Sinclair.

"Maybe you should go and see your family doctor," Rick encouraged.

I agreed. I actually hoped there would be something physically wrong with me so that perhaps some medical procedure would improve my state.

As I sat in Dr. Tasoo Kim's office waiting for my name to be called, I noticed a pamphlet on depression. I was terrified as I read, feeling like I was looking in a mirror. It described me to a T. When I went in to see Dr. Kim, he asked me some questions, and then gave me a test to fill out. The questions were not only what I was experiencing physically, but poked and prodded at what I was feeling and even thinking.

A few minutes after I handed in the completed test, Dr. Kim came back into the room, and announced with his thick Korean accent, "You are depressed."

As I said previously, I knew this already and wondered how much I would have to pay for this diagnosis (he ended up giving me a free visit). Before I left the office, Dr. Kim gave me some anti-depressant pills, and said, "These might help you."

I went home and sat on the couch next to my wife, pills in hand. "How did I end up here?" I asked her, tears in my eyes.

Not knowing if I should take the pills, we prayed and asked God for wisdom. I did not want to get into the drug world. I did not want to feel good synthetically but wanted to know the state of my soul even if I felt terrible. It was not long after that that I was reading the biography of a great healing evangelist, Smith Wigglesworth. On one occasion, Wigglesworth was facing a life-and-death illness, and had to make a decision about invasive surgery. Leaning on his faith, he decided against the surgery, proclaiming, "I would rather die trusting than live doubting!"

I knew this was God's word for me regarding the pills, so I threw them in the garbage. I do not mean to imply that those who take those types of medications are in sin or lack faith, as I believe that sometimes these types of treatments can be merciful, but this was God's word for *me.*

I suppose you would think that I immediately began to improve, proving that my enormous faith won the day, and I am worthy of writing the book that is in your hands! Not so, my friend! I was still only on the beginning of a long journey in the school of the Holy Spirit that ultimately lasted almost four years. The worst of my depression lasted for fifteen months.

The days that followed my visit with Dr. Kim were days of striving. Well-trained in the art of Christian disciplines, I assumed that I must do *more* of what I'd already been doing. I concluded that I must pray *more,* read the Bible *more,* memorize *more* Scripture, do *more* "spiritual warfare." So I put on the boxing gloves and tried to earn my freedom, but it would not come for a long time. Instead of getting better, things got worse. I was tormented to the point where I began to ask God to take my life. Even writing about those days makes me shudder.

I tried to function in ministry during those days, but was so debilitated, I eventually had to get out. I remember leading worship at a college conference for 700 students in April, 2001. I was amazed that God was still moving as I led worship, because even while I was onstage, I struggled to concentrate and not to panic. My soul was insane. This was a time when insomnia was at its worst, and I remember staring out a window at 3:00am from the 15th floor at the street below, my heart racing with anxiety. The next day, a speaker that I now consider a close friend and mentor, Michael Cavanaugh, pulled me aside, and said, "What is going on? You don't look so good." When I shared with him what was happening, he said, "I think it'd be good for you to consider some time off from ministry."

I was out of ministry for six months. Every day was the same. On and on and on, my suffering continued. I would wake up and my heart would be racing with fear that I had to face another day. I would try to find some sense of peace, but would have to endure horrible panic attacks that made me feel as if I was losing control. I would retreat often to my room, and bury my face in a pillow, clenching it with my fists and crying out, "God, where are you?" I hated being around people, and sleep would be welcome so that I wouldn't have to think. The prayers I once prayed, asking God to use me to shake nations, were far, far from me. I was reduced to survival. I was just asking God to help me to function again in the most basic tasks of life, that I might just be a good husband and father. I could have cared less about continuing in ministry. Actually, I had to honestly ask myself, "How can I preach a gospel that hasn't changed me?"

I began to think about other careers, and what I might do with my life after my "sabbatical," because it was looking more and more like it wouldn't be ministry. I didn't know what I would do. I thought of everything from joining the army to studio engineering to small engine repair.

In one final act of desperation, I decided to go on a 21-day fast. I got up every morning, and went to a grove on the shores of the St. Lawrence River just outside of the small town of Waddington, NY. There, I would ask God to heal me. I'd beg Him. It was then that God began to speak to me about my self-sufficiency and the self-sufficiency of my people in America. He led me to a passage in Revelation about the church of Laodicea.

> *"You say, 'I am rich; I have acquired wealth and do not need a thing.' But you do not realize that you are wretched, pitiful, poor, blind and naked." (Revelation 3:17, NIV)*

Laodicea, much like America, had grown in wealth and influence to the point where the inhabitants longer saw their need of God. Their pride drove them away from God and made their hearts black with self-love. I saw the disease clearly. I saw its symptoms in my own life. Guilty. Guilty. Guilty. Nasty, arrogant, self-centered self-sufficiency. But how can you heal this incurable disease?

Deeper and deeper I went into my long fast, and in spite of the knowledge that I was selfish and self-sufficient, my pain remained. Seeing the disease didn't take the disease away.

On Day 13 of my fast, I was in the middle of a three-day retreat on the banks of the Oswegatchie River deep in the fields behind my in-laws' farm in Richville, New York. A violent thunderstorm came through, and I went out by the river's edge and lay down underneath its intimidating canopy. Hard rain pelted my face as the skies turned black. Thunder clapped and the lightning struck all around and I cried out to God for my healing. "I'm not going to move from here until you heal me!" I pleaded. The Lord spoke this verse to my heart:

> *"Since you are precious and honored in my sight, and because I love you, I will give men in exchange for you, and people in exchange for your life." (Isaiah 43:4, NIV)*

I found out the next day that within a mile of me, someone had been struck by lightning.

Encouragements seemed short-lived in those days, as I'd quickly spiral back into the agonies of my condition. On Day 20 of my 21-day fast, I was in a miserable state, and I was furious at God. Why hadn't He saved me? I was done trying to save myself. I was done praying and memorizing and fasting. "I've tried everything, God!" I complained. "I've prayed, I've fasted, I've studied the Bible, I've memorized Scripture!"

As you can see, it was all about me, and what I had done. Indeed I had the disease of self-sufficiency.

At the time, I was sitting in my living room recliner; and out of sheer desperation, I reached over and grabbed my Bible from the end table next to my chair. I flipped open the Bible randomly and just began to read wherever my eyes happened to fall on the page. It was then that I saw a little word that I seen a million times with my natural eyes, but never with my spiritual eyes: *grace*.

It was everywhere. Paul opened his letters with it. He closed his letters with it. It was the theme of his epistles. It was the reason he was persecuted. And I realized that though I was very familiar with this little word, it had become a cliché to me and I had no real grasp as to the magnitude of its meaning. It certainly did not mean as much to me as it meant to Paul the Apostle! I thought grace was for Billy Graham crusades and sentimental hymns.

The more I read, the more it dawned on me that I had stumbled upon a truth that was absolutely central and foundational to the Christian life. And the more I read, the more I realized that I was ignorant to what is probably the most significant key to living a successful and victorious Christian life. It was then that it occurred to me that after all of my striving, maybe God would not fix me *because* of me, but *in spite* of me. Now that my efforts were finished, I sensed that I only had one hope left: God Himself. God had me right where He wanted me. It was as if I was arriving at the end of Romans 7 crying out, "Who will rescue me from this body of death? Thanks be to God — through Christ Jesus our Lord!" I was about to enter Romans 8. My deliverance would be an act of God, and not the result of my commitment to Christian disciplines, discovering in counseling what went wrong in my childhood, or finding the secret demon in my life. I began to see that my responsibility was to trust, and God's responsibility was to work in me.

In the days that followed, I began to devour the Scriptures, and I became obsessed with God's grace. Over the next nine months, I studied Galatians 5 and Romans 8. I went word by word and line by line, not moving on to the next word, phrase, or verse until I grasped what the Scriptures were teaching.

I began to see a Christianity that was more about God's work in me, and less about my work for God. I began to see the cross not merely as a model of self-denial, but as the object of my faith and the source of my strength. I began to see that God didn't want me to *be* righteous, but He wanted to *be my righteousness!* I began to look into the eyes of my Judge and see a Father. Somehow the revelation of my own depravity and weakness became an ally, leading me to grace, because *grace is for sinners.* I began to see that God had sustained me and was sustaining me by His power, that my salvation was eternally secure because it depended upon Christ's keeping power and not my willpower. I began to see that God's chief aim was not my happiness, but His glory. I began to see that God was sovereign in all things, was the Lord of the Wilderness, and that the enemy had no power over me.

Soon, like faint cherry colors on a morning sky as the sun rises after a long black night, my world began to change. Grace was changing me. I sensed His compassion over me, and His favor and love constantly.

One day, I was reading Ephesians 1, where Paul introduced the letter by saying, *"Paul, an apostle by commandment of the Lord Jesus Christ."* That's when it struck me, that Paul didn't say, "An apostle because I feel like it" or "An apostle because I took a spiritual gifts test and I'm really good at apostling." He said, "...by commandment of the Lord Jesus Christ." I was still struggling with the idea of getting back in the saddle of ministry, and now the Lord was showing me the way. He wanted me to serve Him not on the basis of my feelings, but on the basis of faith. He wanted me to return to ministry not because I felt like it, but solely as an act of obedience to His commandment: *Derek, an evangelist by commandment of the Lord Jesus Christ.*

On that word alone, I stepped back into ministry, trusting the Lord and His grace to empower me to serve.

As I walked out of the wilderness, the Lord gave me two commands to deal with the depression. The first was, "Stop crying, for you are free" and the second, "Stop praying for your deliverance, for I've heard your prayers."

Regarding the first, I continued to have panic attacks several times a day, when I would spiral (albeit temporarily) into a state of hopelessness, again weeping in my bedroom. God spoke to my heart that as long as I continued crying, I was sending a message to the fear, and indeed, to the devil, that I was taking him seriously. Resisting the urge to cry, and by faith, beginning to act like a healed man would be part of my healing.

Regarding the second, I'll draw from an illustration with my children. Often times in church, my son Reese will ask my wife for a Cheerio. My wife will agree to the transaction, but tell my son to wait a few minutes until the right time. Inevitably, Reese will ask again within two minutes. "Just wait, my sweet Reese," my wife will patiently answer.

Again, within two minutes, dying of starvation and malnutrition, little Reese will ask again for the Cheerio. Finally, my wife will say, "My dear son, I heard you the first time. Don't ask again!"

What was it that caused Reese to ask the second or third time? *Unbelief.*

Now, the lesson here is not that we pray once and never need to ask again, but that we ask until there's a witness in our hearts that our cry has been heard, and is as good as answered.

When the Lord spoke this to my heart, I knew that I need not ask again for my healing any more than my little Reese needed to ask two more times for a Cheerio. God had heard my cry. I'd begged and pleaded and cried out for months on end. Would I think God cruel and deaf to those cries? My prayers had gotten through. In fact, if I did pray again, I am convinced that it would have been unbelief, just as it was for Reese.

The Lord tested me on this.

In November 2001, I went to lead worship at a men's conference in northern New Jersey. During one of the evening sessions, a pastor from Guatemala named Hector Nufio (who has since become a friend) brought an excellent word on the life of Joseph and his request to his prisonmates (and ultimately to God), "Remember me."

Hector said that "remembering" is the process of gathering or re-*membering* thoughts until the picture is clear, and so this prayer is a request for God to put us back together.[7]

When he invited the men forward for prayer, I went forward, and fell on my face before God. I said, "Lord, I know You've heard

---

[7] The sermon was delivered by Pastor Hector Nufio from Guatemala, pastor of Elim Central in Guatemala City.

my prayer, but..." I so badly wanted to ask for the Cheerio one more time. "...if I could just ask you again..."

And so I did. "Please God...fix me...remember me."

The Lord knows our weaknesses and was merciful to me. No sooner had I prayed than one of the pastors on the prayer team came over and put his hand on my shoulder. Leaning down, he whispered in my ear, "The Lord says to you, 'I have heard your prayer.'"

I was shocked and profoundly encouraged. It was exactly the word my spirit needed to hear. All doubt and anxiety fled from my heart. Then, as if on cue, the Hector began to prophesy from the platform. "I feel like the Lord is telling me that there is someone here that has gone through a terrible time of darkness, and you have lost your passion for ministry and even for life. You have even requested that the Lord would take your life. And the Lord says..." He shouted the next part with a raspy tone and thick Latin American accent, and drove it deep into my heart. "...I will never answer that prayer! I will restore your joy! I will restore your desire to live! I will restore your passion for ministry!"

And here I stand several years later. I never thought I would say this, and in fact, I told God that I wouldn't, but I am so thankful for that wilderness season, and all that I went through. God, in His great mercy, allowed my kingdoms, empires, idols, and man-made religion to fall—all the things I once trusted in and placed my identity in—so that I would arrive at my final destination, Christ Himself.

I can see now the severity of the root in my life. The violence of the dark trial indicated the depth of the root. All the suffering I went through was required to tear out the root of man-made religion and self-sufficiency! And now I wouldn't trade the trial for the finest diamonds in the world, for I was given the true riches of His Word.

People want to know how I escaped the jaws of severe depression, and I tell them all the same thing. "You shall know the truth, and the truth shall make you free" (John 8:31-32). Day after day, I felt my spirit renewed by God's grace. I sensed His compassion over me, and His favor and love constantly. I like to say now that I have not been restored, but *transformed.* I am not what I was before. I had what I've come to call a "grace conversion."

My wife experienced a revelation of grace at the same time I did as we walked through the wilderness together. So powerful was our grace conversion that, for a time, we wondered if we were even saved before 2001! Then I read Galatians 5:25, which says, "If we live in the Spirit, let us also walk in the Spirit."[8] The word *live* basically refers to being born again, and the word *in* basically implies an act of dependence. So Paul is basically saying, "If you were born again by trusting in the Spirit of God, then continue to live by the same principle of dependence for the rest of the Christian life."

I think sometimes we believe that grace is something we receive at salvation and then we move on to "deeper revelations" in the rest of the Christian life, but here Paul is teaching us that the grace that *saved* us is the same grace that will *sanctify* us. And he asks the Galatians, "Are you so foolish? Having begun in the Spirit, are you now being made perfect by the flesh?"[9]

Before my grace conversion, I was a champion of spiritual disciplines. The problem was not the act of doing those things, but the motive of the heart. I had begun to depend on those things, and not on God's grace, for my standing before God. I was depending upon my performance instead of the cross. But when His grace appeared, I could see that "all my righteous deeds were like filthy rags,"[10] and I had only one hope of success as a follower of Jesus. *His grace at work in me.* The grace that gave me salvation at the beginning is the same grace that saved me from depression and anxiety, and it's the same grace that will bring me home.

Matthew 4:1 says that "the Spirit led Jesus into the wilderness."[11] What a comfort to know that when we find ourselves in dry and arid places or dark valleys, God is the Lord of our Wilderness, not Satan. God, in His sovereignty, leads us to

---

[8] NKJV
[9] Galatians 3:3, NKJV
[10] Isaiah 64:6
[11] NKJV

those places that He might reveal Himself to us. David wrote that God revealed His acts to Israel and His ways to Moses.[12] As I walked through the valley, I began to learn God's ways. I saw God as sovereign; I saw His Father's heart; I saw that perseverance is the great secret of the kingdom, not the absence of suffering.

As I began to apply the truths of grace to my life and ministry, I began to understand that embracing the truths of grace completely altered the way I made disciples. Under law, we impose rules and behaviors on our disciples, suggesting that sustained obedience will result in Christian character and nearness to God. Under grace, we must teach young men and women the gospel, and what it means to be in Christ. Then holiness and intimacy with God become a product of believing truth.

I was appalled as I considered the fruit of my ministry before my grace conversion. I saw little long-term fruit, and only disciples in bondage who were reaping the only thing they could reap from my teaching: destruction, death, and deeds of the flesh. Divorce, atheism, adultery, fornication, rape, prison—these were among the fruits borne in my disciples, who had once committed themselves to wholeheartedly serve Christ.

As I was discovering grace and coming out of the Dark Night of the Soul,[13] I began to evaluate what I taught and believed, and I had to ask myself: What's the difference, ultimately, between what I believe and teach, and what Islam believes and teaches? Islam teaches a radical adherence to rules, laws, and disciplines just as I had, and with better results at that! I knew that Christ is ultimately the difference, but how do you apply Christ to sanctification? If we merely apply Christ as an example of self-denial, then ultimately, the walking out of our faith is no different than that of radical Muslims: We work our hardest to keep the Law.

Here lies the whole point of this book. I'm weary of seeing young men and women who want to serve God walk away because all they ever learned to do was to live under law. No one has taught them how to live under grace. Part of the problem

---

[12] Psalm 103:7

[13] A phrase coined by St. John of the Cross.

certainly lies in the fact that many Christians who are making disciples do not understand grace.

When those frustrated with living under law walk away from the Lord, the self-righteous will look and say, "There they go, backsliding from Christ." But let me suggest, dear saint, that many do not fall away from Christ, but *from dead religion*. Whether it is the fault of the hearer or teacher, I don't know fully, but we must commit ourselves as teachers and disciplers to leading our people in the way of grace. We must disciple them by grace. It's not just *a* way, it's the *only* way.

CHAPTER 2
Grace Conversions

"I once was blind but now I see." — John Newton, *Amazing Grace*

What is a *grace conversion?* It is the life-altering shift of the believer's confidence from self-sufficiency to the sufficiency of the grace of God. This is not merely a theological adjustment, because sometimes the person can already regurgitate the theology of grace without truly experiencing it. A grace conversion is the work of the Holy Spirit to thoroughly convince the heart that the flesh is hopelessly helpless, and that God's grace is enough.

From the days of the Scriptures until now, God has been leading His children to a revelation of Himself. Throughout church history, we see again and again the story of ordinary men and women who are transformed by grace. This transformation always seems to be preceded by a poor soul in a state of self-sufficiency, followed by an inner or external trial of extreme pressure that forces the soul into seeing the grace of God as the only solution.

For so many, the journey is the same. Beginning with self-confidence, the path winds along the treacherous, stony pass of frustration, discouragement, and suffering, finally turning onto the smooth plains of grace and peace. The summary of the experience of those who have discovered God's grace might be as follows:

I will.

I can't.

He can.

We begin with the desire to serve Him and cry out, "I will!" But our strength and willpower end, and we confess, "I can't." Then God renews our strength, lifts our gaze upward, and we say, "He can!"

In the Bible, we see it in Moses, who committed the self-sufficient act of slaying the Egyptian soldier. His heart was in the right place in that he wanted to liberate Israel from oppression, but his actions were those of a man taking it upon himself and not trusting God. He spent 40 years in the desert, and finally a broken man emerged ready to lead God's people.

We see it in Abraham, who acquired his Ishmael through an impatient act of mistrust in God's promise. It was years later when the old man finally rested from his strivings that Isaac was born.

In Church history, we see it in Augustine, who after facing the failures of his youth and his own efforts to find God, found such a deep revelation of grace that R.C. Sproul wrote, "He said that mankind is a *massa peccati*, a 'mess of sin,' incapable of raising itself from spiritual death. For Augustine man can no more move or incline himself to God than an empty glass can fill itself."[14]

John Bunyan had his own grace conversion, suffering persecution in prison, when he found his Savior to be his All in All. Eventually he wrote in prison the now famous book *Pilgrim's Progress*.[15] The following poem by Bunyan shows the depth of revelation he enjoyed:

> *Run John Run*
> *The Law demands*
> *And gives us neither feet nor hands*
> *Far better news the gospel brings*
> *For it bids us fly*
> *And gives us wings*

PETER

Peter is one of the best biblical studies of the before and after picture of a person who has had a grace conversion. Before, we see a self-sufficient man who convinced himself that he was great and that he could do anything for his Master.

> *But Peter kept saying insistently, "Even if I have to die with You, I will not deny You!" And they all were saying the same thing also. (Mark 14:31, NASB)*

---

[14] From the essay titled "Augustine and Pelagius" by R.C. Sproul, © 1996 *Ligonier Ministries*.
[15] Bunyan, John (1628-1688), *Pilgrim's Progress*. Public Domain.

Yet, in spite of his willpower, we ultimately see a before picture of a man who denied Christ, full of fear when the rubber hit the road, and weak in the face of his enemies.

> *Then he began to curse and swear, "I do not know the man!" And immediately a rooster crowed. (Matthew 26:74, NASB)*

Then came a series of events that affected all of us. Jesus Christ died. He rose again. He ascended to heaven. He sits at the right hand of the Father. The day of grace arrived. He sent the Holy Spirit.

Now we see a different Peter. Peter had seen the risen Christ. Jesus restored him. Peter finally understood grace. He was filled with the Holy Spirit. On the Day of Pentecost, Peter was provoked to speak to the crowds of people, among whom were some of the very murderers of Christ. The very people of whom Peter was so afraid when he denied Christ were now standing before him as he preached.

> *"Therefore let all the house of Israel know for certain that God has made Him both Lord and Christ — this Jesus whom you crucified." (Acts 2:36, NASB)*

He was bold. He was unafraid of death. The one who could not admit to a servant girl that he knew Christ no longer feared anything. When faced with the possibility of his own martyrdom, Peter seemed at ease with the idea, longing to be with his Lord.

> *"I consider it right, as long as I am in this earthly dwelling, to stir you up by way of reminder, knowing that the laying aside of my earthly dwelling is imminent, as also our Lord Jesus Christ has made clear to me." (2 Peter 1:13-14, NASB)*

Peter was a new man. He had a grace conversion. He knew that Christ had been *with* him and was now *in* him; that his entire DNA had been altered as he partook of divine nature.

"For by these He has granted to us His precious and magnificent promises, so that by them you may become partakers of the divine nature, having escaped the corruption that is in the world by lust." (2 Peter 1:4, NASB)

The self-sufficient one had been converted to grace. Christ had become his All in All. He had become a new creation living with divine nature inside. He had completed the journey of, "I will. I can't. He can."

Many more in the centuries that followed would have transformations similar to Peter's as the gospel was preached and published. But like Peter, many would have to experience the dark before the dawn before their grace conversions.

THEY FOUND THE SECRET

V. Raymond Edman, in his profound book *They Found the Secret*, teaches, *"The exchanged life.* Hudson Taylor first used the term to describe what it means to know Christ as our sufficiency in all things. Taylor is but one of the many Christian luminaries who have discovered Christ as the secret to abundant living. John Bunyan, Andrew Murray, Amy Carmichael, Oswald Chambers, Charles Finney — behind the varied lives and personalities of these and other men and women lies a common theme, a pattern that leads from desperation to the abundant life Jesus promised."[16]

Edman delves deeper, "The details of their experiences are usually quite different yet as we listen to their stories and watch their lives, either in our reading or in our contact with them, we begin to see a pattern that reveals their secret. Out of discouragement and defeat they have come into victory. Out of weakness and weariness they have been made strong. Out of ineffectiveness and apparent uselessness they have become effective and enthusiastic.

"The pattern seems to be self-centeredness, self-effort, increasing inner dissatisfaction and outer discouragement, a

---

[16] V. Raymond Edman, *They Found the Secret.* Zondervan, Grand Rapids, MI. © 1984 Zondervan: back cover text.

temptation to give it all up because there is no better way, and then finding the Spirit of God to be their strength, their guide, their confidence and companion—in a word, their life."[17]

The following is a "before and after" snapshot of the effects of grace in the soul.

Before	After
self-righteousness	revelation of Christ's righteousness
self-sufficiency	God-sufficiency
mastered by sinful nature	mastery over sinful nature
bondage	freedom
striving	resting
elusive joy	joy in the Lord
confusion and anxiety	peace

HUDSON TAYLOR

The following is from a letter that the great missionary Hudson Taylor sent to his mother as he wrestled with the depravity of his own soul. He was thirty-seven at the time:

"I cannot tell you how I am buffeted sometimes by temptation. I never knew how bad a heart I had. Yet I do know that I love God and love His work and desire to serve Him only in all things...Often I am tempted to think that one so full of sin cannot be a child of God at all; but I try to throw it back, and rejoice all the more in the preciousness of Jesus...Do pray for me. Pray that the Lord will keep me from sin, will sanctify me wholly, will use me more largely in His service."[18]

Not long after, Taylor had a deep revelation of God's grace and wrote to his sister:

---

[17] Ibid, pg. 12.
[18] Ibid, pg. 18.

"As to work, mine was never so plentiful, so responsible, or so difficult; but the weight and the strain are all gone. The last month or so has been perhaps, the happiest of my life; and I long to tell you a little of what the Lord has done for my soul. I do not know how far I may be able to make myself intelligible about it, for there is nothing new or strange or wonderful – and yet, all is new! In a word, 'Whereas once I was blind, now I see....'

"When my agony of soul was at its height, a sentence in a letter from dear McCarthy was used to remove the scales from my eyes, and the Spirit of God revealed the truth of our oneness with Jesus as I had never known it before. McCarthy, who had been much exercised by the same sense of failure, but saw the light before I did, wrote (I quote from memory): 'But how to get faith strengthened? Not by striving after faith, but by resting on the Faithful One.'

"As I read, I saw it all! 'If we believe not, He abideth faithful.' I looked to Jesus and saw (and when I saw, oh, how joy flowed!) that He had said, 'I will never leave you.' 'Ah, there is rest!' I thought. 'I have striven in vain to rest in Him. I'll strive no more. For He has promised to abide with me – never to leave me, never to fail me!'"

Taylor, like all those that experience a grace conversion saw that it was "not by striving after faith, but resting on the Faithful One." This is a great work of grace to give the heart eyes to see, and receive this mighty revelation. Perhaps Taylor could have even preached something to this effect before his grace conversion, but somehow, God makes it a reality when the eyes of our heart are opened.

MARTIN LUTHER

Martin Luther also recounts his own conversion from religion to grace. After making a vow in a thunderstorm to become a monk in 1505, Luther sought peace for his own soul as he dedicated himself to the monastic life in a German monastery, but peace was elusive as his excessive introspection nearly drove him mad. He became painfully aware of his own depravity and found himself lost in depression. Johann von Staupitz, his superior in the Roman Church, was so concerned for Luther's sanity that he encouraged Luther to start an academic career to take his mind off of his dark obsessions. Luther said of Staupitz, "If it had not been for Dr. Staupitz, I should have sunk in hell."[19] Luther later says of this time, "I lost touch with Christ the Savior and Comforter, and made of him the jailor and hangman of my poor soul."[20]

Around 1512, God was merciful to Luther, opening his eyes to the light of the gospel. Later in life, he wrote about the darkness and light he experienced during this season:

> *"Meanwhile, I had already during that year returned to interpret the Psalter anew. I had confidence in the fact that I was more skillful, after I had lectured in the university on St. Paul's epistles to the Romans, to the Galatians, and the one to the Hebrews. I had indeed been captivated with an extraordinary ardor for understanding Paul in the Epistle to the Romans. But up till then it was not the cold blood about the heart, but a single word in Chapter 1, "In it the righteousness of God is revealed," that had stood in my way. For I hated that word "righteousness of God," which, according to the use and custom of all the teachers, I had been taught to understand philosophically regarding the formal or active righteousness, as they call it, with which God is righteous and punishes the unrighteous sinner.*

> *"Though I lived as a monk without reproach, I felt that I was a sinner before God with an extremely disturbed conscience. I could not believe that He was placated by my satisfaction. I did not love, yes, I hated the righteous God who punishes sinners, and secretly, if not blasphemously, certainly murmuring greatly, I was angry with God, and said, 'As if, indeed, it is not enough, that miserable sinners, eternally lost through original sin, are crushed by every kind of calamity by the Law of the decalogue, without having God add pain to pain by the gospel*

---

[19] "Johann von Staupitz," on *Augnet*, page ID 890.
[20] Kittelson, James. *Luther The Reformer*. Minneapolis: Augsburg Fortress Publishing House, 1986, 79.

and also by the gospel threatening us with his righteousness and wrath!' Thus I raged with a fierce and troubled conscience. Nevertheless, I beat importunately upon Paul at that place, most ardently desiring to know what St. Paul wanted."

"At last, by the mercy of God, meditating day and night, I gave heed to the context of the words, namely, 'In it the righteousness of God is revealed, as it is written, "He who through faith is righteous shall live."' There I began to understand that the righteousness of God is that by which the righteous lives by a gift of God, namely by faith. And this is the meaning: the righteousness of God is revealed by the gospel, namely, the passive righteousness with which merciful God justifies us by faith, as it is written, 'He who through faith is righteous shall live.' Here I felt that I was altogether born again and had entered paradise itself through open gates. There a totally other face of the entire Scripture showed itself to me. Thereupon I ran through the Scripture from memory. I also found in other terms an analogy, as, the work of God, that is what God does in us, the power of God, with which He makes us wise, the strength of God, the salvation of God, the glory of God.

"And I extolled my sweetest word with a love as great as the hatred with which I had before hated the word 'righteousness of God.' Thus that place in Paul was for me truly the gate to paradise. Later I read Augustine's <u>Of the Spirit and the Letter</u>,[21] where contrary to hope I found that he, too, interpreted God's righteousness in a similar way, as the righteousness with which God clothes us when he justifies us. Although this was heretofore said imperfectly and he did not explain all things concerning imputation clearly, it nevertheless was pleasing that God's righteousness with which we are justified was taught."[22]

---

[21] Saint Augustine (354-430): *Of the Spirit and the Letter*. Translated by Peter Holmes and Robert Ernest Wallis, and revised by Benjamin B. Warfield. From *Nicene and Post-Nicene Fathers, First Series, Vol. 5*. Edited by Philip Schaff. (Buffalo, NY: Christian Literature Publishing Co., 1887.)

[22] This selection is taken from *Preface to the Complete Edition of Luther's Latin Writings* by Martin Luther, written in Wittenburg in 1545.

So powerful was Luther's conversion to grace that he would soon after nail *The Ninety-Five Theses* to the church doors in Wittenberg, igniting a Reformation that would affect the history of the known world.

GEORGE WHITEFIELD

God's chief vessel during *The Great Awakening* of America in the 18th Century was George Whitefield. He preached powerfully throughout the states, and his booming voice could carry to crowds of 30,000 people without a microphone. His revelation and message of God's grace was profound and powerful, shaking a nation. But typical to all of God's giants is a grace conversion.

In 1739, en route by ship from England to America, Whitefield had many days to examine himself. He had preached many days in England, and had become very popular. Now he asked God to search his heart.

Whitefield was soon convicted of his pride: "I am blind. I am full of self-pride and self-love." He prayed, "Oh, that these inner conflicts may purify my polluted, proud and treacherous heart!"[23]

Biographer Arnold Dallimore writes of this time, "Indeed, so severe became his self-reproach that he had thoughts of leaving the ministry...He even came to the place where he looked upon himself as unfit to continue his correspondence [to friends]; 'I feel myself so wretched and miserable, so blind and naked in myself,' he confessed, 'that Satan would tempt me to write to no one.'"

Dallimore later adds, "But though God gave Whitefield thus to grasp something deeper of the nature of sin, even more did He give him to understand in a new and fuller way the exceeding riches of His grace."[24] Whitefield himself writes of this time:

> *"I underwent inexpressible agonies of soul for two or three days, at the remembrance of my sins and the bitter consequences of them. All the while I was assured that God had forgiven me, but I could not forgive myself for sinning against so much light*

---

[23] *George Whitefield* by Arnold Dallimore: The Banner of Truth Trust: Carlisle, Pennsylvania. pg. 402
[24] Ibid, pg. 403

and love. I felt something of that which...Peter [felt] when, with oaths and curses he had thrice denied his Master. At length my Lord looked upon me, and with that look broke my rocky heart, and I wept most bitterly...Were I always to see myself such a sinner as I am, and as I did then, without seeing the Saviour of sinners, I should not be able to look up.

"The latter part of the week, blessed be the Lord, He has restored me to the light of His countenance, and enabled me to praise Him with joyful lips."[25]

Dallimore concludes, "Whitefield's whole outlook, both theological and in relationship to the daily Christian life, was affected by this deeper understanding of Divine grace."[26]

CORRIE TEN BOOM AND OTHERS

Our dear sister, Corrie Ten Boom, who suffered so much during World War II, was mercifully and tenderly led to grace through dark places. A watchmaker in Holland, she and her family helped Jewish refugees by hiding them from the Nazis in their house. Betrayed by a friend, she found herself in a Nazi concentration camp with her sister Betsy. After watching her sister die a slow death, and never seeing her beloved father again, she struggled to forgive the man who betrayed her and the cruel Germans who mistreated her and her family. Finally, when her heart seemed hopelessly in the clutches of hatred, the light of grace came. Eventually, she would travel the world and preach forgiveness, calling herself "a tramp for the Lord." Corrie once said, "Sometimes you don't know that Jesus is all you need until Jesus is all you have."

Even as I write these words, the tears fill my eyes again as I remember the sorrows of so many of God's followers, and yet the goodness of God to lead them to green pastures. On and on the list goes, and on and on the stories go; and as we walk with God,

---

[25] Ibid, pg. 404
[26] Ibid, pg. 404

stand in the midst of fire, and trust God when all seems bleak and the sun seems it will never rise, we shall be among them.

The change is profound, and primarily internal, where no one sees but God. But for the soul converted to grace, everything changes. That which was dead becomes alive; that which was merely a mental assent becomes an experience; that which was such hard labor becomes a joy; and that which was thought to be a part becomes the whole: knowing God. Great Evangelist A.B. Simpson says it all in a poem he wrote titled, "Himself."

> *Once it was the blessing, now it is the Lord*
> *Once it was the feeling, now it is His Word*
> *Once His gifts I wanted, now the Giver own*
> *Once I sought for healing, now Himself alone*
>
> *Once 'twas painful trying, now 'tis perfect trust*
> *Once was a half salvation, now the uttermost*
> *Once 'twas ceaseless holding, now He holds me fast*
> *Once 'twas constant drifting, now my anchor's cast*

CHAPTER 3
Fallen From Grace

"You have been severed from Christ, you who are seeking to be justified by Law; you have fallen from grace."
– Paul the Apostle (Galatians 5:4, NASB)

This is an interesting Scripture. Paul is speaking to the church in Galatia, to his own early church disciples, and he makes this outrageous diagnosis of their spiritual condition: *You have fallen from grace.* If this was the analysis of an apostle over early church believers, then you will not mind if I say that many modern Christians also suffer with this same condition.

The Galatian church had been infiltrated with a notorious band of heretics called the Judaizers, who made the claim that all Gentile converts must believe in Jesus, plus be circumcised. In essence, they were suggesting that through Christ *now we could keep the Law,* and so we must live under it. Circumcision would be the starting point, as it was the basic requirement for all Jewish people from the days of Abraham.

Was this such an outrageous request?

God, after all, had Himself commanded circumcision to Abraham. It would seem to be the doorway of access into the devout life of a good God-follower. I'm sure the Judaizers reasoned, *"Wouldn't Jesus at least expect us to obey that law?"* Even if we're exempt from other laws, surely He didn't mean *that* one.

"This is my covenant with you and your descendants after you, the covenant you are to keep: Every male among you shall be circumcised. You are to undergo circumcision, and it will be the sign of the covenant between me and you. For the generations to come every male among you who is eight days old must be circumcised, including those born in your household or bought with money from a foreigner – those who are not your offspring. Whether born in your household or bought with your money, they must be circumcised. My covenant in your flesh is

45

to be an everlasting covenant. Any uncircumcised male, who has not been circumcised in the flesh, will be cut off from his people; he has broken my covenant." (Genesis 17:10-14, NIV)

Can't you hear the logical and persuasive arguments of the Judaizers in their teachings? "This shall be the sign!" I can hear them say. "Does God have to be any clearer?"

The Galatians, mesmerized by their persuasive words, would nod. Then a Judaizer would give the punchline. "The Scripture is clear: 'Any uncircumcised male, who has not been circumcised in the flesh, will be cut off from His people; he has broken my covenant.' Brothers and sisters, you *must* be circumcised!"

The crowds, moved with counterfeit conviction, would begin to make their painful plans to obey this Old Testament law.

Paul didn't just disagree. He was so furious at these false teachers that he made the statement, "I wish that those who are upsetting you would castrate themselves!" (Galatians 5:12, NIV) He also adds, "Again, I insist that everyone who allows himself to be circumcised is obligated to obey the entire Law."

What the Judaizers didn't understand was that Jesus came to bring a *circumcision of the heart.*

"For he is not a Jew who is one outwardly, nor is circumcision that which is outward in the flesh. But he is a Jew who is one inwardly; and circumcision is that which is of the heart, by the Spirit, not by the letter; and his praise is not from men, but from God." (Romans 2:28-29, NASB)

Paul was so upset because these false teachers had removed his disciples from grace. They'd taken their focus from God's love and the completeness of the cross, and put their focus back on their performance. It was a "Jesus plus" gospel. Jesus *plus* circumcision. Jesus *plus* works. In essence, they were suggesting through their teaching that the cross was not enough to save them, but they needed to *add* to the cross through their works.

Charles Spurgeon wrote, "Paul assured us that the two principles of grace and [personal] merit can mix no more than fire or water; that if a man is to be saved by the mercy of God, it must be the mercy of God and not by works; but if man is to be saved by works, it must be works entirely and not by mercy mixed in, for mercy and works will not blend together."[27]

The plain fact is, when you depend upon your performance and not the work of the cross, you are basically saying to God, "The cross was not good enough for me." The minute we claim to have good standing before God based on our works, we make the blood of Jesus meaningless, as Paul wrote, "I do not nullify the grace of God, for if righteousness comes through the Law, then Christ died needlessly" (Galatians 2:21, NASB).

Jesus declared, "It is finished." He did not say, "It is half finished" or "It might be finished." He paid the whole price and drank the entire cup of God's wrath. The Son of God died like a sinner so that sinners could live like sons of God.

"It seems so simple!" you might say. "How did I lose sight of this?" Before we blame false teachers, let us remember that we were born with a false teacher within our own hearts. Our *flesh* is a sufficient enough false teacher to lead us astray into legalism and confusion, and destroy all spiritual life within! Our flesh wants to do everything (legalism) or nothing (license) for God, and will constantly be tempting us to place our faith in the wrong object.

THE OBJECT OF YOUR FAITH

Ivan Q. Spencer, founder of the worldwide ministry Elim Fellowship, once said, "What basis do you have to expect anything from God? The basis is Calvary and Calvary is the manifestation of God's love."

Having faith is not enough. We must have faith in the correct *object*. Paul taught the Galatians to make the object of their faith the grace of God given through Christ's death on the cross. The Judaizers taught the Galatians to make the object of their faith *circumcision*. Paul taught that access to the Father came through

---

[27] Charles Spurgeon, *Grace*

47

faith in grace. The Judaizers taught that access to God came through the works of the Law. The Galatians had *fallen from grace.*

Everyone has faith in something. We all trust in some worldview, philosophy, creed, or religion that we believe is worthy of building our lives upon. So the question we should ask is not, "Do you have faith?" Really, the question should be, "What is the object of your faith, and will it produce for you that which it is promising?"

Years ago, my brother-in-law, Jeremy Moore, received a G-Shock watch from my sister for Christmas. He insisted that it was unbreakable, as the commercials had advertised. At the time, I was a centerfielder for a college baseball team, and I asked him, "So you're telling me that if I throw your watch against that wall that it won't break?"

Confidently, he asserted, "That's what I'm telling you."

"Okay," I challenged, "give me the watch."

He hesitated.

"C'mon," I coaxed, "you said it won't break. Let's go ahead and see!"

His pride overcame him, and he agreed to the challenge. He handed me the watch, and said, "Give it your best shot."

I took the watch, and gave him one last opportunity to recant. "You're sure?" I asked. "Last chance."

He folded his arms and waited for the show. "It won't break."

I wound up like I was gunning a ball to home plate from centerfield, and rifled the watch against the wall. It smashed into about 500 pieces.

Jeremy was shocked (or maybe I should say "G-shocked"). Looking at the metal, glass, and springs on the floor, he said, "Hey man! That's my watch!"

"That *was* your watch," I corrected.

You see, Jeremy had faith. That wasn't the question. The problem was that the object of his faith did not produce for him what it had promised to produce!

In the book of First Corinthians, chapters 1 and 2, Paul reveals the only true and worthy object of faith for the believer.

> *"For the message of the cross is foolishness to those that are perishing, but to us who are being saved it is the power of God." (1 Corinthians 1:18)*

> *"For Jews request a sign, and Greeks seek after wisdom, but we preach Christ crucified." (1 Corinthians 1:22-23a)*

> *"For I determined not to know anything among you except Jesus Christ, and Him crucified." (1 Corinthians 2:2)*

Paul here is explaining that the only object of faith for the believer that will produce what it promises is *the cross of Christ*. Christians may place their faith in many different objects—some put faith in prayer and Christian disciplines, some in rituals, some in denominations, some in signs and wonders, some in eschatology or their position on Israel, some have faith in faith, and some even have faith in their study of Scripture.

Jews request a sign and Greeks seek after wisdom.

In the modern church, these could be charismatics and evangelicals. *Charismatics look for signs and evangelicals seek after wisdom.* Some charismatics believe if they could just have the right experience, get the right spiritual gift, visit the right revival, get the right "anointed" speaker to lay hands on them, then they would be transformed. Evangelicals believe if they could just study the Bible the right way, find the meaning of the right Greek word, sit under the right teaching ministry or find the newest idea by a hot Christian author, they would be transformed. But Paul says it's neither. The answer is *Christ crucified*. For "to those who are the called, both Jews and Greeks, Christ the power of God and the wisdom of God."[28] Christ becomes both power and wisdom to the one who puts his faith in the cross. Jesus said, "You search the Scriptures, for in them you think you have eternal life; and these are they which testify of Me."[29]

There is only one object of faith able to bring power into our lives to overcome sin and live victorious Christian lives: *the cross of*

---

[28] 1 Corinthians 1:24, NASB
[29] John 5:39, NKJV

Christ. Unless a believer's faith is fixed on what Paul the Apostle called "Jesus Christ and Him crucified," he will live a defeated Christian life, no matter how fervent his devotion may seem.

I must say something more at this time about faith, for there is much teaching today about the importance of faith, often (I believe) at the expense of grace. We are in danger of putting our faith *in faith.* Charles Spurgeon had something to say about this when he said, "Faith is the channel, and not the fountainhead, and we must not so much look to it as to exalt it above the divine source of all blessing which lies in the grace of God."[30]

Here Spurgeon likens grace to be like a brook flowing over a rock that a man dying of thirst could not reach because of a small chasm. So the thirsty man found a pipe and reached it across the chasm into the brook, and the water flowed down the pipe to the thirsty man. What saved the man? Was it the pipe or the water? Though the pipe played an important role, it was the water that saved the thirsty man. If all he had was the pipe, he still would have died of thirst. Let us not put our trust in the pipe of faith, but only use it to access the true source of life, God's amazing grace.

This trusting in the cross of Christ is a twofold work. First, we must cease to trust in ourselves and must be convinced of our own spiritual bankruptcy and helpless state, that we are thoroughly incapable of saving ourselves in any way. Secondly, we must see the perfection of Christ's sacrifice. That He did not pay half the price for our redemption, but He paid all of it when He said, "It is finished."[31] He drank every drop of the wrath of God for sins that was upon us, fully redeeming us from the curse.

When we see these truths, we begin to recognize that it is not about what we can do for Him, *but what He has done for us!* We cease to look to our own works or efforts to impress God, gain a status with Him, or achieve His favors; we see that we are complete in Christ and have access to the Father through the blood of Christ. John put it this way: "But as many as received Him, to them He gave the right to become children of God."[32]

---

[30] Charles Spurgeon, *All of Grace.* © 2008 Biblio Bazaar: pg. 36
[31] John 19:30, NKJV
[32] John 1:12a, NKJV

I like that. We have *the right* through Christ to be called the children of God. And because we are His children, we also have a right to our inheritance as children of God. Jesus Christ took the punishment for our sins, and therefore, we have a right to freedom, and to "righteousness and peace and joy in the Holy Spirit."[33]

WHAT DOES IT MEAN?

Now let's return to the key phrase that influenced this chapter: *fallen from grace*. When we make the object of our faith our performance or anything other than the cross, we have *fallen from grace*.

What, exactly, does this phrase mean? Does it mean we have backslidden into a damnable state? Not quite. I don't believe it speaks of salvation, as if we have fallen away from the faith and are hell bound. I believe it speaks of falling away from *the way of grace*. In other words, though we are trying to live for God, we have disconnected from the power source, and ultimately will not see the fruit of the Spirit in our lives.

It's like saying to a man who is rowing a sailboat, "You're not competing in *the way of the sailboat*." Surely the man will get some distance in his own strength, but will eventually run out of strength, and will eventually lose the race. He's still in the race, and still has full access to all the tools needed to race properly, but has "fallen from the sailing way."

It's like saying to a lumberjack who is trying to use a hacksaw on a redwood, "You are not working in *the way of the lumberjack*. You are now ineffective and useless to this company as long as you insist on functioning in this way."

Thankfully, we have the Church, the Scriptures, and the Holy Spirit, all three of which point the way back to grace, and all three of which God is working through to call us back to authentic Christian living — the way of grace.

---

[33] Romans 14:17, NKJV

CHAPTER 4
Discovering the Searching Heart of God

"For the Father is seeking such to worship Him."
—Jesus (John 4:23b, NJKV)

A quick glance at this remarkably profound statement by the Lord Jesus, and we learn two things about God and His nature: 1) He is a Father, and 2) He has a searching heart. Indeed, these two are one, for it is a father's heart that is the seeking heart. What father who has lost his child does not immediately bring his life to a screeching halt that he may dedicate himself entirely to finding the one he loves?

Until the believer understands these attributes of God, he cannot fully experience all that God has given through Christ. It is impossible to grasp discipleship by grace without grasping the nature of God. Central to every grace conversion is looking into the eyes of the Judge and finally seeing a Father. Michael Cavanaugh said, "Without a revelation of God's love, it's impossible to walk in any level of victory." Indeed it is. Grace causes you to see that God acted first, reaching for you when you were helpless to reach for Him; seeing this places your confidence solely in what God has done for you through the cross, not what you can do for Him; soon the eyes of the heart are opened by grace to who you are in Christ; who you are in Christ is a loved child of God; seeing your sonship causes you to see the Father; seeing the Father causes you to see and access your inheritance; seeing your inheritance causes you to walk in your destiny. I've noticed all these truths being intertwined. There is a system of truths and doctrines that grace weaves together.

So when you look at God, do you see a Father or Judge?

Do you believe that you found God (or must still find Him), or that God found you?

THE SEARCHING GOD

A.W. Tozer called it "the doctrine of prevenient grace," stating that "before a man can seek God, God must have first sought the man."[34]

I think that sometimes we get an idea that God is off in heaven somewhere, completely disinterested in us, and that if we'll pray loud enough and long enough, maybe we'll get His attention. Yet this is not the God that is described in the Bible.

The Bible paints a picture of a God who is more interested in us than we are in Him; a God who is looking for us *harder* than we've ever looked for Him. Consider these verses:

> "*For the eyes of the Lord run to and fro throughout the whole earth, to show Himself strong on behalf of those whose heart is loyal to Him.*" (2 Chronicles 16:9a, NKJV)

> "*For the Son of Man has come to seek and to save that which was lost.*" (Luke 19:10, NKJV)

> "*For the Father is seeking such to worship Him.*" (John 4:23b)

Over and over again, the Bible paints a picture of a searching, seeking God. Even back in the garden of Eden, when Adam and Eve fell from grace, God came into the garden looking for Adam, and called out, "Where are you, Adam?"

Ashamed of his nakedness, Adam hid from the presence of the Lord.[35]

I believe that God has been calling out to mankind ever since. And here we see the truth of it, that God has sought for man long before we sought for Him. Perhaps the entire Old Testament is the story not of man's journey to find God, but God's journey to find man. Tirelessly, patiently, relentlessly, God has pursued man. His journey led Him right to a cross, where finally a Way was made for God to pour out His love upon lost mankind.

---

[34] A.W. Tozer, *The Pursuit of God* (Camp Hill, Pennsylvania: Christian Publications). © 1982, 1993 by Christian Publications, Inc., p. 11
[35] Genesis 3:9-10

GOD HUMBLED HIMSELF

Elim Bible Institute teacher Sylvia Evans once said that God humbled Himself in three ways for mankind. First, God became a man. Isn't that enough of a demonstration of His love? But He didn't stop there. Second, He was born in a manger. God, the Designer of Life, could have come to earth any way He wished! But He did not come as high priest, the Emperor of Rome, or a son of nobility. He was born next to donkeys and goats. Isn't that enough for man to see God's love? But He didn't even stop there. Third, He died the most humiliating, brutal death a man in that day could die: Crucifixion on a Roman cross. Why would God do this? So that no man on this earth can say, whether of high or low position, "He didn't come for me."

All of this reminds me of a time when I was six years old, and my parents took my siblings and me to a fireworks display at a local fairgrounds in Albany, New York. When the fireworks display ended, and the mob of humanity began to migrate back to its vehicles, my father left me in the crowd, thinking I was with my mother back at the car. But there I was, six, short, and scared in the middle of a sea of people. Paralyzed with fear, I stood and looked up at the giants. "Daddy?" I called out, but he was gone.

"Daddy!" I called out again, terrified and crying.

Soon, a kind old man came by and, seeing my poor state, asked me, "What's the matter, son?"

"I lost my Dad!" I explained through my tears.

"Aw," he said with compassion, "come on with me. I'll help you."

The old man took me to a small pavilion in the middle of the fairgrounds and introduced me to some people. They asked me my name, and moments later, an announcement went out over the PA system of the entire fairgrounds, "Would the father of Derek Levendusky please report to Lost and Found. We have your son!"

Here's my dad's side of the story. He, along with my siblings, meandered back to the car separately from my mother, who'd gone before him. When he got to the car, he asked my mother, "Where's Derek?"

"He was with you!" said my mother.

55

My father was stunned. "What? No! I thought he was with you!"

My father is normally a calm, quiet-natured, sometimes socially shy man who doesn't like to rock the boat—except on that day. Something primal took over my father, as he turned back toward the mob of people and screamed, "Dereeeeek!"

He rushed toward the crowd, pushing people, and knocking some of them out of the way, ever yelling my name: "Derek!"

Surely people wondered at how rudely he was acting, but he didn't care. He was looking for me.

There I was, back at the pole, looking out into the sea of people, whimpering my father's name: "Daddy! Daddy?" I wondered if he even knew if I was lost.

Suddenly, the crowd parted, and there was my father. Now, I may be exaggerating this a bit, but I think *Little House on the Prairie* music started just then over the PA, and in slow motion, I ran into my father's arms!

You see, on that hot summer night back in 1978, once my father realized I was lost, the rest of his life shut down. Only one thing mattered: finding me. He was looking for me the whole time. And he was searching for me harder than I was searching for him. Now I want you to understand this: God is like my Dad.

The moment man fell in the Garden, God's heart began to search for us as He called out, "Adam, where are you?" Then "the Lord God made garments of skin for Adam and his wife and clothed them" (Genesis 3:21, NASB). What had to happen for garments of skin to be made? An animal had to die. Do you see it? God was sending a message to humanity that it was already in His heart to send His own Son to the cross; the Lamb of God who would be slain for the sins of the whole world, and would cover our nakedness with His grace. The Father heart of God could not stand by. He would act.

GOD DID

There are many who would heap commandment after commandment, ritual after ritual, on the necks of Christ's followers, instructing them that such is the way to God. But one simple statement will annihilate such legalism.

> *"For what the Law could not do in that it was weak through the flesh, **God did** by sending His own Son in the likeness of sinful flesh..." (Romans 8:3a, NKJV)*

Do you see those two words? *God did*. It is not man who made, or will ever make, the way to God, but *God did*. God made the way Himself to man. He found us. He reached out to us. He did the work for us. He did it. God saw the absolute helplessness of man and scaled the walls we could not, being so *weak*.

There are many who would consider themselves seekers, and they will tell of their great efforts through prayer, fasting, and studying of Scripture to "find God." But He doesn't need to be found. We do. We must first understand the nature of God, that He is the Ultimate Seeker. Any true passion, devotion, or determination we have is due to the simple fact that we have become partakers of His divine nature.[36] If we are seekers, it's because He lives within us. When we seek Him, we are only becoming more like Him! We "find" Him when He finds us accepting our helpless state, and depending on His all-sufficient grace for our pursuit of Him.

We cannot even begin this journey without a spark of His grace to light the fires of faith and passion. As Jesus taught us in John 6:44, "No one can come to Me unless the Father who sent me draws him, and I will raise him up at the last day."

Is this grace available to all men? Some may debate this until Jesus returns, but suffice it to say that if Jesus sent His followers into all the world to preach the gospel to every creature, then every creature who hears is a candidate for grace.

The one who will not see God as the First Seeker, and the One who grants us grace to seek Him, will never experience a true divine passion for knowing Him. That one is only left with the helplessness of His own flesh to reach out to God, and is incapable

---

[36] 2 Peter 1:4

of sustaining true spiritual fervor for God. The one thing we can do is *depend* on God's grace and power.

The paradox is remarkable, isn't it? To find Him, He needs to find us first. To run after Him, we must rest in our faith. To seek Him fervently, we must earnestly embrace our helplessness to do so. To achieve godliness, we must perceive lowliness. To obey relentlessly, we must depend endlessly.

THE GOD OF THE FAR OFF ONES

In Ephesians 2:13, Paul wrote, "But now in Christ Jesus you who once were far off have been brought near by the blood of Christ."[37]

Paul is writing here to Gentile believers, describing their condition throughout the chapter:

"aliens from the commonwealth of Israel"[38]
"strangers from the covenant of promise"[39]
"no hope"[40]
"without God in the world"[41]
"far off"[42]
"strangers"[43]
"foreigners"[44]

Paul is desperately trying to get the reader to understand how far off the Gentiles were from God. If God needed to redeem His own people Israel, how far away were the Gentiles, who were not counted among the promises of the Old Testament? This term "far off" basically denotes being as far away from its object as possible. The Gentiles were separated from God in *every* way: legally, spiritually, and ethnically. So far off were the Gentiles that they

---

[37] NKJV
[38] Ephesians 2:12, NKJV
[39] Ibid.
[40] Ibid.
[41] Ibid.
[42] Ibid.
[43] Ibid.
[44] Ibid.

were completely ignorant that God even was, and utterly disinterested in discovering if it was so!

All this begs the question, "Why would God be even remotely interested in anyone in this state?"

"Man's extremity is God's opportunity!" the great Welsh intercessor Rees Howells used to say.[45] God is most glorified when He chooses to redeem the most desperate, the most foolish, the most hopeless, and the weakest among us.

Why do you think that God chose the most unlikely and unqualified to do His exploits? People like Gideon the Afraid, David the Small, Peter the Sinful, Deborah the Hesitant, and Moses the Murderer. God is most glorified in our weakness.

Why do you think God allowed His people to find themselves in the most desperate of circumstances? Like the Israelites at the Red Sea; like Gideon and his 300 men against tens of thousands of Midianites; like twelve frightened disciples against a world system that just crucified their leader! God is most glorified in our weakness.

Why do you think God chose a tormented soul like Martin Luther to lead the Reformation? A simple man like George Muller in England to feed the mouths of ten thousand orphans? A weak old woman in India named Teresa to inspire the world? God is most glorified in our weakness.

And finally, why do you think Jesus quoted this passage in Isaiah about His ministry?[46]

> *"The Spirit of the Lord is upon Me, because He has anointed Me to preach the gospel to the poor; He has sent Me to heal the brokenhearted, to proclaim liberty to the captives and recovery of sight to the blind, to set at liberty those who are oppressed; to proclaim the acceptable year of the Lord." (Isaiah 61:1-2, NKJV)*

God is most glorified in our weakness.

---

[45] Norman Grubb, *Rees Howells, Intercessor.* © 1997 CLC Ministries.
[46] In Luke 4:17-21

According to this passage, who did Jesus come for? I see five kinds of people: the poor, the brokenhearted, the captives, the blind, and the oppressed. Now hear me well—unless you're one of those, this book has no message for you. And unless you're one of those, Christ Himself has no message for you.

So now we see why God chose you and me. He wants to be glorified in this generation! Paul wrote that God chooses the weak and foolish things of the world to shame the strong and the wise.[47] God wants to be glorified!

Author John Piper wrote, "The most passionate heart for God in all the universe is God's heart."[48] God knows that the greatest thing He can do for us, and for mankind, is to glorify His name in us, for when we worship God, we fulfill our greatest duty, and enjoy our greatest calling.

THE SPRINGHEAD OF WORSHIP

I want to deliberately provoke wonder and awe in you at God's amazing grace. I want to deliberately provoke you to passionate worship! Are these truths not among those that inspire the deepest love, the deepest gratitude, and the deepest worship? That God pursued us, while we were yet in sin and far off, to a cruel cross, and redeemed us from the curse!

John wrote, "We love Him because He first loved us."[49] He first loved us. This is the reason John had for giving worship to Him. God's choosing of us, God's love for us, *causes us* to love Him. The greatest case John could make for us to worship God was that God loved us first. A revelation of God's love opened up the fountains worship in John's life!

Jesus said, "You did not choose Me, but I chose you."[50] Search for a reason why God chose you and loved you. Go ahead and ponder it; search your heart, search your merit, mine your character and seek for a logical reason—you will find none. The

---

[47] 1 Corinthians 1:27
[48] John Piper, *Let the Nations Be Glad* (Grand Rapids, MI: Baker Academic). © 1993, 2003 by Desiring God Foundation, p. 21
[49] 1 John 4:19, NKJV
[50] John 15:16, NKJV

only place to land is thankfulness, praise, and worship for unmerited and unbounded grace!

Paul tells the Romans that "while we were still sinners, Christ died for us."[51] He goes on to say, "Much more then, having now been justified by His blood, we shall be saved from wrath through Him."[52] One of the great messages of Romans is that if God sought us and gave Himself for us when we were far off from Him, how much more should we have confidence that He will strengthen us *now that we believe!* How can we not worship Him? Here worship ceases to be a duty or command, and becomes an overflow of true thankfulness and wonder! This is where we understand that we don't *have* to worship Him, we *get* to. Since God loved us first, we love Him. Since God sought us, we seek Him.

---

[51] Romans 5:8b, NKJV
[52] Romans 5:9, NKJV

Discipleship by Grace

CHAPTER 5
Blessed Helplessness:
The Doctrine of Sin

*"God can do a lot with a little; He can do more with less;
and He can do everything with nothing."*
–Anonymous

One day, I wanted to teach my children about God's grace, and so I told them to go to the bottom of the staircase in our house. It was my three oldest daughters, Grace, Joye, and Esther. "If you can make it up the stairs," I told them, "I'll take you down to the store and buy you whatever candy you want." They confidently began their trek up the steps, and I stopped them. "Hang on," I explained, "you are not allowed to touch the walls or the steps."

They looked confused and somewhat dismayed because the candy, which for a moment had seemed so close, now seemed so far away. My daughter Joye tried to get a running start so she could leap up the steps. She didn't even make it halfway. Dismay turned to distraught as they talked and schemed, but could not come up with a solution, and desperately wanted the candy. "Daddy," they finally said, "there's no way to do it!"

"Yes, there is," I insisted. "Why don't you pray now and ask God for wisdom?"

They joined hands and prayed fervently. After all, candy was in the balance. Suddenly, almost as if I could see the Holy Spirit speak to Gracie, she looked up at me and smiled. "Daddy," she asked, "can you come down here and carry me up the stairs?"

I smiled back. "Yes!" Then I walked down the steps, lifted up my daughter, and carried her up the steps to the top. She did not touch the walls or the steps.

"Daddy!" Joye called. "Can you carry me?"

I carried her up. She did not touch the walls or the steps.

Then Esther.

"Don't ever forget this," I told them. "This is a picture of God's grace at work in your life. You are helpless to complete the journey yourself, but He will carry you!"

This is why a revelation of our helplessness must precede a revelation of grace. If we will disciple by grace, we must understand and teach these things. Before we look at the how, my hope is to convince your heart that these truths are as sure as the sky is blue.

DO THE THINGS YOU DID AT FIRST

When I walked through the wilderness season, I asked the Lord to help me understand this passage: *"Yet I hold this against you: You have forsaken your first love. Remember the height from which you have fallen! Repent and do the things you did at first."* (Revelation 2:4-5)

"Lord," I prayed, "what are 'the things you did at first'?"

It was not long after that that I noticed my wife breastfeeding Esther, one of our daughters, when she was still a newborn. Little Essie flopped around, completely helpless, and at the mercy of her mother's strength, just like she had been since the day she was born. *Do the things you did at first.* Suddenly, it dawned on me. The first thing my daughter did when she was born was come out in a helpless state, and completely depend upon her mother.

Do the things you did at first.

I see it! The first thing we did when we came to Christ was fall helpless at his feet, like Mary Magdalene the prostitute, and depend fully on His grace! It is our helplessness that brings us to His grace.

To truly understand the power of grace, the depth of God's love, and the wonder of the cross, we must have a thorough understanding of two doctrines, the doctrines of sin and grace. I'd like to spend the next two chapters looking briefly at each one.

THE IMPORTANCE OF DOCTRINE

Maybe you're reading this, and you are young in the Lord or young in years, and are intimidated by words like "doctrine." I certainly have no desire or intention to talk over anybody's head (not even sure if I'm qualified to talk over anyone's head). I believe that it is essential for believers young and old to know what they believe, and if you will grasp the doctrines of sin and grace, you will be on your way to living a full and victorious Christian life! I wish I understood these things sooner than I did. Not understanding these truths led to defeat in my life.

When I was in college, a friend and mentor named Paul Brown challenged me to know what I believed. At first, I failed to see how important this was. Unfortunately, many Christians pooh pooh doctrine as if it's a cold thing left only for archaic institutions or lifeless fundamentalism. I could not disagree more. Paul said to Timothy, "Watch your doctrine closely."[53] Author Neil Anderson said, "Good doctrine precedes a good experience." [54]

There's a difference between understanding doctrine and being doctrinaire. God does not want us to be puffed up or religious, but He does want us to understand His Word.

How careful must we be to understand doctrine when Jesus Himself said that a little leaven leavens the whole lump? If we allow even a small amount of bad thinking or bad teaching to pollute our understanding of grace, we can destroy all spiritual life within! Furthermore, Peter warned that false teachers would operate among us.[55] That's right: radio, TV, books, DVDs, and the internet are inundated with teachers, and we'd be fools to think that false teachers—those who lead us away from grace—do not move among us.

So what do we believe about sin and grace? So let's take a look at these all-important truths. If you are secure in good doctrine, it does you well to review these pillars of truth.

GOD IS HOLY

To really understand the Doctrine of Sin, one has to have an appreciation for the holiness of God. Holiness is the absence of sin. That alone should explain why a fallen man is hopeless without Christ. Since God lives in the absence of sin, how can any one of

---

[53] 1 Timothy 4:16
[54] Neil Anderson is the author of *Victory Over Darkness* and *The Bondage Breaker*
[55] 2 Peter 2:1

us fellowship with God? If I bring *even one* sin into the presence of God, He no longer lives in the absence of sin! That's why James said, "For whoever keeps the whole Law and yet stumbles in one point, he has become guilty of all" (James 2:10, NASB).

A few years ago, I was asked to speak at a conference, and holiness was a large part of the topic I was asked to speak on. I felt that it would be important for me to define it during my message. For days I worked on it, tweaking it, altering it, tweaking it again, but I couldn't settle on a definition that did it justice. Finally, I complained in my heart to the Lord, "How am I supposed to define an indefinable word?"

Then I sensed the Lord smiling and say to me, "That's part of the definition."

Holiness is the indefinable and indescribable nature of God, encompassing His sinlessness, His power, and His glory. A.W. Tozer said this about the holiness of God:

> *"Neither the writer nor the reader of these words is qualified to appreciate the holiness of God. Quite literally a new channel must be cut through the desert of our minds to allow the sweet waters of truth that will heal our great sickness to flow in. We cannot grasp the true meaning of the divine holiness by thinking of someone or something very pure and then raising the concept to the highest degree we are capable of. God's holiness is not simply the best we know infinitely bettered. We know nothing like the divine holiness. It stands apart, unique, unapproachable, incomprehensible and unattainable... Holy is the way God is. To be holy He does not conform to a standard. He is that standard."*[56]

THE DOCTRINE OF SIN

In the early 20th Century, an English newspaper ran a column called "Daily Mail," and solicited responses from readers to the question, "What's wrong with the world?"

---

[56] A.W. Tozer. *The Knowledge of the Holy.* (San Francisco: Harper Collins, 1961), pp. 104-5.

Christian writer and apologist G.K. Chesterton wrote the following response:

Dear Sir,

I am.

Yours sincerely,

G.K. Chesterton

In Romans 7:18, Paul wrote, "For I know that nothing good dwells in me, that is, in my flesh."[57]

This is the starting point of understanding grace.

If you believe this verse, then you must believe that all good things come from God, and no good things come from you. As my personal motto goes: "Jesus is my everything and I am my nothing."

So then, crucial to embracing grace is embracing your own depravity without it. Without Christ, we are completely and absolutely hopeless, helpless, destitute, poor, blind, naked, dead, and any other word that would further help us to despair in ever trusting ourselves. We must see sin as a thing and not just a deed. It is something alive in us, rotting us to the core, and keeping us in bondage and prison without heaven's assistance.

Even Anton LaVey, founder of the Church of Satan, understood his unregenerate nature and bent toward sin. The only difference between LaVey and a Christian (in regard to the Doctrine of Sin) is that LaVey reveled in his sin. He said, "I've never presented myself as having spoken directly to Satan or God or being in touch with any sort of divinity or having any sort of spiritual mandate. I just feel that what I'm doing is part of my nature."[58]

---

[57] NASB

[58] "Sympathy For the Devil" by Lawrence Wright in a series on religious leaders entitled "True Believers" for the magazine *Rolling Stone*. *Rolling Stone* is the property of Straight Arrow Publishers, Inc.

A lot of teachers that call themselves "grace teachers" feel that including discussions on sin will undermine their message, and keep the hearer from confidently embracing grace. In fact, I recently heard that one well-known author and teacher refuses to mention even the word "sin" in his messages! This is a tragedy, as I believe that it's impossible to understand the Doctrine of Grace without first understanding the Doctrine of Sin. Grace doesn't make any sense without a deep conviction of sin. Furthermore, I believe that if grace teachers won't teach on sin, we leave the doctrine solely in the hands of fire-and-brimstone preachers and legalists. How truly tragic this is!

John Stott said, "Before we can see the cross as something done for us, we have to see it as something done by us."[59]

The plain truth is that you *cannot* understand grace without understanding sin. Grace *doesn't make sense* without a clear understanding of sin. Why call Christ "Savior" if you have nothing to be saved *from*? How tragic the times become when preachers deny the soul the sweetest joys of our faith by concealing and neglecting the truths that make our gospel such great news. The gospel will never be great news if it is not preceded by the *awful and dreadful* news that mankind is fallen and "the whole world lies in the power of the evil one" (1 John 5:19b, NASB).

One of the great rules of Bible study is, "If you want to know what the Bible says, find out what the Bible *also* says."

There are truths in Scripture that co-exist together. One without the other is incomplete. The truths synergize each other, creating power and life when the harmony of the two truths is understood. I've heard this concept called *binary truths.*

Sin and *grace* have such a relationship. When we understand these binary truths, finally the cross makes sense.

It all began in the garden of Eden, when Adam and Eve sinned after God had said, "Of every tree of the garden you may freely eat; but of the tree of the knowledge of good and evil you

---

[59] John Stott, *The Cross of Christ*, p. 63

shall not eat, for in the day that you eat of it you shall surely die."[60]

Now we know from the Bible story that neither Adam and Eve, nor mankind, died physically in that moment (though they eventually would), but their death was broader and more thorough than that. The curse of Sin killed us in every way. The Doctrine of Sin may be understood in five ways:

1. The death of our position before God

We are no longer children of God, but children of wrath,[61] aliens and strangers,[62] and unknown by the One that matters most.[63] A million good deeds can't change the fact that we are not members of God's family. We are positionally eliminated from His household. Do you think that you would be a member of my family if you came to my house and did some housework? Of course you wouldn't. So how do you become a member of my family? By being born, adopted, or married into my family. That's why Jesus said we must be "born again."[64] It doesn't matter how many chores you do around God's house — singing in the choir, sweeping the floor, or putting money in the offering — you must be born into His family spiritually, because as things stand without Christ, you are dead.

2. The death of our innocence

We are lawbreakers guilty of death.[65] No man can stand before God and call himself righteous or holy. There are no good people in heaven, just forgiven people. Even the best of saints apart from Christ are filthy in His eyes. The Scripture says, "There is no one righteous, not even one" (Romans 3:10, NIV).

Yes, that includes you.

---

[60] Genesis 2:16a-17, NKJV
[61] Ephesians 2:1-3
[62] Ephesians 2:19
[63] Matthew 7:23
[64] John 3:3
[65] Romans 3:20-23

"God gives you the same grace He gives prostitutes and addicts," preaches friend and speaker Darrell Scott.[66] So in God's eyes, without Christ, none of us is any different than a prostitute, an addict, or serial killer. We all stand guilty before God and need grace.

It reminds me of a story I read from a revival that happened in Africa in the early 1900's. There was an old saintly African man walking up a hill to a church meeting when he turned and saw next to him what looked like Jesus carrying a huge weight on His back. The old man knew it was Jesus, and said, "Jesus! Are you carrying the weight of the world's sin up this hill?" Jesus said to the old man, "No, just yours."

Hell is not unfair, but is the logical and righteous consequence for every one of us. As I've stated before, God is holy and by definition holiness is the absence of sin. How can any one of us claim the right to stand by His side in heaven based on our own merits? One sin would corrupt holiness and make it unholy. Our crimes against God's laws only leave one option: We are worthy of eternal separation from God.

3. The death of our nature

We have no good thing in our flesh, but are spiritually bankrupt. Many people, when they think of sin, begin to think of what bad things they might have done within the last week. But the Bible teaches that our hearts are desperately sick beyond understanding.[67] Therefore, sin is not an incident, but a state; a condition. Our DNA is corrupt. We are habitual sinners and cannot stop sinning without a miracle of the heart. Even the one who claims to have achieved a righteous state externally would be embarrassed if his thoughts were broadcast on the wall for all to see, for even our thoughts cannot escape the symptoms of our nature. The gospel message, then, does not call a man to "do better" but raises him from the dead.

---

[66] Darrell is the father of Rachel Scott who was killed in the Columbine school shootings of 1999.
[67] Jeremiah 17:9

70

4. The death of our strength

Without Christ, man is helpless and hopeless to change or save himself. Jesus taught in the Beatitudes, "Blessed are the poor in spirit, for theirs is the kingdom of heaven."[68] To be poor in spirit is to recognize the poverty of one's own condition. This verse might be read, "Blessed are those who recognize their helplessness."

Could Jesus be more clear than when He said, "Without me you can do nothing"?[69]

Our only hope is a dying and resurrected Savior.

5. The death of our bodies

Adam and Eve eventually died physically.

If we are free from the curse of the Law, then why do our bodies still die? Death is a punishment for sin, and we are no longer under sin, so why must we die?

We must understand the scope of salvation. The Scripture teaches that we are saved, are being saved, and shall be saved, all at the same time. The Holy Spirit makes us fully confident that we *are* saved, for 1 John 3:2 says, "Beloved, *now* we are children of God." Then the Scriptures teach that we *are being* saved, as 1 Corinthians 1:18 says, "For the word of the cross is foolishness to those who are perishing, but to us who *are being* saved it is the power of God."[70]

Finally, the Scriptures teach that *we shall be* saved, as Matthew 10:22 teaches that "the person who endures to the end *will be saved*." And Romans 8:23 says, "And not only this, but also we ourselves, having the first fruits of the Spirit, even we ourselves groan within ourselves, waiting eagerly for our adoption as sons, the redemption of our body."

What's the point? Our salvation is a settled issue in the heart of the Father, so we are fully saved in essence, though in the process of salvation, our salvation is not complete. We have received the deposit of our salvation in the Holy Spirit's

---

[68] Matthew 5:3
[69] John 15:5, NKJV
[70] NASB

indwelling,[71] though our bodies are still under the curse of the fall and will die. Yes, God is able to work in these bodies, but pending Christ's return, these bodies will eventually die. One day, we will be given glorified bodies, and the final enemy of Death will be destroyed forever, completing the journey of our salvation. (Hallelujah!)

The appetites and tendencies of our natural bodies are still given to sin (sexual appetites, food, addictive substances, depression, chemical imbalances, etc.), and though we are responsible to have self-control and wisdom, these appetites and tendencies are not part of the new man in Christ. This is why Paul separated himself from his sin nature by saying in Romans 7:17, "So now, no longer am I the one doing it, but sin which dwells in me."[72] He understood that sin and death were working in the members of his body, and that the inner man being formed by Christ was an entirely different creature.

This is also why we will not be completely like Christ until we see him face to face.[73] Until these bodies die and are renewed, we are still facing residual symptoms of the Fall of Man.

DEAD

How do we summarize all this? Let me say this plainly. We are *dead*. "And you were dead in your trespasses and sins" (Ephesians 2:1). We do not need to improve our behavior. We need to be resurrected. We do not need to try harder. We need a miracle to change us into something we could never be on our own. For us, attempting to fulfill the Law in our own strength is no different than expecting a corpse to run a marathon.

God never took our merits into consideration when He gave Himself for us. It is precisely because we are dead that He acted. The cross would have been unnecessary had we been able to save ourselves.

---

[71] Ephesians 1:13
[72] NASB
[73] 1 Corinthians 13:12

I have a friend who had a person tell him, "Pastor, I just feel so hopeless!" He answered what he always does: "Friend, you're not hopeless enough."

The "behave and pray" message is insufficient to save a dead man, seeing that a dead man is incapable of accomplishing anything. We need more than willpower. We need the miracle of divine regeneration.

GETHSEMANE

So there Jesus was, in the Garden of Gethsemane, confronted with the reality that man was dead and could not redeem Himself, and that He alone — the sinless One — could sacrifice Himself for our sins. He alone could bear the wrath of God for sins, and make a way to the Father. He was in agony when He prayed, "O My Father, if it is possible, let this cup pass from Me; nevertheless, not as I will, but as You will."[74] He came back only moments later and said, "O My Father, if this cup cannot pass away from Me unless I drink it, Your will be done."[75]

Here we see two things. First, if there were another way to the Father apart from the sacrifice of Christ on the cross, surely God the Father would have spoken up then, when Jesus said, "If it is possible..." But God did not speak up. His silence should teach us one thing: *That it was not possible.* Jesus is the only way to the Father! Many unbelievers (and maybe even believers) are angry that the Bible makes this claim. Yet they criticize from the presumption that mankind *deserves* to go to heaven. After seeing the depraved state of man I've described, we should all see that no one *deserves* to go to heaven or to have a relationship with God.

The world thinks it has a right to be angry that anyone would claim that Jesus is *the* way, but what the cross teaches us is to rejoice that there is *a* way! That there is any way at all to the Father should cause us to live in ceaseless praise, not dark suspicion! These fleshly suspicions, criticisms, and objections all stem from total ignorance of the Doctrine of Sin. Not understanding these

---

[74] Matthew 26:39, NKJV
[75] Matthew 26:42, NKJV

things will keep us from understanding the cross or God's grace at all.

Second, we see that Jesus was willing to drink "the cup" of the cross. What was the cup? Was it the pain of whips, thorns, and nails? I don't believe so. Author and pastor C.J. Mahaney wrote, "In this garden, our Savior is beginning to confront as never before the ultimate and deepest agony of Calvary—an agony that will go infinitely beyond any *physical* suffering..."[76]

He later writes, "This cup contains the full vehemence and fierceness of God's holy wrath poured out against all sin, and we discover in Scripture that it's intended for all of sinful humanity to drink. It's your cup...and mine."[77]

Finally, Mahaney concludes, "That's why there's shuddering terror and deep distress for Him at this moment. In the crucible of human weakness He's brought face to face with the abhorrent reality of bearing our iniquity and becoming the object of God's full and furious wrath."[78]

Seeing our hopeless and miserable condition; seeing the terrible eternal danger we were facing; seeing God's righteous judgment and wrath for sin will help us see the beauty of the cross. "The glory of the gospel is this," says R.C. Sproul, "The One from whom we need to be saved is the One who has saved us."[79]

GRACE ACTS FIRST

If what I've written in this chapter is true; if we are dead without Christ, and if "nothing good dwells in me, that is, in my flesh,"[80] then if we will do *anything* to please God, grace must act first. What can a dead man do? *Without Jesus we can do nothing.* Anything good that we think, do, choose, or plan is preceded by an act of grace by a loving God that draws us into it.

---

[76] C.J. Mahaney, *Christ Our Mediator,* (Sisters, Oregon: Multnomah Publishers, Inc.) © 2004 Sovereign Grace Ministries, p.53.
[77] C.J. Mahaney, *Christ Our Mediator,* (Sisters, Oregon: Multnomah Publishers, Inc.) © 2004 Sovereign Grace Ministries, p.54.
[78] C.J. Mahaney, *Christ Our Mediator,* (Sisters, Oregon: Multnomah Publishers, Inc.) © 2004 Sovereign Grace Ministries, p.55.
[79] R.C. Sproul, *Saved from What?* (Wheaton, Illinois: Crossway Books, 2002), p. 109.
[80] Romans 7:18, NASB

John 1:16 says, "And of his fulness have all we received, and grace for grace." What comes before we can walk in grace? An act of grace by God to empower us to receive grace. God gives us *grace for grace*. God is beginning of every good thing in our lives!

It's like little Simba in the movie *The Lion King*. When confronted by hyenas in the elephant graveyard, he begins to growl in the cute tone that wouldn't frighten a rabbit. The hyenas laugh. On his second attempt, a monstrous roar resounds throughout the fray, and the hyenas cower in fear. For a moment, Simba thinks it's he who frightens his enemies, but what he doesn't know is that his father Mufasa is standing just over his shoulder, ready to demolish his enemies. The glory belonged to Mufasa, and not little Simba!

Likewise, so many times, we think it's our effort or our performance or our strength. But what we can't see is the King of Kings standing just over our shoulder. The battle belongs to the Lord!

Grace.

In the next chapter, we'll look at this powerful doctrine, and let our hearts burn within us as we visit this holy place.

"Grace is the very opposite of merit...Grace is not only undeserved favor, but it is favor shown to the one who has deserved the very opposite."
—Harry Ironside[81]

---

[81] Harry Ironside (1876-1951) was a Canadian-American Bible teacher, preacher, pastor, and author.

CHAPTER 6
God Accepts Christ:
The Doctrine of Grace

"Grace takes its rise far back in the heart of God, in the awful and incomprehensible abyss of His holy being; but the channel through which it flows out to men is Jesus Christ, crucified and risen." — A.W. Tozer[82]

R.C. Sproul pondered in his writings that the most perplexing theological question is not why there's suffering in this world, but why God tolerates us in our sin. More so, why would God allow sinners, who by Law deserve death, to be with Him forever? There's only one reason: *Grace.* Why are we not all dead? *Grace.* Why does God accept me? *Grace.*

Grace says:

"I'm complete in Christ."

"I cannot add to the cross."

"The cross was enough to save me to the uttermost."

"I can never perform enough for God, but His performance was enough for me."

"I did not choose Him; He chose me!"

"I am acceptable to God because of the work of Jesus on the cross."

Not too long ago, I had a dream that I was witnessing to an unbeliever who insisted he didn't need to follow Jesus because, he said, "God loves me like I am, and He accepts me as I am." That's when I said something to him in my dream that I'd never thought of before. I said emphatically, "God does not accept *you,* He accepts *Christ!*"

I woke up and realized how biblical this is, as the Scripture came to mind that says, *"To the praise of the glory of His grace, wherein He hath made us accepted in the Beloved"* (Ephesians 1:6).

---

[82] A.W. Tozer. *The Knowledge of the Holy.* (San Francisco: Harper Collins, 1961), Chapter 19: "The Grace of God"

God is not drawn to you or me! He's only drawn to Jesus Christ within us — *the hope of glory!*[83]

In the Old Testament sacrificial system, the high priest would enter the Holy of Holies to meet with the *shekinah* glory of God before the ark of the covenant. On the lid of the ark were two seraphims (angels) facing each other with their wings stretched out toward one another. Their eyes were looking down at the lid, where the high priest would sprinkle the blood of a lamb. This was called "the mercy seat." Look at what God said about the mercy seat:

> *"And there I will meet with you, and I will commune with you from above the mercy seat, from between the two cherubim which are on the ark of the testimony, of all things which I will give you in commandment to the children of Israel." (Exodus 25:22, NKJV)*

There, on the mercy seat, between the seraphims, God's shekinah presence would manifest. What was the presence of God drawn to? *It was the blood of the Lamb!* What were the eyes of the seraphim looking at? *The blood of the Lamb.*

God accepts Christ.

There are many in the Christian faith, however, who continue to look to their own merits and not the blood of Christ, their own works as a basis for approaching God. In fact, some of those who are working the hardest to please God feel the farthest from Him! Why? The Jealous One will not give His glory to another. He will not allow you or me to receive the credit for our relationship with Him.

There are also many in the Church that continue to struggle with a confidence in the love of God. It seems so elusive to them. One day, when we've spun all the plates of prayer, Scripture memorization, and Bible study, we feel good. Another day, a few of the plates crash to the ground, and we feel condemned. But I believe that a deep understanding of the love of God comes from a

---

[83] Colossians 1:27

deep understanding of the cross of Christ. To truly understand the cross, we must understand Sin and Grace.

Now we've looked at the grotesque disease of Sin, and we've seen the ravages of sin upon the body, soul, and spirit. We've looked at death. Now grace makes sense. Now the cross makes sense. The object of our faith will become very clear, very necessary, and very worthy of our absolute trust. It is the believing of His strength in grace that is the essential revelation of the Christian life. I believe the Doctrine of Grace may be understood in four ways:

1. The penalty of sin is broken

"The righteousness of Christ" is ours and we no longer have to face the charges of our crimes.[84] It's as if all the righteousness in Christ's bank account was transferred to yours the moment you believed!

In the fiction I wrote called *The King's Secret,* moments after the orphan Jane of Aldengate is sentenced to death, the king bursts into the courtroom, and announces that he is implementing "The Posterity Law"—a law originally created for kings to give themselves in exchange for the crimes of their children to preserve the royal posterity. King Noel announces that he will give his life for the orphan girl Jane. The judge tells the guards to remove Jane's chains and put them on the king.

So it is with Christ.

He has chosen to implement the "The Posterity Law" and the King of Kings has given Himself for you, removing the penalty for your sins and the chains that bound you as a prisoner.

2. The power of sin is broken

Romans 6:22 says, "But now that you have been set free from sin and have become slaves to God, the benefit you reap leads to holiness, and the result is eternal life."[85]

The divine nature works inside of us now, giving us victory over our sinful natures (2 Peter 1:4). Commentary writer Kenneth

---

[84] 2 Corinthians 5:21
[85] NIV

Wuest called it "The Double Cure": the penalty *and* power of sin are broken! [86]

Evangelist and Bible scholar A.W. Pink once said, "The nature of Christ's salvation is woefully misrepresented by the present-day evangelist. He announces a Savior from hell rather than a Savior from sin. And that is why so many are fatally deceived, for there are multitudes who wish to escape the Lake of Fire who have no desire to be delivered from their carnality and worldliness." [87]

God wants us free from the power of sin in every way — inwardly and outwardly.

When I say that the power of sin is broken, I do not mean that sin is *absent*, for until we see Jesus, our being fully conformed to Him will not be complete. [88] When Paul speaks of being dead to sin, [89] he was not speaking of death of the sin nature itself, but death to our *relationship* to sin. Sin is no longer our master, [90] or has mastery over us, but we gain dominion over it. There is the presence of both the sin nature and the divine nature, God's divine power in us dominating our sinful tendencies and appetites.

Imagine that you were part of a crew on a ship that was controlled by a cruel captain who had unjustly taken the ship to sea. This captain mistreats you and the other crew members, physically and verbally abusing you, forcing you into hard labor. One day, a new captain ambushes the ship and takes control, throwing the cruel captain into the dungeon below. You can still hear the old captain shouting, but he is no longer in control.

The Bible says, "For sin shall not be your master, because you are not under law, but under grace" (Romans 6:14, NIV). The old captain is no longer our master. He is not dead, but our relationship to him has changed. He is no longer our master.

---

[86] Kenneth Wuest's commentary on The Book of Romans, © 1961 Wm. B. Eerdmans Publishing Co.
[87] A.W. Pink, "The Nature of Christ's Salvation Misrepresented by the Present-day 'Evangelist'"
[88] 1 Corinthians 13:12
[89] Romans 6:11
[90] Romans 6:14

Romans 8:2 describes it a different way. It contrasts a battle between "the law of sin and death" and "the law of the Spirit of life in Christ Jesus." The word "law" here does not speak of a law like an Old Testament law, or legal regulation, but speaks of an *inward working principle.* In other words, instead of habitual sinning, we become habitually holy.[91] There is a coexistence of two laws that are in direct contrast to each other, the law of the spirit of life in Christ Jesus being superior to the law of sin and death, much like the law of aerodynamics and the law of gravity. The laws of gravity and aerodynamics coexist, but the law of aerodynamics "trumps" the law of gravity. For further discourse on the laws of gravity and aerodynamics, ignore the author, whose knowledge on the topic is comparable to an aardvark's knowledge of music theory. I still look up in the sky at airplanes and ask my wife, "How do they do that?"

When you find someone who is living a victorious Christian life over sin, the world (and sometimes the Church) will likewise look at that one and wonder, "How do they do that?"

3. The position of sin is broken

We have become children of God and can enjoy our inheritance in Christ (Galatians 4:6-7, Ephesians 1:18). I suppose I'll have to call it "The Triple Cure": the penalty, power, and position of sin are broken!

Scripture makes it clear this wasn't always the case. Paul teaches us that we were once "children of wrath."[92] We were objects of God's holy judgment. How could those born in sin fellowship with a God who is Himself the essence of purity and holiness? Christ's blood made a way. The wrath and judgment were poured out on Christ, executed on our behalf. As I mentioned in an earlier chapter, John describes our position before Christ as a *right* to those who believe on Jesus:

---

[91] From author and speaker Neil Anderson, excerpt from video series on the book of Ephesians.
[92] Ephesians 2:3

> *"But as many as have received Him, to them He gave the right to become children of God, to those who believe in His name." (John 1:12, NKJV)*

So the greatest promise of the New Testament becomes not riches, mansions, or even eternal life, but *access to God*. This is the great treasure of our inheritance.

At the end of the Civil War, there was a soldier who had a problem only the President could fix. So the soldier went to the White House in an attempt to see Abraham Lincoln, but he was denied access at the gate. Dejected, he sat on a nearby bench and wept. Soon, a little boy came by and saw the soldier crying. When he asked the soldier what concerned him, the soldier poured out his soul to the young listening ear. After hearing his story, the boy had compassion and said to the man, "Follow me!"

The soldier followed the boy right through the White House gate, past the guards, and right into the White House! The boy barged into the Oval Office, and Abraham Lincoln turned and asked the boy, "Yes son, how can I help you?"

"Father," said Abraham Lincoln's son, "this man needs your help."

Like Abe Lincoln's son, believers in Christ have access to the Father! Yes, now we have become His children, and we can approach His throne with confidence![93] We have access to His presence; we can enjoy Him, walk with Him, talk with Him, know Him. We have access to an inheritance reserved for His children;[94] to righteousness, peace, and joy in the Holy Ghost,[95] to deliverance from our enemies,[96] to healing,[97] to the love of God,[98] to freedom.[99] These things belong to you in Christ. You must grasp this: Because you are a child of God, and because of the

---

[93] Hebrews 4:16
[94] Ephesians 1:18
[95] Romans 14:17
[96] 1 John 3:8
[97] Luke 4:18
[98] Romans 8:39
[99] Galatians 5:1

blood of the sacrificial Lamb, *you have a right* to your inheritance in Him!

If you were contacted by a lawyer who told you that your rich uncle left you a million dollars in his will, wouldn't you want it? What if the lawyer told you that though it was yours, someone stole it. Wouldn't something rise up in you that says, "I will get back what is mine!" How much more your inheritance in Christ? You have a right to it and someone is trying to steal it.

The greatest part of our inheritance is the ability and privilege of knowing God. He Himself becomes our greatest reward. As pastor and author Michael Cavanaugh once said, "The One who knows me the best loves me the most." Unending Love; stubborn, relentless, unwavering, unconditional, ever-present Love! What a God! What a Savior! Can I say it better than John when pondering the riches of our position in Christ?

> *"Behold what manner of love the Father has bestowed on us, that we should be called children of God!" (1 John 3:1a, NKJV)*

4. The presence of sin shall be broken

Finally, with a hearty "Hallelujah!" I want to tell you that one day, thanks to Christ's work on the cross, even the very *presence* of sin shall be broken! Since "we have become the righteousness of God in Christ" (2 Corinthians 5:21), we shall live "in the beauty of holiness." As I've said, holiness is the absence of sin. Therefore, we will no longer have to battle sin. It will be done away with the old man, and only the new man in Christ shall live. What a day that will be! No more struggling with fear, or lust, or hatred, or depression, or sorrows!

I suppose I'll have to adjust my vocabulary one more time and call it "The Quadruple Cure." His grace truly is amazing!

DEFINING GRACE

So how do we finally define grace? That might be important to clarify as we continue a book together called *Discipleship by Grace!*

After reviewing the truths of grace in this chapter, I think we can see that grace has a two-part definition. The first part is what most people would quote when asked to define grace: *unmerited favor*, that God showed us mercy and love while we were yet in sin. The second part, however, is rarely understood: *unmerited power*. So, for example, grace isn't simply the kindness of God to pardon sin (unmerited favor), but it's the empowerment to stop sinning (unmerited power). It's not just forgiveness for losing your temper, it's power over your temper.

Author Jerry Bridges put it this way: "Grace...expresses two complementary thoughts: God's unmerited favor to us through Christ, and God's divine assistance to us through the Holy Spirit."[100]

Friend and author Rick Mills says, "Sometimes people confuse mercy and grace when they say something like, 'By God's grace, my sins are not held against me.' In reality, it's His mercy. God's grace is power to overcome the world."

In a sentence, grace is God's unrelenting and unmerited love, favor, and power for His children. My hope for the rest of this book is to examine the depths and heights of amazing grace, to show its fruits in our lives, and to see how it affects every area of the Christian life.

PUT ON THE LORD JESUS CHRIST

You may be asking, "If we have received such a great deliverance, then why are so many Christians living defeated? Why am *I* living defeated?"

Just believe.

God has not been deficient in supplying all that we need for life and godliness.[101] In fact, He has already supplied it in Christ. We must apply it to our lives. The Bible tells us to "put on the Lord Jesus Christ" (Romans 13:14).

---

[100] The Practice of Godliness, NavPress, 1996, p. 98-99. Used by permission of NavPress – www.navpress.com. All rights reserved.
[101] 2 Peter 1:3

If I gave you a tie and money to enjoy a nice restaurant, but you forgot your tie and cash, in my mind, I've met your need. You need to put on your tie and grab your wallet.

Put on the Lord Jesus Christ.

If I gave you a new car, and you never drove it, complaining to your friends that you had no way of getting around, you would be failing to see reality. You need to grab the keys and take advantage of what you have been given.

Put on the Lord Jesus Christ.

If you were treading water in the middle of the ocean and I threw you a life jacket, you would be wrong to continue to pray for a life jacket. You would need to use what I've provided.

Put on the Lord Jesus Christ.

God has made the way through Christ for us to live confident and victorious Christian lives.

GRASPING GRACE

I recently shared a message on grace to a group of young missionary leaders, and one young man came up and said, "I loved every word, and hated every word."

Grace does have that effect, doesn't it? It offends the flesh, and inspires the spirit.

Paul wrote of this phenomenon, "But I, brethren, if I still preach circumcision, why am I still persecuted? Then the stumbling block of the cross has been abolished" (Galatians 5:11, NASB).

When someone hears the message of grace, the flesh will be provoked to doubt and anger. Why? Because the flesh wants to do all the work, and when our eyes are opened to grace, our flesh must bow to it. It makes us *stumble* and then makes us *humble*, because we realize that our merits or efforts alone won't achieve the standard. So God did it Himself.

Just after my grace conversion, I was talking to a close friend about God's amazing grace, and I could tell he knew he needed a revelation of grace, so he said to me, "Man, I've really got to try to get a hold of that!"

I smiled gently and said, "And there lies the problem, my brother. You're still *trying* when Jesus said, 'Only believe.'"[102]

THE GOSPEL OF DONE

Michael Cavanaugh says of the Doctrine of Grace, "So many are trying to live the gospel of *do* when true freedom comes in realizing that the New Testament teaches the gospel of *done*."

Not long ago, during family devotions, I wanted to teach my children this idea of *do* versus *done*, so I put a blanket on the family room floor, and told my children that the blanket was a ship, the carpet surrounding it the water. I knelt on the "ship" and began to cry out, "Dear God, please save me from drowning! I don't want to die!"

Then I asked my kids, "What's wrong with this picture?"

"Daddy," said my daughter Joye, "you're not drowning."

"That's exactly right!" I told her. "Yet this is how many Christians live their lives, constantly asking God to do something He's already done!"

Likewise, Paul Harvey, on his radio program *The Rest of the Story,* told the tale of a man who was convinced he was too sick to walk, and lay in his bed as a paralytic for over forty years. Finally, a doctor examined him and discovered that *there was nothing wrong with him.* It was all in his mind. How many believers live like this? Thinking they are defeated by sin, they live as slaves though Christ has already made them free!

Jesus didn't say, "It is almost done!" He said, "It is finished."

Oh, what wonderful and glorious words rang from the cross on that dark and beautiful night.

It is finished.

This is why the gospel is called *good news.*[103]

This is why Jesus came *to proclaim liberty to captives and freedom to prisoners.*[104]

The prison doors are open! They don't need to *be* opened. They *are* open! The work is done, and now we simply must believe

---

[102] Mark 5:36, NASB
[103] The word "gospel" literally means "good news."
[104] Isaiah 61:1

and walk by faith. We must be *transformed by the renewing of our minds.*[105] That's what I'd like to discuss in the next chapter, but first some thoughts on repentance.

REPENT AND BELIEVE

Mark 1:15 says, "The time is fulfilled, and the kingdom of God is at hand; repent and believe in the gospel."[106]

The Scriptures teach us to "repent and believe." Before we continue in this book, I want to deliberately provoke you to question your salvation and see if you are in grace, as the Scriptures teach us: "Test yourselves to see if you are in the faith; examine yourselves! Or do you not recognize this about yourselves, that Jesus Christ is in you-- unless indeed you fail the test?" (2 Corinthians 13:5, NASB).

Have you trusted in yourself, your works, your performance, or anything other than the cross of Christ for your salvation? If so, I want to encourage you to *despair* of any of those things ever saving you, or of you ever having any hope of saving yourself. Fix your hope completely on Christ, and repent of your self-sufficiency. Place your faith strictly, solely, and completely on Christ and Him crucified.

For those of you who are confident you have trusted in grace for your salvation, what about your sanctification? "Are you so foolish? Having begun by the Spirit, are you now being perfected by the flesh?" (Galatians 3:3, NASB)

I also want to deliberately provoke you examine yourself and see whether or not you have *fallen from grace.* If so, turn from your self-love, your selfish pride, your self-sufficiency and place all your hopes in the cross just as you did at the beginning.

If you are convicted, you must stop reading now and allow the Holy Spirit to minister to your heart and begin the grace conversion, for the rest of this book will be meaningless if you do not attach yourself to the Vine.

---

[105] Romans 12:2
[106] NASB

May we never again seek to lean on our own strength, trust in our own righteousness, strive in our own performance, or bow down at the altar of another idol.

May God give all of us grace for grace.[107]

"God welcomes me into His presence not on the grounds of my Christian progress, the depth of my knowledge, the amount of my activity, or the degree of my victory, but only by the blood of Jesus!"
— Michael Cavanaugh

---

[107] John 1:16

CHAPTER 7
Princes with Amnesia

*"And be not conformed to this world: but be ye transformed by the
renewing of your mind, that ye may prove what is that good,
and acceptable, and perfect, will of God."*
— Paul the Apostle (Romans 12:2, KJV)

*"But as many as received Him, to them He gave the right to become
children of God, even to those who believe in His name."*
— John the Beloved (John 1:12, NASB)

Being a father of five, I've become somewhat of an expert on
watching children's movies. A few years ago, my kids went
through a *Toy Story* phase, and I watched the movies multiple
times. There's a scene in Toy Story 2 where Woody meets up with
"Woody's Round Up Gang." The only problem is that Woody
didn't know he was part of "Woody's Round Up Gang." When the
old Prospector realizes this, he says to Woody, his grandfatherly
eyes full of pity, "Why, you don't know who you are, do you?"
One day, watching this film with my kids, God began to speak to
me about the Church. *You don't know who you are, do you?*

Not long ago, this story printed in *Newsweek*:

WEST VIRGINIA PRINCESS[108]

Sept. 25, 2006 issue- It's something that every little girl
fantasizes about ... that the phone will ring and the voice
on the other end of the line will tell her she's not the
lonely, gawky girl that she thought she was. That she is, in
fact, a princess.

And that's exactly what happened to Sarah
Culberson. In 2004, 28-year old Culberson, a biracial
woman who had been adopted by a white family in West

---

[108] Soukup, Elise, *Newsweek:* "West Virginia Princess"

Virginia as a baby hired a private investigator to find her biological father. (Her mother, she had been informed a few years earlier, had died of breast cancer.) The investigator called back within three hours; the information he yielded was a shocker: her father was a member of the ruling family of the Mende tribe in the Southern Province of Sierra Leone. She was, by birthright, a princess. "I just about fell off my seat," says Culberson, an aspiring actress who had trained in San Francisco. "I mean, a princess. To be totally honest, it was really cool."

Sarah was a princess even when she didn't know it. She was the daughter of a king, and yet it wasn't until she was 28-years-old that she finally learned the truth.

Likewise, you have the right to be called a child of God. You are worthy of being called a child of God because your worthiness is not based on you but on Jesus Christ and Him crucified! It is no longer based on what you do or how you feel.

Let's imagine that there is a foreign prince named Benjamin, and he journeys to New York City. Let's say that as he's getting off the plane, he hits his head and gets amnesia, forgetting who he is and where he's from. Now let's say that I'm walking in downtown New York and find poor Benjamin eating garbage in an alley, and I say to him, "Hey there! Prince Benjamin? What are you doing eating garbage in this alley? You're the son of a king!"

Let's say he said to me, "I'm the son of a king? A prince? I don't *feel* like a prince!"

Would he be any less the son of a king *because he didn't feel like it?*

Of course not!

His royal status should not be based on his feelings, but on the truth. He's the child of a king because reality says *it is so*. Truth is not based on his subjective emotions. Likewise, Jesus said, "You shall know the truth, and the truth shall make you free."[109]

---

[109] John 8:31, NKJV

Paul wrote that the believer should be "transformed by the renewing of your mind."[110]

What the New Testament teaches is that those who are in Christ are like princes and princesses with amnesia. When we come to the Father through faith in the blood of Christ, we need to learn, through Scripture, who we are. And then we live out who we are by faith.

So many believers are trying to learn what to *do* to be better Christians, but I am convinced that the Scriptures tell us what to *believe* before they tell us what to *do*. The *doing* will flow from the *believing*.

Let's go back to poor Prince Benjamin again. If Benjamin would *believe* what I told him—that he is a prince—then he would begin to *act* like a prince. He would stop eating garbage, come out of the alley, and begin to change the way he lives. The *doing* flows from the *believing*.

It is precisely here in this point I am making that many fall away from the faith. Some never learn who they are in Christ, and spend their whole Christian life trying to perform their way into the kingdom, striving to become what they already are. It is my prayer that more leaders would disciple by grace than by Law, teaching young believers who they are in Christ instead of teaching them how to behave. Discipleship, our own or others', is not merely reformation of behavior, but is the renewing of the mind!

Reforming behavior never changed anyone's heart. But a changed heart will reform behavior. Therefore, God deals with the heart and mind first, and then the doing becomes natural. That's why Paul wrote that "faith comes by hearing and hearing by the word of God" (Romans 10:17). We must hear the truth before faith is ignited that will enable us to truly live the Christian life.

Unfortunately, I find it far more common for leaders to base discipleship merely on a set of rules or behaviors. If grace is not the foundation of all Christian behavior, this only creates a

---

[110] Romans 12:1, NASB

performance-driven culture that drives the followers toward spiritual exhaustion, the leader toward control and domination.

There has never been more confusion than there is today about how to live the Christian life. False teachers are everywhere, as are ignorant teachers. I often find myself evaluating teachers by saying, "It's not what they said. It's what they didn't say."

This is precisely why we should all be students of the Word of God ourselves. We should all be self-feeding disciples so that we can recognize bad teaching, and filter all teaching through the truths of grace. Then we can stand fast.

When Paul tells us to stand fast,[111] I believe that he is teaching us that we should never allow the devil, false teaching, or even our own flesh, to steal away the confidence that we *are* God's children, and that we have become "the righteousness of God in Christ."[112] It is believing that when God brought us home, he didn't condemn us to the barn, but brought us to His table.

SONSHIP

After the Book of Acts, the focus is more on sonship than discipleship. The theme of the Scriptures becomes more about knowing who you are instead of what to do.

> *"And because you are sons, God has sent forth the Spirit of His Son into your hearts, crying out, 'Abba, Father!' Therefore you are no longer a slave but a son, and if a son, then an heir of God through Christ." (Galatians 4:6-7)*

Verses like these edify us and give us the confidence in who we are in Christ. But how confident should we really be? A quick glance at a few things in this verse will do well to encourage our faith.

First, I want us to understand this word *crying*. The original Greek word is *krazo,* and has no accurate translation because the word is actually *onomatopoeia*—a word that is spelled like it

---

[111] Galatians 5:1
[112] 2 Corinthians 5:21

sounds. Words like *BANG!* and *POW!* are onomatopoeia. *Krazo* is like that. It's actually the same word used for the croak of a raven. This should teach us the absolute confidence and passion we should have in calling God *Father*. There's nothing sheepish about it!

Second, we need to understand this word *Abba*. Preserved in the original Greek, this wonderful word appears here exactly as it was in the original Greek texts. *Abba*. Exactly as Christ Himself said it in the Garden of Gethsemane when He called out to His Father. *Abba*. This little word teaches us the intimacy of the relationship with God that we've been granted through Christ. Again, there is no precise translation for *Abba* so it's been preserved in its original form in the biblical text. It implies the intimacy of "Daddy" and the reverence and respect of "Father."

Recently, a friend of mine went to Israel, where he was on a beach, enjoying the sunny day, when a little boy went running after his father and called out, "Abba! Abba!"

There it is! *Abba* is the cry of a little child to his tender and strong father. This little boy provides for us the perfect picture of our relationship with our heavenly Father. Yet sometimes we have "religiousized" the word Father in our Christian rituals, disciplines, and traditions. With as much piety as we can muster, we say, "Our Father, Thou art in heaven on high, etc." Somehow, the term "father" has lost its impact on our hearts.

Evangelist D.L. Moody was sitting on the platform in one of his Chicago crusades waiting to preach, when a clergyman stood up to pray. "Almighty God," he began, "we know that Thou dost look upon us from Thy throne, and we beseech Thee to hear our petition. We cast ourselves on Thy mercy, and..."

At this point, D.L. Moody had enough. He walked across the platform, pulled on the clergyman's robe, and whispered, "Just call Him Dad and ask Him for something!"

During my grace conversion, I realized that I had religiousized the term "Father;" so to retrain my mind, I began to call God "Dad." It felt very awkward at first, but as the days went on, the Abba cry began to rise in my heart.

Finally, I want you to see that the above verse does not say, "Because you are sons, God has sent forth the Spirit of His Son into our hearts, and *now you can raise the dead.*" Or, "*...now you speak in tongues.*" Or, "*...now you preach the gospel.*"

None of that here.

The evidence of the Holy Spirit in the heart is a rich and deep inner confidence that we are children of God. So deep is the conviction that a cry comes out, croaking as unashamedly as a raven, "Daddy God! Abba Father!"

Misguided teachers would have us believe that the evidence is some great act or radical adherence to God's laws or some other thing, but the greatest evidence of your salvation is an inner *certainty* that you are God's child. It's called "the witness of the Spirit."[113]

It was precisely this *witness of the Spirit* that was the theme of the 18th Century Revival in England, led by John Wesley. When he experienced it at Aldersgate, he called it "a heart strangely warmed."

Wesley says, "The testimony of the Spirit is an inward impression on the soul, whereby the Spirit of God directly witnesses to my spirit, that I am a child of God; that Jesus Christ hath loved me, and given himself for me; and that all my sins are blotted out, and I, even I, am reconciled to God."[114]

SLAVE OR SON?

So are you a slave or son? I should probably rephrase that because we both know what God's Word says you are. Do you *feel* like a slave or a son? There is a great difference in the Christian experience between the one who walks as a slave versus the one who walks as a son. Here's a comparative list of slaves and sons.

Slaves	Sons
-Sleep in the barn	-Sleep in the house
-Eat in the shed	-Eat in the dining room
-Don't want to be there	-Belong there

---

[113] Romans 8:16
[114] Part of John Wesley's printed sermon "The Witness of the Spirit"

-Have to work for their status	-Are born loved
-Are afraid of the owner	-Play with the owner
-Are not intimate with the owner	-Know the owner intimately as father
-Work out of fear	-Work out of love
-Are not heirs, will inherit nothing	-Are heirs, will inherit everything
-Have no ownership in the business	-Share their father's business
-Reward comes from hard work	-Reward comes from relationship
-Work to be blessed	-Blessed, so they work
-Have limited or no access	-Have full access
-Do all under law	-Do all under grace
-Are religious	-Have relationship
-See God as Judge	-See God as Father

WORSHIP AT THE THRONE OF GRACE

These principles greatly affect our worship. I believe that God wants to move us from the song "Holy!" to the song "Daddy!"[115] He wants us to approach His throne with confidence as sons and daughters, on the basis of the blood of Jesus, and worship Him with great joy!

Wherever you find a church or movement that does not have a revelation of the Father heart of God, you only find the song, "Holy." And you often find depressed, discouraged, and exhausted Christians who are trying to hard to please God, but perpetually falling short. Often the worship services in these environments are like funeral services, or like the prophets of Baal cutting themselves to get God's attention. Where's the joy?

It grieves me when I'm in a church or conference where there is no joy or confidence in the worship. As children of God, we should be enjoying our heavenly Father as redeemed sons and daughters!

---

[115] Galatians 4:6-7

I get the picture that when we are in heaven, we'll all be worshiping God together with the angels, singing, "Holy, Holy, Holy is the Lord who was and is and is to come!" After a few millenniums, you or I will say, "Hey, wait! Listen to my song for Him!" And we'll begin to sing, "Abba! Father!" as the angels look on baffled, wondering what that's like.[116] We know God in a way the angels do not.

John wrote, "By this, love is perfected with us, so that we may have confidence in the day of judgment; because as He is, so also are we in this world" (1 John 4:17, NASB). How many people do you know that associate the word "confidence" with "Judgment Day"? Most would speak of fear, punishment, death, damnation, and hell. But to John ("the disciple Jesus loved"), he thought of "confidence." That's the work of grace in the heart, convincing us that we are children of God, that He would never hurt us, that we have access to His presence, and that we can come *boldly* with joy before Him.

A few years ago, I went to China along with my pastor and spent five days with forty leaders of the underground church in a remote setting. These leaders represented about half a million Christians. When worship began, I was very moved by the haunting minor melodies, and asked the interpreter there with us to translate the lyrics. "This one's about God's holiness," he told me. They began another song. "What's this one about?" I asked. "This one's about the fear of the Lord," he explained. Then they began another and he said, "This one's about trusting God in the midst of suffering."

After a few days of this, I asked the interpreter, "Do they have any songs about the Father heart of God?" He struggled to remember one.

During that time, the other minister on the trip with me was teaching a message called, "Hindrances to Receiving the Holy Spirit." One of the points he made was, "One of the reasons we don't receive the Holy Spirit is because we have a sense that, 'I am not worthy.'"

---

[116] 1 Peter 1:12

At this, the interpreter stopped translating, and said directly to my pastor, "Just so you know, this is the big one." Then he translated it and the room was filled with gasps and whispers. For days, these dear Chinese believers wrestled with this idea, and struggled to receive this teaching.

I also struggled with my concept of the Chinese believers. I always had the idea that the Chinese believers were spiritual giants, and spiritual superiors to the inferior faith of American Christians. But after this experience, I wrote in my journal, "My romantic picture of the Chinese church has fallen." Though they were superior and had a greater grace in the area of suffering and understanding whole-hearted Christianity, many of the movements like this one desperately needed a revelation of grace and the Father heart of God. Perhaps their communist system had given them a harsh view and model of leadership, and that affected the home and the church, where they struggled to see God as a tender, loving Father.

This deep sense of unworthiness, and view of God as the Lawgiver, greatly hindered their worship, and their ability to enter into a deeper experience with the Holy Spirit. Please pray for the saints in China, that they would have a great revelation of Abba.

FALSE HUMILITY

I think that sometimes we think that God is impressed when we cower in His presence, bemoaning our miserable condition as wretched sinners saved by grace. We cry "Holy" in our songs, and remind our arrogant hearts how miserable our sinful state really is. We hear the distant call to approach the "throne of grace with confidence,"[117] but stay afar, attempting to please the Lord with our humility.

Do you really think this pleases the Father?

This is not true humility, but false humility. The one who disqualifies himself because of his sins is unwittingly suggesting

---

[117] Hebrews 4:16

that the cross is enough to save him. He believes he must earn his standing with God. Such "humility" does not please the Father.

As a father of five children, what do you think would please me more on Christmas morning? — If my child accepts the gift I give to him, or if he rejects it, citing his poor behavior during the previous year? What blesses me as a father is when my son takes the gift, rips it open all the while grinning with anticipation, and then shrieks with excitement and joy as he sees what's inside!

God has offered us the gift of righteousness through the blood of His Son Jesus,[118] and through Him the right to be called children of God.[119] He has invited us to a place of intimacy and adoption. Do you think He is pleased when in the name of humility, after all He's done to make a way, you *reject* this gift?

On February 27, 1993, I asked my would-be wife, Heidi Jo, to marry me. I invited her to a place of intimacy in my life. What would bless me more: If she said, "No, I'm unworthy" or if she said, "Yes"?

God is blessed when we say *yes*, and accept His gift of adoption on the basis of the blood of Jesus, and don't reject it on the basis of our own unworthiness. Listen to what King David said: *"What shall I render to the Lord for all His benefits toward me? I will take up the cup of salvation, and call upon the name of the Lord"* (Psalm 116:12-13, NKJV).

What an interesting way to answer the question "What shall I render" with the answer, "I will
take." David recognized that what would bless the Father the most would be to *take* from Him the cup of salvation. Likewise, what blesses God most is that we believe His word and embrace sonship.

Neil Anderson said, "I believe that not understanding who you are in Christ is the source of every spiritual conflict."[120] I'm now convinced this is true. If we don't understand our sonship, we'll walk in condemnation, never knowing our inheritance in Christ and all the benefits and blessings we have as children of

---

[118] 2 Corinthians 5:21
[119] John 1:12
[120] Heard this quote in a video series by Neil Anderson called *Spiritual Warfare.*

God. Dear brothers and sisters in Christ, may God cure your amnesia and renew your mind. You are God's daughters and sons.

"I see that there is a place for us in Christ where we are no longer under condemnation, but where the heavens are always open to us."
—Smith Wigglesworth[121]

[121] Smith Wigglesworth, *The Teachings of Smith Wigglesworth: Ever Increasing Faith and Faith That Prevails.* © 2007 Wilder Publications.

CHAPTER 8
Dead Languages and Cliches

"The Holy Spirit's tangible presence is the evidence of justification by faith." —Randy Clark[122]

As I said in an earlier chapter, good doctrine precedes a good experience. It's not new or special revelations that save us, but the good old-fashioned tried and true doctrines of the faith. Paul wrote in Philippians 3:1, "Finally, my brethren, rejoice in the Lord. To write the same things *again* is no trouble to me, and it is a safeguard for you."[123]

As we look at church history, we'll find that all of the genuine and great moves of God were birthed and sustained by the preaching of the simple doctrines of our faith. It's not that they hadn't been preached or taught previously, but in revival, these truths come alive to the heart and transform massive numbers of hearers.[124] God uses His servants not to introduce a new profound truth as so many are attempting to do today, but He uses them to "say something true in a new way."[125] What I'm speaking about is preaching the gospel. I'm not referring to evangelistic messages spoken at a Billy Graham crusade, but the hallmark and pillar truths of our faith that make us who we are. Christian artist Rich Mullins once sang of these truths, "I did not make it, no, it is making me."[126]

This being the case, why are so many Christians running after signs and wonders, overly fascinated with peculiar manifestations like being "slain in the Spirit," gold dust or gold fillings, or chasing "the glory cloud"? Why are others running after the latest idea, attending conferences the current hot author or radio teacher

---

[122] A quote from a message Randy Clark preached at the EF Leader's Conference in May of 2007.
[123] NASB, emphasis added
[124] I look at some of these historical moves of God in the chapter titled "True Revival."
[125] From Michael Cavanaugh in his seminar *The Art of Biblical Preaching.*
[126] Rich Mullins song "Creed"

may be putting on? And why are so many Christians and even some preachers completely ignorant of (or at least neglecting) the vocabulary of the Scriptures that form the doctrines that introduce the saving grace of Christ?

To grow in our understanding of discipleship by grace, we do well to understand the terminology that builds the precious doctrines of the faith. For the sake of this chapter, I'll call these terms *dead languages*. Many of today's teachers don't use these terms and phrases anymore. For example, if you say the phrase "justification by faith" to most Christians, they'll think you're trying to talk over their heads, that you've been in the seminary too long, or that you've been reading too many commentaries! But a quick study of terms or phrases like this one will open the eyes of our hearts to a vista of transforming truth.

Other terms and phrases have simply become cliches — overused terms or phrases that have lost their meaning. *You're saved by the blood of the Lamb! You're in Christ, dear saint!* Those sentences are loaded with truths that have become clichés. Our solution is not to drop the terminology, but to revisit the truths that make the words so powerful!

I'd like to spend the rest of this chapter looking at some of these terms. These definitions are my own, though based on Scripture. I am sure a scholar may find some points of deficiency, but I've written what has encouraged and enlightened me.

Righteousness

Righteousness is moral perfection and holiness; a guiltless position before God, and in fact, it is itself the very character of God residing inside of a believer. It is not acting right most of the time, as a common person would think of it, but it is the complete absence of sin and its criminal sentences, resulting in an acceptable condition before God.

Because God lives in the absence of sin, He is completely *righteous*. He is morally perfect. Logic alone, then, will tell us why it is impossible for a man to go to heaven. We are *unrighteous*. If unrighteousness mixes with righteousness, then the righteous become unrighteous. James 2:10 says, "For whoever keeps the

102

whole Law and yet stumbles at just one point is guilty of breaking all of it."

Since God defines righteousness as moral perfection, then even stumbling at one point will cause true righteousness to cease and become unrighteousness. *Who then can be saved?*

Only by grace do we enter!

Imputed Righteousness

Imputed righteousness is Christ's righteousness charged to the account of another; reckoned righteousness that arrives upon conversion, and long before the believer is fully righteous in behavior or inward conversation. This is the righteousness that is constant while our sanctification is being completed. Consider this verse: "He made Him who knew no sin to become sin for us that we might become the righteousness of God in Christ" (2 Corinthians 5:21). This verse teaches that all the righteousness in Christ's bank account was transferred to yours, and therefore, through Christ, our sins are wiped away and we are now as righteous as Jesus in the eyes of God the Father.

Amazing grace!

"But I still struggle with sin!" one may tell me.

"Yes," I would answer, "but Christ's righteousness was *imputed* to you, and therefore God sees you as righteous."

So then, righteousness is not just a thing, but a *position* before God. It is a place we can stand.

Many believers are praying for something they already have.

"Oh God," they say, "make me holy!"

You are holy, my brother, my sister.

"Oh God, I want to please You!" they cry.

He is pleased with you because you are in Christ.

Once there was a prince who went to his father and asked him for permission to join the fighting men of the kingdom in foreign battles. His father the king consented, only asking that upon returning by sea, that he would fly the white flag high if he had survived.

The day came when his son's vessel was spotted on the horizon. The king ran out to the cliffs and looked for the white flag. Though his son had survived, he'd forgotten to raise it. Overtaken with despair, the king cast himself from the cliffs upon the rocks below.

Many believers are like that king. Though we are made righteous through Christ, we do not know it or believe it, and spiritually cast ourselves upon the rocks.

Imparted Righteousness

Imparted righteousness is Christ's righteous character being formed in the believer during the process of sanctification. It is the visible righteousness that is conferred during the process of discipleship. Angry Alan becomes kind and loving. He has received imparted righteousness. Depressed Dawn becomes joyful. She has received imparted righteousness. Lusting Leonard stops looking at pornography. He has received imparted righteousness.

People often confuse imputed and imparted righteousness and get tangled up in condemnation and insecurity in their relationship with the Lord. They mistakenly believe that their standing with God is based on *imparted righteousness* when it is solely based on *imputed righteousness;* so they begin to depend upon their works as the basis for God to accept them.

Justification

Justification is the judicial act of God by which He pardons all the sins of those who believe in Christ, and accounts, accepts, and treats them as righteous in the eye of the Law, as conformed to all its demands.

The whole concept of justification is based on the belief that all of humanity will stand before God in judgment, and that our sins will condemn us apart from saving grace. David said in Psalm 130:3, "If you, O Lord, kept a record of sins, O LORD who could stand?"[127]

Paul shouted the good news from the rooftops when he said, "In the gospel a righteousness from God is revealed, a

---

[127] NIV

righteousness that is by faith from first to the last, just as it is written; the righteous will live by faith" (Romans 1:17, NIV).

Though the condition of the pardoned is called righteous, the actual pardon from sin is a legal term called justification. We see it in verses like Romans 5:9: "Much more then, having now been justified by His blood, we shall be saved from the wrath of God through Him."[128]

Because it is a legal term, it is not based on our feelings, but a legal decree. In the fiction I wrote called *The King's Secret*, young orphan Jane of Aldengate is pardoned for a terrible crime, though she still *feels* guilty. Returning to the judge, she asks that he reinstate her crime, believing herself still to be a criminal. After Jane pleads her case, the wise judge pulls out the legal document that declares her *Not Guilty* and says, "Jane, I know you *feel* guilty, but I have here in my hand a legal document that says, 'Not Guilty.' So the plain fact remains, your feelings are inconsequential when the legal document declares you innocent. The Law has been satisfied."

The legal document is the word of God!

There are some also who confuse justification and sanctification. As author C.J. Mahaney writes: "Justification is being *declared* righteous. Sanctification is being *made* righteous—being conformed to the image of Christ. Justification is our *position* before God. Sanctification is our practice. You don't *practice* justification. It happens once for all, upon conversion…[the legalist] confuses his ongoing participation in the process of sanctification with God's finished work in justification."[129]

This justification is *complete*, dealing with our past, present and future sins. This is not merely a state of innocence, but a state of *righteousness* before God. When faith is properly applied, this justification removes all guilt. A drunk driver may rearend your car, and as a Christian you can forgive him, but still he is guilty. Justification actually removes the guilt.

---

[128] NASB
[129] C.J. Mahaney, *The Cross-Centered Life*

Hymn writer Augustus M. Toplady, author of the famous hymn *Rock of Ages,* wrote these beautiful words on justification:

> *Nothing in my hands I bring,*
> *Simply to thy cross I cling;*
> *Naked, come to Thee for dress;*
> *Helpless, look to Thee for grace;*
> *Foul, I to the fountain fly;*
> *Wash me, Savior, or I die,*
> *Rock of Ages, cleft for me,*
> *Let me hide myself in Thee.*

Justification by Faith

Where justification is the legal decree, *justification by faith* is how we attain it; justification by faith is the biblical description of the means of salvation. Justification does not come by the works of the Law, but by the faith a believer has in the work of the cross. Romans 5:1 says, "Therefore, having been justified by faith, we have peace with God through our Lord Jesus Christ."[130]

The Greek word for "justified" is *dikaioo* which literally means "to render righteous or such he ought to be; to declare, pronounce one to be righteous." This is a legal term speaking of acquiring a righteous position, gaining a good standing, gaining innocence, and escaping a sentence of death. Brothers and sisters, justification by faith means that your standing with God has already been *settled*. When Jesus said "It is finished," it meant that He satisfied every legal demand at the cross. Having put our faith in the cross, the legal judgment is taken away by Christ's wounds.

Having been justified by faith.

It's past tense. It's a done deal. The person that understands justification by faith realizes that they need to stop begging God for what they already have and rest in the finished work of Christ.

This is not positive thinking, but *biblical* thinking!

Paul writes, "This is the only thing I want to find out from you: did you receive the Spirit by the works of the Law, or by hearing with faith?" (Galatians 3:2, NASB).

---

[130] NASB

Hearing with faith? This means we hear the promise of God, and then place our faith in the promise and not in our own works. We stake all on the hope that salvation will come through the grace God has promised, and cease looking inward for an answer.

You know that it's possible to hear without faith. Let's say I told you I'd pick you up at 4:00pm and you didn't believe me. You would be anxious and struggle to find peace because you doubted my word. *Hearing with faith.* If you did believe me, your soul would be serene, and you would see my face as I promised at 4:00pm. To embrace justification, it must be coupled with faith, just as Paul wrote in the above Scripture, "Therefore, having been justified by faith..." (Romans 5:1a, NASB). Hearing the promise, trusting the promise, and trusting the Promiser gives us peace in the soul and peace with God.

The Reformers called it *sola fide,* or "faith alone." In other words, we cannot depend on our works to save us, but faith in Christ's redeeming work *alone* will save us. So important is understanding this, that Martin Luther said, "Justification by faith alone is the article where the church will stand or fall."[131]

The 16th century theologian Wilhelmus `a Brakel said, "Justification is the soul of Christianity and the fountainhead of all true comfort and sanctification. He who errs in this doctrine errs to his eternal destruction."[132]

Justification by faith does not mean that we are trusting in our faith to save us; we are justified by the grace in which we are putting our faith. This is the most important concept in the New Testament. Not understanding justification by faith will ultimately be the demise of the Christian. Understanding it and walking in it will be the victory of the Christian.

Martin Luther longed for justification by faith, and when he found it, shook the world for Christ. The doctrines of the Great Awakening were centered on *justification by faith.*

A few years ago, I spoke a message called "Justification By Faith" at Elim Bible Institute during *Spiritual Emphasis Week.* As I

---

[131] Martin Luther, *Treatise on Good Works.* Published in 1520.
[132] Wilhelmus `a Brakel, *Brakel, Vol. 2.* p.341

taught the material, I sensed that some were struggling with it, but that the Holy Spirit was working deeply in others.

Just last fall—over a year after I'd spoken—one of the students sought me out and told me, "I wanted you to know that when you spoke the message on 'Justification By Faith' last year, I had a major breakthrough in my walk with the Lord, and I haven't been the same since! It's become such a passion of mine that I actually spoke a message by the same title just last week at my home church and used your notes. Hope you don't mind."

How could I mind when all I did was borrow from the great teachers and writers before us?

Regeneration

Regeneration is the new birth; that work of the Holy Spirit by which the soul, previously dead in sins, is created anew in Christ unto righteousness. As I wrote about in the chapter *Blessed Helplessness: The Doctrine of Sin,* we are dead and made alive, not merely unfortunate and given a little assistance. Ephesians 2:1 says it plainly: "As for you, you were dead in your transgressions and sins."[133]

Salvation

Salvation is the redeeming act of God to rescue us from sin and its eternal consequences. Salvation is what Jesus purchased for us by His blood when He took our sin on Himself.

As I've previously discussed, salvation is now, is now coming, and shall come. The salvation we all enjoy here on the earth is only a taste of what's to come, and is only in part, as our salvation will not be completed until we escape the fires of hell on Judgment Day.

Since this threefold salvation is taught by Scripture, and the Bible also teaches that we are "saved by grace," then we must assume that grace applies to all echelons of salvation. We are saved by grace at the beginning ("we are saved"), in the middle ("we are being saved"), and at the end ("we shall be saved"). My

---

[133] NIV

point is that when we understand the scope of salvation, we can apply grace properly to all of it. Many believers see their sanctification as a separate experience from salvation, yet if we understand sanctification as synonymous with "are being saved," then we see that the role of grace is perpetual. Grace is as important in salvation as it is in sanctification, because salvation includes sanctification! We need to see sanctification as part of our salvation.

The gospel of salvation needs to be understood, not as that which saves us from hell, but that which saves us from sin. Hell is just a consequence of the sin. There are many who fall away from the faith because they have believed a gospel that teaches them they'll be saved from hell, but they never learned salvation from sin. The salvation that God freely offers, as we discussed in "The Doctrine of Sin," rescues us from the penalty and power of sin.

Central to the teaching and understanding of salvation is the belief that there is something we need to be saved *from*. Salvation has no meaning if we don't understand that we have fallen from God, are slaves to sin, and that we are criminal lawbreakers in heaven's eyes. We are "children of wrath,"[134] enslaved to death and hell. This point may be the sad reason why much of today's evangelism does not yield fruit that remains. Unbelievers are not taught that they have broken God's laws, nor are they taught that they can be delivered from sin.

Salvation is available to all men *today*. Jesus said, "Him that comes to me I will in no wise cast out" (John 6:37, NKJV). The Bible also says, "Now is the time of God's favor, now is the day of salvation" (2 Corinthians 6:2, NIV).

If more people would see that the gospel does not just improve our lives, but saves us from the wrath of God, the punishment of hell, and the power of our sins, we would never stop praising God, and our zeal for evangelism would be unquenchable!

---

[134] Ephesians 2:3

Sanctification

Sanctification is the work of the Holy Spirit in carrying on to perfection the work begun in regeneration. It is growing in our faith, and is, in fact, the process of becoming more like Jesus. It is not merely the reforming of behavior, but an ever-increasing revelation of Christ, His grace, and who we are in Christ.

I used to think that Christlikeness was basically the process of going from *bad* person to *good* person. In other words, I get saved out of sin, I learn what a Christian acts like, and then get *sanctified* – I act more and more like Jesus. What I have seen in Scripture and in experience, however, is that sanctification is the process of going from *self-sufficiency* to *God-sufficiency*. In other words, we go from self-trust and self-dependence to full dependence and trust in God. Christlikeness equals *God-sufficiency*. Holy behavior does not equal Christlikeness, but is simply a product of it. Therefore, the more I trust and depend upon God's grace and His Holy Spirit, the more I will see true sanctification happen in my life. Otherwise, all I'm doing is temporarily reforming my behavior, and not truly changing on the inside. If we define sanctification (or Christlikeness) as holiness, we will never achieve it. We must make our goal a greater understanding and dependence upon the grace of God. Holiness will be the fruit of this dependence.

Maybe what I just said fries your circuits or shoots your sacred cow. Sorry about that. The example Jesus left us was *God-sufficiency*. So, to be like Him is to be God-sufficient. Come on — how many times have you said, when someone tells you to be like Jesus: "Yeah, but that was Jesus!"

In other words, "Jesus was God and I'm not God, so there's no way I can ever live in victory over sin." With this thinking, we believe somehow that this gives us permission to disqualify ourselves from ever truly being like Jesus in this world.

It is true that Jesus was unlike anyone ever born. The math doesn't even compute. He was 100% God and 100% human. Huh? That's 200%! That's right — He was the only 200% being that ever lived. He was fully God and fully man at the same time.

That said, let me ask you some questions. Since God is omniscient (all-knowing), was Jesus omniscient? No, He wasn't. How could He be when He said in Matthew 24:26, "No one knows when that day or hour will come—not the angels in heaven, nor the Son, but only the Father"?[135] And since God is omnipresent (everywhere at once), was Jesus omnipresent? No, He wasn't. How could He be when Mary said to Him at Lazarus' grave in John 11:32, "Lord, if you had been here, my brother would not have died"?[136] And since God is omnipotent (all-powerful), was Jesus omnipotent? No, He wasn't. How could He be when the Bible says in Mark 6:4-6, "He could not do any miracles there, except lay his hands on a few sick people and heal them. And he was amazed at their lack of faith"?

What am I saying? To understand this mystery, we have to understand Philippians 2:6-8:

> *"Who, being in very nature God, did not consider equality with God something to be grasped, but made himself nothing, taking the very nature of a servant, being made in human likeness. And being found in appearance as a man, he humbled himself and became obedient to death—even death on a cross!"*[137]

This passage teaches that Jesus was fully God, but *emptied Himself* of the benefits of that position so that He could live *by faith* and become our Champion of God-Sufficiency. This is exactly why He said in John 5:19, "I tell you the truth, the Son can do nothing by himself; he can do only what he sees his Father doing, because whatever the Father does the Son also does."[138]

Here we begin to understand God's goal of our sanctification. He wants us to be like Christ the Son, fully surrendered and yielded to the strength of His spirit, and fully dependent upon Him for all things.

---

[135] International Standard Version (ISV)
[136] NIV
[137] NIV
[138] NIV

Atonement

Atonement is a covering; implying that by a Divine propitiation the sinner is covered from the just anger of God. "We all, like sheep, have gone astray, each of us has turned to his own way; and the Lord has laid on him the iniquity of us all" (Isaiah 53:6, NIV). Jesus sacrifice "covers" us so that, in a sense, God can no longer see our sin, but only the righteousness of Christ.

Just like Adam and Eve's nakedness was covered with garments of skin,[139] implying that an animal had to die for their sins to be covered, so the Lamb of God was slain for the sins of the whole world, covering our sin from the sight of the Father. In reality, the sins aren't merely covered in the sense that they are still there but concealed, but they are *removed* by the blood of Jesus, absorbed in His wounds. Thank You, Father!

As I mentioned in a previous chapter, Romans 13:14 says, "But put on the Lord Jesus Christ."[140] Like a covering, we must, by faith, put on the garment of atonement, believing that Jesus' sacrifice has covered our sins. So when we stand in worship or prayer, we must *put on the Lord Jesus Christ*. When we face our own shame and condemnation, we must *put on the Lord Jesus Christ*.

Consider this story:[141]

> *A young nun once claimed to have had a vision of Jesus. Her bishop decided to test her truthfulness and ordered that the next time she had a vision she should ask Christ what the bishop's primary sin had been before he became a bishop.*
>
> *Some months later the nun returned and the bishop asked if she had asked Christ the question, to which she affirmed that she had. "And what did he say?" the bishop asked, apprehensively.*
>
> *"Christ said..." and the nun paused a moment... "He said, 'I don't remember.'"*

---

[139] Genesis 3:21
[140] NASB
[141] Donald Deffner, Seasonal Illustrations, Resource, 1992, p. 94.

Atonement. Our sins are removed in Christ.

One final footnote to these thoughts on atonement is that this "covering" doesn't simply shield our sin from God's view, but this covering actually takes the sins away. We are covered by the sacrifice of Christ, and beneath the covering, nothing is there. Our sins are gone!

Propitiation

Propitiation is a substitute; referring to Christ Jesus assuming our obligations and removing our guilt, covering it, by the vicarious punishment which He endured. Jesus was a substitute for you! The following story illustrates the idea of propitiation.

A few years ago, in northern California, there were two friends that lived as roommates in an apartment. One was named Larry Johnson, and the other was named Phil Jones.

Phil Jones led a woman to Christ that had been the girlfriend of a biker from a notorious biker gang in the area, and she chose to leave the biker gangs. Her boyfriend was furious at Phil Jones, because she wouldn't sleep with him anymore. So he found out where Phil Jones lived and went to his house to "teach him a lesson."

When the biker arrived at Phil Jones' apartment, Phil was inside the house napping while his roommate Larry read a book in the warm sun on the porch.

The biker, his engine blaring loudly, pulled into the driveway, got off his motorcycle, and screamed at Larry, "Where's Phil Jones?"

Larry knew this situation was not good. He put his book down and walked to the front of the porch, silently asking God for wisdom.

"Where's Phil Jones?" the biker yelled again, approaching the stairs to the porch.

113

Larry stood at the top of the stairs as the biker reached the top step and towered over him. Larry could see the hatred and rage in his eyes as he fumed one last time, "Where's Phil Jones?"

In a moment of time, what was in Larry's heart came out. Looking up into the eyes of the biker, he said, "I'm Phil Jones."

The biker attacked quickly, beating him and kicking him until Larry lay bleeding on the ground.[142]

The Bible says, "But God demonstrates his own love for us in this: While we were still sinners, Christ died for us" (Romans 5:8, NASB). Do you know what Jesus did on the cross? In effect, He said, "I'm Phil Jones." And you can insert your name in there, because Jesus did that for you. He is the propitiation—the substitute—for our sins. The only difference between the above story and what Jesus did for you is that Larry did it for his dear friend, and Jesus did it when we hated Him.

In Christ
In Christ is the hallmark and centerpiece of Paul's teaching. He mentions it almost fifteen times in Ephesians 1:1-14. What does it mean?

This powerful phrase summarizes the gospel, and the fact that our access to the Father and our inheritance as children of God is *in Christ*. This is especially important to understand in discipleship because it establishes our *position* before God as the foundation of our Christian life, not our *works*. In fact, Paul eventually teaches that our works come from our position in Christ when he says, "For we are His workmanship, created *in Christ Jesus* for good works, which God prepared beforehand so that we would walk in them" (Ephesians 2:10, NASB, emphasis added). If we fail to understand this, we'll think our works determine our position, not our position determining our works!

In Christ.

---

[142] Other evangelistic stories like this one can be found and downloaded at www.isaiahsix.com.

114

"For you have died and your life is hidden with Christ in God" (Colossians 3:3, NASB). Again, encompassing propitiation and atonement, this pillar of truth teaches that grace "hides" us in Christ, and that when God looks upon us, He only sees His Son because we are *in Christ*.

So why so downcast, oh my soul? Put your hope in God!

If you are in Christ, you are as righteous in the eyes of God as Jesus Himself. This is the beauty of imputed righteousness! God accepts you because He accepts Christ the Son, therefore God's love for you is equal to that which He has for His own Son.

Excuse me, I need to go worship for a few minutes.

Born Again

Born again is the new birth of the inner man that happens when a person puts his faith in the cross to save him. "Jesus answered and said to him, 'Truly, truly, I say to you, unless one is *born again* he cannot see the kingdom of God'" (John 3:3, NASB).

Unfortunately, this phrase has become a cliché in and out of the church, conjuring up images of hippies and flower children in the 1960's. *Born again* has become a noun or an adjective, when it is in fact a verb.

"Are you one of those born agains?"

"What kind of Christian am I? I'm a born again Christian."

But *born again* is not something I am; it's something that happened to me!

It speaks of the experience of regeneration, when the new man was created, and I was made spiritually alive in Christ Jesus.

You can't be born again by attending a church, doing good deeds, filling out a commitment card, or merely going to an altar. It is a miracle of the heart where that which is dead becomes alive.

Let's say that I visit my friend Seth Goodson's house with the intention of becoming a Goodson. So I ask him for a list of chores, and he sends me on my way, where I heartily perform all my duties. When finished, let's say that I announce to Seth, "I am now a Goodson!"

He would say, "Sorry, it doesn't matter how many chores you do. To be a Goodson, you must be born into my family."

So it is with the new birth. We cannot earn our way into God's family. We can only be *born* into it. Then the new creation arises by the breath of God, and we live in this world as citizens of heaven. We are no longer slaves to sin, but alive to God through Christ Jesus!

So powerful and so real is the new birth that Paul actually makes a distinction between sin which dwells in him, sometimes called "the old man," and the new man in Christ: "So now, no longer am I the one doing it, but sin which dwells in me" (Romans 7:17, NASB). In a sense, when faced with the failure of his flesh, he basically says, "Look, this is not the real me! This is part of my flesh, but not the real Paul that Jesus has created through the new birth."

When we understand the new birth, we begin to see this divine distinction, and no longer accept the identity, weaknesses, and shame of the old man as part of who we really are. We "consider [ourselves] to be dead to sin, but alive to God in Christ Jesus."[143]

Revelation

Revelation is the opening of the eyes of the heart to truth. This knowledge can be previously known in the mind, and mental assent given to it, but when revelation comes, it is understood in a way that transforms.

The Greek word for revelation is *apokalupsis*, meaning "to make an appearance," signifying the removing of a veil. Imagine the magician, hiding something under a black cloth on his hand, and then suddenly pulling the cloth away, revealing a bouquet of flowers. Suddenly, you can see what was hidden. It has *made an appearance*. Revelation.

Imagine if Rick had not seen his long-lost sister Joan in 30 years, and that he drove to JFK airport in New York City to reunite with her. Let's say that he arrived with a friend at 1:15pm, and Joan's plane was scheduled to land at 1:30pm. At 1:35pm, Rick and his friend look at the "Arrival" monitors, and see that her

---

[143] Romans 6:11, NASB

plane has landed safely. "Rick," his friend would say, "Joan is in this airport."

"I know," Rick would answer, and even though he mentally understands this, he is not emotionally moved even remotely close to the way he will be when he sees Joan face to face. A few minutes later, he sees Joan walking down the airport concourse, and his tears begin to flow as he runs toward her. They embrace, and now Rick really knows that *Joan is in the airport!*

Joan has *made an appearance*. Revelation.

In the same way, we can hear messages, understand doctrine mentally, recite creeds, and regurgitate catechisms, but without *revelation,* we are incapable of truly seeing or experiencing the power of the truth. We can understand that Joan is in the airport, but not understand that Joan is in the airport. When it comes to Scripture, only the Holy Spirit is capable of opening our eyes. We are helpless to open the eyes of our own hearts. In John 16:13, Jesus says, "But when he, the Spirit of truth, comes, he will guide you into all truth. He will not speak on his own; he will speak only what he hears, and he will tell you what is yet to come."[144]

This is what Paul prayed for when he lifted up the believers in Ephesus: "I keep asking that the God of our Lord Jesus Christ, the glorious Father, may give you the Spirit of wisdom and revelation, so that you may know him better. I pray also that the eyes of your heart may be enlightened in order that you may know the hope to which he has called you, the riches of his glorious inheritance in the saints" (Ephesians 1:17-18, NIV).

What's interesting about this is that Paul actually commended them just before he said this when he wrote, "For this reason, ever since I heard about your faith in the Lord Jesus and your love for all the saints, I have not stopped giving thanks for you, remembering you in my prayers" (Ephesians 1:15-16, NIV). These were early church believers that had been converted and taught by Paul himself, and they had faith and love that Paul thought was worthy of a public commendation. All this, and yet *still needed the eyes of their hearts opened.* Paul understood that there is always a

---

[144] NIV

greater revelation of God, and that his preaching was useless if the Holy Spirit did not breathe on the truth and turn it into revelation.

Often, people who have grace conversions have experiences where they will suddenly grasp a truth in a life-changing way, though they had given mental assent to the idea for years. Remember what Hudson Taylor wrote to his sister as he described "the exchanged life"? "As I read," he wrote, "I saw it all! 'If we believe not, He abideth faithful.'"[145]

What does he mean by *saw it all?* Revelation. *Apokalupsis.*

Thanks be to God, who will not leave us lost and dull in understanding! Through His precious Holy Spirit, He will lead us to the truth. He constantly invites us to experience revelation.

> *"Call to me and I will answer you and tell you great and unsearchable things you do not know." (Jeremiah 33:3, NIV)*

> *"Then you will call upon me and come and pray to me, and I will listen to you. You will seek me and find me when you seek me with all your heart." (Jeremiah 29:12-13, NIV)*

> *"Ask and it will be given to you; seek and you will find; knock and the door will be opened to you." (Matthew 7:7, NIV)*

---

[145] V. Raymond Edman, *They Found the Secret.* Zondervan, Grand Rapids, MI. © 1984 Zondervan: pg. 18.

CHAPTER 9
Cross-Centered Living:
Applying the Message of the Cross

"Abide hard by the cross and search the mystery of His wounds."[146]
— "Prince of Preachers" Charles Spurgeon

I've titled this book *Discipleship by Grace,* and I've been discussing grace now for many chapters, but let's stop and remember that a discussion about grace is really a discussion about the cross. There are many who preach and teach "grace" without preaching and teaching the cross. We have no right to talk about grace unless it is married to the message of the cross. They are one and the same. The message of the cross is not just a feel-good, God-loves-you-no-matter-what message. It is a glimpse into how serious God is about sin, how committed He was to redemption, and how great His love is for us. The cross is where mercy and justice kissed. God didn't just give us a pass. He damaged His Son to pay for it.

Because of this, God wants us to live "cross-centered lives" (and I thank author C.J. Mahaney[147] for that phrase). This means that we continually determine to make the cross the object of our faith, and that we live our lives drawing all our strength and satisfaction from it. A cross-centered life is a grace-centered life. A grace-centered life is a cross-centered life.

The Jealous One pursued us to a cross and became the Wounded Savior. Now the Wounded Savior lives, and He ever makes intercession for us at the right hand of the Father.[148] What greater hope do you have than the redeeming sacrifice of Christ? What greater promise than access to God? What enemy can stand against you? "Who shall separate us from the love of Christ?"[149]

---

[146] Charles H. Spurgeon, *Morning and Evening,* January 4, evening meditation.
[147] C.J. Mahaney wrote the book *The Cross-Centered Life.*
[148] Romans 8:34
[149] Romans 8:35, NKJV

C.J. Mahaney wrote, "Cross-centered lives begin with cross-centered days."[150] So how do we apply these truths to our daily lives?

1. Repent

In the earliest preaching of the gospel from the mouth of Jesus, we see that simple message is still the same today: "Repent and believe" (Mark 1:15, NASB).

We must start with repentance. Recognizing out helplessness, we fall at our Master's feet like "the sinful woman" in Luke 7, and turn away from our sin.

Here is one remarkable note about repentance, however. We must not simply repent from our wicked works, but our *good works*. Author and pastor Tim Keller said, "The main thing separating you from God is not your sin, but your damnable good works!"[151]

We must cease to trust in them, renounce them as Paul did and "count them but rubbish" (Philippians 3:8b, NASB). Keller also said, "Pharisees repented of their bad deeds and were still Pharisees."[152]

When we see the glory of grace, we see the depravity of our sin natures, the arrogance of our self-sufficiency, and renounce sin and self-salvation.

2. *Never* graduate from the cross

Polycarp, a disciple of John the Beloved, wrote, "Wherefore, leaving the foolishness of the crowd, and their false teaching, let us turn back to the word which was delivered to us at the beginning."[153] We never graduate from the cross, but the same one that saved us at the beginning still saves us today.

Why do we have so many tangents in the Body of Christ? *The cross has ceased being enough for us.* So we move to end-time

---

[150] Mahaney, C.J., *The Cross Centered Life* (Sisters, Oregon: Multnomah Publishers, Inc., © 2002 by Sovereign Grace Ministries), p. 25
[151] Tim Keller, pastor of New York's Redeemer Presbyterian Church in Manhattan said this in a sermon on renewal at *The Leadership Summit 2009*.
[152] Ibid.
[153] The Epistle of Polycarp to the Philippians

prophecy, to an infatuation with Israel, to manifestations of spiritual gifts, to an obsession with faith, to politics, etc. The cross ceases to become beautiful to a Church that does not understand its role in the Christian life.

We never graduate from the cross. The same cross that saved us is the same one that will keep us. We must always be certain that the cross is the object of our faith and the source of our strength. One commentary writer puts it, "We never move on from the cross, only into a more profound understanding of the cross."[154] It is there you will always find strength, and it is there you will maintain your confidence in who you are in Christ.

The same cross that saved you at the beginning is the same cross that will save you today. The same cross that saved you from the penalty of sin when you first believed is the same cross that will save you perpetually from whatever enemy of your soul attacks your faith. The cross that brings salvation from hell also brings salvation from anger; from fear; from doubt; from loneliness. God's grace and His spirit will carry us until the end of the journey.

One of my favorite Bible teachers, an Englishman named Edgar Parkins who went to be with the Lord in the late 1980's (I've only heard him on recordings[155]), once told a story about a return voyage he had on a ship from Africa to England. He said that when they came near the port bay where the ship would dock, a terrible storm came upon the sea. Navigating the shoals would be difficult under such conditions. Local provision had been made, however, that when such conditions would arise, the port authority would send out what they called a "harbor captain" to take over the controls of the vessel, and navigate the ship through dangerous waters safely to port. There would be a formal handing over of the steering wheel in the control room by the ship's captain to the harbor captain. Once the ship's captain surrendered control, he would have to quietly stand in the background, ceasing

---

[154] David Prior, *Message of 1 Corinthians: Life in the Local Church* (Downers Grove, Illinois: InterVarsity Press, 1985), p.51.
[155] These recordings can be ordered from the bookstore at Pinecrest Bible College in Dolgeville, NY.

all attempts to convene control or authority, yielding to the harbor captain.

During the storm Parkins spoke of, after the harbor captain took control, Parkins went out onto the deck of the ship and looked out at the stormy sea. There he saw the first buoy, which was marked *Alpha*. The harbor captain steered the ship along further, and Parkins saw the next buoy marked *Beta*. Then came *Gamma*. On and on the harbor captain led the vessel, said Parkins, from *Alpha* to *Omega* until the ship was brought safely to port. Parkins said that the Holy Spirit is like the harbor captain, guiding us from the beginning until the end of our Christian experience.

The Holy Spirit is drawn to the cross, and as we keep our eyes on Christ's work, the Holy Spirit will guide us through the storms of life until we see Jesus face to face.

3. Fight the fight of *faith*

The Scriptures do not teach us to fight *sin*, but teach us to *"fight the good fight of faith."*[156] The Bible does say *"in your battle against sin"* but then teaches us that the battle lies in keeping our faith in Christ, not in finding the willpower to defeat our own weaknesses. First John 5:4 says, "…this is the victory that overcomes the world, even our faith." In other words, we cannot defeat our own sins. Only Christ can do that. Our responsibility is to make sure that our faith is always enduring, and is always centered on the cross. Doing so will cause all of our enemies to be defeated. Listen to John 3:14-15:

> *"And as Moses lifted up the serpent in the wilderness, even must the Son of Man be lifted up, that whoever believes in Him should not perish but have eternal life."* – *Jesus in John 3:14-15, NKJV*

A.W. Tozer explains this mystery in his book *The Pursuit of God*,[157] first reminding the reader of the Old Testament story to

---

[156] 2 Timothy 4:7, paraphrase; see also 1 John 5:4
[157] A.W. Tozer, *The Pursuit of God* (Christian Publications: Camp Hill, PA), © 1982, 1993 by Christian Publications, Inc., pg. 79-91

which Jesus is referring. In the book of Numbers, Israel had become discouraged in the wilderness and spoke against the Lord. The Lord's anger burned against Israel for their sin, and He sent a plague of deadly snakes upon them. Moses interceded and God gave the command for Moses to fashion a bronze serpent, nail it to a pole, and raise it high in view of all the people, "and it shall be that everyone who is bitten, when he looks at it, shall live."[158] Moses obeyed, "and so it was, if a serpent had bitten anyone, when he looked at the bronze serpent, he lived."[159]

So the symbol of the enemy that destroyed them was nailed to a pole so they could look at it. Do you know what a foolish command it seemed to be for the Israelites, when bitten to look at the pole? Wouldn't it make more sense to fight off snakes and suck out poisonous venom? If there were 500 deadly snakes in your room right now, and I told you not to worry about it, and that looking at me would keep you safe, you'd think I was insane. It would take *faith* to do such a thing.

Jesus says the cross is like that. He was nailed to a pole with the symbol of our enemy — sin — in his own wounds. And like the story of Moses and the Israelites, if we'll stop trying to fight off our sins, and behold the Lamb with our faith, we'll be free of them. On this principle, Tozer says, "Our plain man, in reading [John 3:14-15]...would notice that *look* and *believe* are synonymous terms. 'Looking' on the Old Testament serpent is identical with 'believing' on the New Testament Christ. That is, the *looking* and *believing* are the same thing. And he would understand that, while Israel looked with their external eyes, believing is done with the heart. I think he would conclude that faith is the gaze of the soul upon a saving God."[160]

Tozer later adds, "The man who has struggled to purify himself and has had nothing but repeated failures will experience real relief when he stops tinkering with his own soul and looks away to the perfect One. When he looks at Christ, the very things

---

[158] Numbers 21:8, NKJV
[159] Numbers 21:9, NKJV
[160] A.W. Tozer, *The Pursuit of God* (Christian Publications: Camp Hill, PA), © 1982, 1993 by Christian Publications, Inc., pg. 83

he has so long been trying to do will be getting done within him. It will be God working in him…"[161]

And so this is how we fight the fight of faith. Keep believing that His grace is enough and that the cross is sufficient to meet all your need. Keep resting in the finished work of Christ and not your performance.

4. Be moved by what you believe, not by what you *feel*

Evangelist Smith Wigglesworth once said, "I'm not moved by what I feel. I'm not moved by what I see. I'm moved by what I believe."

Part of maturity in Christ and growing in grace is not being moved by our feelings, but by what we believe. We must believe and live out what God's Word says about us and not give in to the ups and downs of our emotions, which often betray reality.

When young pilots are being trained, they are taught to trust their gauges, and not what they may feel in the cockpit. The G-forces on the body are so radical that what a pilot feels may not be accurate. You can think you're crashing and be flying perfectly straight, and conversely, you can feel like you're fine, and be flying straight into the ground. In stormy conditions, believing the gauges is critically important. I remember seeing a report when JFK Jr. died a few years back that indicated that this may have been the reason for his plane crash.

When we choose to believe in the love of God, we trust our gauges.

When we choose to believe that we can approach the throne of grace with confidence, we trust our gauges.

When we choose to trust in the cross and not our works, we trust our gauges.

Satan would have us to live on the roller coaster of our feelings. We're up, we're down. We're in, we're out. But truth will stabilize our souls and set us free. When we live out truth, our feelings will follow our will. Eventually, you will find that even

---

[161] Ibid, pg. 85

your soul will conform to the will of God when you choose to be moved by truth and not feelings.

5. *Remember* that your part is to trust and God's part is to work[162]

Practically, applying the message of the cross is a matter of striving to trust. Working hard to rest. A paradox? Yes, and I welcome you to the kingdom of God. To return to an earlier illustration, we must make certain that the object of our faith is always fixed on the finished work of Christ. *Not* on our disciplines, our denominations, or our dead works. If our dependence is on an object of faith other than Christ's work, we will reap failure and defeat.

This Scripture has to be one of my favorite verses in revealing the paradox of grace: Hebrews 4:11 says, "Let us labor therefore to enter into that rest."[163] There it is, dear friends. *Labor to rest.* This is our gospel! We must work diligently and strive to make sure that we're resting in the grace of God!

This is the same idea that is captured in the oft-misunderstood Scripture: *"Work out your salvation with fear and trembling; for it is God who is at work in you, both to will and to work for His good pleasure"* (Philippians 2:12-13, NASB). Most people I know actually use this verse as an objection to what I teach on grace. "Hey!" they say. "What about the verse that says, 'Work out your salvation...'" but they never remember the next part! *For it is God who is at work in you both to will and to work for His good pleasure.* In other words, Paul is warning, "You better make sure that you're trusting in grace and not the works of the Law! Be afraid that you have trusted in yourself!"

I recently heard of an American pastor who visited China to minister to some leaders of the underground church. On one occasion, the American pastor asked a Chinese pastor, "You've met enough Americans over the years—what do you think the problem is with the American Church?"

---

[162] This principle and its phrasing are from the book *The Christian's Secret of a Happy Life* by Hannah Whitall Smith. Ballantine Books © 1986.
[163] NKJV

"Very simple," answered the Chinese pastor. "American Christians are *committed* and not *surrendered.*"

I would agree with that assessment.

Commitment has its place under grace, but is not the foundation of our faith. *Surrender* is. *Commitment* means, "I will do my best and try my hardest." *Surrender* is about letting go of control.

> "*The wind blows where it wishes and you hear the sound of it, but do not know where it comes from and where it is going; so is everyone who is born of the Spirit.*" (John 3:8, NASB)

Here Jesus likens the life of faith to something that's more like a sailboat than a rowboat. A rowboat is a man straining at the oars, trying to get across the sea in his own strength, but eventually he fails because his arms are too weak and the journey is too long. This is not the picture of Christianity that Jesus presents. He calls us to trust Him, put up our sails, and let the power of the wind of the Spirit be the strength that moves the vessel.[164]

Not understanding the role of trust in Christ can be deadly to a believer's faith. As I mentioned in the introduction, C.J. Mahaney wrote, "Very small errors in a person's understanding of the gospel seemed to result in very big problems in that person's life."[165]

Recently, when I ministered in a church in western New York, I met a young man who had just returned from Israel. He was a spiritual mess. He'd gotten involved with a group that taught that now that they were Christians and had the Holy Spirit, they had the power to keep the Law of Moses, and the Jewish customs, feasts and festivals. Attempting to do so had nearly driven him

---

[164] I wrote a song titled "In the Wind" that is based on this principle. All *Derek Joseph & Isaiah Six* music can be purchased on www.isaiahsix.com.

[165] C.J. Mahaney, *Christ Our Mediator*, (Sisters, Oregon: Multnomah Publishers, Inc.) © 2004 Sovereign Grace Ministries, p.40. This statement actually came from one of Mahaney's friends in ministry, who made the statement in a letter describing a situation he had encountered with a young woman in his church.

insane, and he returned to the United States to try to get his life back together. He was burned out, tired, and hopeless. His only hope is a revelation of grace.

I encourage the reader to study the object of your faith in Scripture, and to read books such as the one you have in your hands that will further your revelation of grace, your ability to discern legalism, and deepen your confidence to depend on Christ to be your All-Sufficiency.

6. *Commune* continually

As I previously discussed, access to God is the great promise of the New Covenant, as Paul encourages us in Ephesians 3:12, that "we have boldness and access with confidence through faith in Him."[166]

I used to think that prayer was something you do for a few minutes in the morning. Now I understand that prayer is far more than running a laundry list before God. It is living in the presence of God. It is communion with His presence. Prayer becomes a joy and a lifestyle, as you no longer feel confined by a ritual or a discipline, but can converse always with the One who is with you always! Whether it is requesting our daily bread, or the silent awareness that He is there, communion with His Spirit should be enjoyed by God's children. I would include worship in the same discussion. Under the new covenant, worship ceases to be a once-done act, and becomes a lifestyle that constantly magnifies God. I discuss this later in the book.

The blood of Jesus has torn the temple veil in two,[167] meaning that God's presence has come out of the Holy of Holies and now resides in the hearts of His people! So now "whatever you do in word or deed, do all in the name of the Lord Jesus, giving thanks to God the Father through Him."[168]

David said that God's praise would be continually on his lips,[169] and Paul taught us to pray without ceasing.[170] How can we

---

[166] NKJV
[167] Matthew 27:51
[168] Colossians 3:17, NKJV
[169] Psalm 34:1

possibly do this if worship and prayer are disciplines or rituals, a servicing of a list of songs and requests? Lock ourselves in a room or monastery all day long? How about *taking God's presence with us wherever we go!* That's our gospel.

How can we do this? By believing in the work of the cross that gives us bold and constant access to the Father!

Often, when my wife and I are traveling together in a car, time will go by without us having any conversation. When you are not intimate with someone, silence can feel threatening and awkward, but when you are intimate with someone, you don't feel the need to constantly be talking to one another in order to feel comfortable or validate the relationship. My wife and I are aware of each other's presence, and yet we are not talking all the time. So it is with communion. You don't need to be talking to God all day to be in His presence, but you can cultivate an awareness of His presence. You can know that He's in the seat next to you by developing what A.W. Tozer called "the gaze of the soul."

The Messiah Jesus pursued us to a cross and became the Wounded Savior. Now He lives and ever makes intercession for us at the right hand of the Father.[171] What greater hope do we have than the redeeming sacrifice of Christ? What greater promise than access to God? What enemy can stand against us? "Who shall separate us from the love of Christ?"[172]

7. *Be honest* with God

As I went through the wilderness and learned more of God's ways, one of the things I learned was that God wants us to be honest with Him. I used to think that if I was honest with God, He'd be mad at me! During my depression, I thought He'd want me to get up in the morning and make positive confessions like, "I will be joyful today, for the word of God says that the joy of the Lord is my strength!'" I'd try it, but each day I'd look back and see a trail of failure and misery again. It was like I was turning truth

---

[170] 1 Thessalonians 5:17
[171] Romans 8:34
[172] Romans 8:35, NKJV

into a ritual, and instead of believing it, attempted to use it as some magic Bible wand.

Then the Holy Spirit led me to the Old Testament, and the writings of the prophets. I was shocked by how raw and honest they were with God. Look at the several Scriptures below:

"How long, O Lord? Wilt Thou forget me forever? How long wilt Thou hide Thy face from me?" —David (Psalm 13:1, KJV)

"Would that God were willing to crush me; That He would loose His hand, and cut me off." —Job (Job 6:9, NASB)

"O God, why have you rejected us forever?" —Asaph (Psalm 74:1, NASB)

Question: Did God really forsake Asaph and Israel *forever*? Of course not! Then why did God let him say something like that in the Bible?—I thought the Bible was all true! What Asaph said *is* true in the sense that he was being real and honest with God about what he felt, in spite of the fact that his view was inaccurate.

The plain truth is this: You can't be intimate with someone with whom you can't be honest. Many who read this book will be among those who desire to know God intimately, and many more who will consider themselves as those who are intimate with God. And yet, among those same readers are those who do not know how to be honest with God; who do not know how to pour out their soul to the Father. Irreverence is when we are blasphemous, or disrespectful to God. But honesty is learning to take the aches, pressures, pain, and questions, and pour them out at the feet of the Father.

I've heard many believers talk about the heart of David. But what is the heart of David? I believe it is the heart that approaches God like a son approaching a father. It is an intimate heart, and it is exactly what I'm speaking about in these pages—an honest heart. It's no coincidence that David is among the fellowship of the honest that I've referenced above. David knew how to pour out his soul to God in prayer and in worship. This is the heart of David.

Another man we can observe is Jeremiah the prophet. Jeremiah was known as "the weeping prophet." He simply knew that bottling up his agonies did not please or impress God, but he knew how to pour them out before Him, becoming one of the great intercessors of the Old Testament. Take a look at this broken man:

> *"For these things I weep; my eye, my eye overflows with water; because the comforter, who should restore my life is far from me. My children are desolate because my enemy has prevailed." (Lamentations 1:16, NASB)*

> *"I am the man who has seen affliction by the rod of His wrath. He has led me and made me walk in darkness and not in light. Surely He has turned His hand against me time and time again throughout the day." (Lamentations 3:2-3, NASB)*

> *"Why has my pain been perpetual, and my wound incurable, refusing to be healed? Wilt Thou indeed be to me like a deceptive stream with water that is unreliable?" (Jeremiah 15:18, NASB)*

Can you believe Jeremiah said some of those things? If it wasn't in the Bible, I would think that some of it is unbiblical! But God allowed Jeremiah to be honest with Him, and allows all of us to see it printed in the pages of His Word. God teaches us here that honesty is the only way to intimacy. Honesty comes before intimacy. Being real comes before genuine relationship.

Notice that Jeremiah isn't blaspheming God, nor is he disrespecting His presence with folly or mockery, but he's asking honest questions, and discussing his pain and misery with God.

Isn't that how you got saved? Wasn't honesty *essential* at the beginning? If you had a true revelation of the gospel, you said something like, "Lord, I am a *sinner,* and I need a *Savior!*" You knew that God was pleased with your honest confession of weakness and brokenness, and you were convinced that He accepted you based on your plea for mercy.

If this is how we came to Jesus, then why do we dismiss honesty from the rest of the Christian life? Honesty was the doorway to grace when you began, and it is the doorway to grace now.

Surely some here will say, "What about faith?" They'll wonder what role faith has in our thinking, or in the framing of our perspective. To answer this simply, I do not believe that faith pretends or ignores reality. Faith is the ability to see the reality, and still believe that God is sovereign. Faith is the vehicle that gets you to the feet of the Father, where you can pour out your soul to Him.

In wilderness season, I began to realize that though I'd wanted intimacy with God, I did not really know God, and I never would if I didn't learn to be honest with Him. So I began to be honest with Him through my prayers, journal writings, and songs. This experienced, I began to find great freedom, approaching Him more as an understanding Father than as a cold and cruel Judge. The song I wrote titled "Who Would Have Known" is just such one of those songs.

> *I come weak*
> *I come broken*
> *This is my offering*
> *For my name can't be counted with the strong*
> *I come empty*
> *I come hungry*
> *And I thank You for Your mercy*
> *Let Your grace be my story and my song*[173]

Recently, in a busy traveling season of ministry, I found myself worn down by the rigorous pace and schedule. Traveling to a meeting alone in a car, I told the Lord, "Well, Lord, I guess You're going to have to use me this time *in spite of me!*"

The Holy Spirit spoke to my heart, "Since when has the agreement ever been that I've used you *because* of you?"

How stupid I can be sometimes.

---

[173] "Who Would Have Known" from the album *Jealous One*, words and music by Derek Joseph Levendusky, © 2003 Prophet Hall Music.

"Even on your best day," whispered the Holy Spirit, "it's always been grace!"

8. *Stop* and pray

One of the most practical ways I can apply the message of grace to my life is through using my weaknesses, temptations, and failures as a catalyst to turn me to grace. These become opportunities for God to teach me His grace and glorify His name in my life.

The most practical way to do this is to *pray* when faced with your weaknesses. Sounds too simple, doesn't it? It is simple! Since access to God is the great promise of the New Covenant, prayer becomes the great privilege of the New Testament, because prayer is accessing God. Prayer is the first act of dependence you can do when living a cross-centered life. The minute you pray is the minute that you are admitting that you are too weak to shoulder this one alone. Why do you think a prideful person often won't pray? They do not want to admit they need help.

C'mon, guys. This is the same pride that keeps us from asking for directions when we are driving. We know we can figure it out without help, right? So what do we do? We drive into oblivion and end up staring at cows on dirt roads rather than stop and ask for directions! We do not want to admit our need.

I'm telling you that the only way to apply grace is to *admit you are lost and stop and ask for directions.* For example, there have been times with my kids when the demand and chaos build up to a boiling point. Though I was previously convinced that I had achieved a Christlike state (if you believe that I'll sell you a bridge in Brooklyn too), I now see that I am very unlike Him! What do I do? *Stop and pray.* "Lord," I say, "I am beside myself and I'm about to blow my top. I do not have the patience in my flesh to keep me from a meltdown, so I simply ask for Your grace right now. Amen!"

I've never had a moment when I've been willing to stop and pray that God hasn't deposited enough grace to meet my challenge. You know what my real challenge is? *I don't stop and pray!* How foolish am I? At times, I've been amazed at myself at how often I don't ask for help! Either I forget, or I'm too prideful to *stop and ask for directions!* We all have to develop the blessed instinct and habit of stopping to pray for grace.

9. *Check* your motivation

Why are you fasting? Why are you reading your Bible? Why are you praying? Why do you feel compelled to do evangelism? These are all good things, but God is more interested in the motive of the heart than in the action itself!

Consider Galatians 5:6, where Paul wrote, "For in Christ Jesus neither circumcision nor uncircumcision means anything, but faith working through love."[174] This powerful verse is teaching us what really matters to God. It's not the act of circumcision; it's the motive behind it. Had some received circumcision in an attempt to keep the Law of Moses? Then it was a self-sufficient act of self-righteousness! It was *dead works.* Had some of the Jews done it as an act of love? It was *worship.* All that matters is *faith that works through love.*

What exactly does this phrase mean?

Sometimes I understand the Bible not by what it says, but by what it *doesn't* say. It doesn't say, "Faith that works through *fear.*"

"Oh dear!" says the fearful one. "I slept in today and didn't pray! Now I can't live in God's presence today because I've disappointed Him so severely with my laziness!"

It also doesn't say, "Faith that works through *pride.*"

"Well, well, well," says the prideful one, "why weren't you at the 5am prayer meeting? I was there, the old intercessor Stella was there, and God was there, but you *weren't* there. Shame on you, sluggard."

You must appreciate the Scriptural vocabulary of legalists. *Sluggard.*

The only commendable faith is *faith that works through love.* Love must be our motivation, because when it is, everything becomes worship and not a legal duty. Everything becomes a joy

---

[174] NASB

to do, because we no longer serve the Lord *to become* children of God. Instead we serve *because we are* children of God.

So this verse might read: "*Neither getting up to pray or not getting up to pray means anything, but faith working through love.*"

There was once a young man in my church who struggled to understand the concept of "do vs. done." He would strive with such diligence that he would often compete with his peers to see who could be more righteous. Once, another young church member asked him about his old shoes, and why he hadn't gotten a new pair. He answered, "These are worn out because I pray so much. As I bend my knees, the creases get worked into my shoes, wearing them down. I can't afford new shoes now, but the damage is well worth the sacrifice."

Yuck. Faith that works through pride.

Another young man met me one cold New York day at the church in his old beat up car, and though it was minus 10 degrees, he pulled into the driveway with the windows down. I asked him to explain this to me, and he said, "There are so many suffering in the world today that it did not seem right for me to enjoy a warm car while I drove over to the church."

Yikes. Faith that works through fear.

No one is drawn to a person motivated by self-righteousness. Not believers. Not unbelievers. Such a person is useless to minister to others. It is through living a cross-centered life that we defeat such a spirit, and can truly serve others in love.

10. *Study* the Word

"*This is the victory that has overcome the world, even our faith*" (1 John 5:4, NIV).

If our faith is the victory that overcomes the world, we'd better get more of it! How, exactly, do we do that? "*So faith comes from hearing, and hearing by the word of Christ*" (Romans 10:17, NASB). "*Then you will know the truth, and the truth will set you free*" (John 8:32, NIV).

Your level of victory, then, is directly proportional to how much truth you know. *Reading* the Bible rarely gives you the deep revelation that results in a strong faith. As a matter of fact, there's little in the Bible about merely *reading* it. There's much more about *studying* the Word and *meditating* on it.

> *"Study to show yourself approved to God, a workman that needs not to be ashamed, rightly dividing the word of truth." (2 Timothy 2:15, NKJV)*

> *"I meditate on your precepts and consider your ways. I delight in your decrees; I will not neglect your word." (Psalm 119:16)*

If you would live a cross-centered life, determine to be one that *studies* the Word of God. Though it's good to listen to sermons and podcasts of other teachers, learn to become a *self-feeding disciple.* Learn to go to the Word, and with the help of the Holy Spirit, discover truth.

11. Let your disciplines be *desire-driven*

After my grace conversion, one of the first things I learned about living a cross-centered life is to let my disciplines be *desire-driven.* God wants our lives to be driven from our passion and zeal for Him, and He wants everything we do to be worship.

> *"Delight yourself in the LORD and he will give you the desires of your heart" (Psalm 37:4, NIV).*

> *"Therefore I say to you, What things soever you desire, when you pray, believe that you receive them, and you shall have them" (Mark 11:24, NKJV).*

What we see here is that God works with the deepest desires of the heart. This does not mean that God gives us whatever we want, but that as we delight in Him, He actually *places* His desires in our hearts. *Delight in the Lord, and He will give you the desires of your heart.*

So then, to discover what the will of God is for the cross-centered person, we must simply look at the deepest desires of our hearts, because *we're only going to want what God wants.* Jesus said,

"If you abide in me and my words abide in you, you can ask for anything you want, and you will receive it" (John 15:7, ISV).

God wants us to experience joy and passion in serving Him. Why? Because it gives God glory. Author John Piper wrote, "God is most glorified in us when we are most satisfied in Him."[175]

This desire principle, then, must be carried over to prayer and Bible study. Our prayers and Bible study must be desire-driven. We must ask in prayer, "What is *really* on my heart?" C.S. Lewis put it this way: "In prayer we must lay before Him what is in us, not what ought to be in us."[176]

When it comes to studying the Bible, we must ask, "What do I *really* want to grow in?" Right now, I'm really asking the Lord to teach me more about marriage and family, so I'm studying Ephesians 5. I'm thoroughly enjoying the experience, and I'm learning a lot as the Holy Spirit guides me into truth. When I had my grace conversion, all I wanted to study was grace, so I spent months in Romans and Galatians. I discuss this further in the chapter "The Role of Discipline."

Even fasting has become a joy. Most people I know hate it, but when it is desire-driven and is done for a purpose about which you're passionate, the whole experience changes. For example, I am so passionate about God's grace that I decided to fast and pray about how to share what I've learned with others. The morning I began, I presented my desires to the Lord, and asked, "How can I have a greater impact and influence in my generation in the area of teaching grace?" The book you are reading is the Lord's answer for that. When the vision for this book came clearly into my view, I was thrilled with the idea of completing it. It was my heart's desire.

Once you see grace, He will be your delight, and you will find great pleasure in your spiritual disciplines and in His will for your life.

---

[175] John Piper, *Let the Nations Be Glad!* Baker Academic & Brazos Press, 2nd edition: © 2003

[176] Walter Hopper, *C.S. Lewis: A Complete Guide to His Life & Works*: HarperCollins, 1998, pg. 382.

CHAPTER 10
Another Jesus, Part 1: Legalism

"But I'm afraid, lest as the serpent deceived Eve by his craftiness, that you should be led astray from the simplicity and purity that is found in Christ...[for one comes preaching] another Jesus..."
—Paul the Apostle (2 Corinthians 11:3, NASB)

When Aaron fashioned a golden calf in Exodus 32, one of the things that offended God the most was that Aaron presented this calf as "the gods that brought you up out of Egypt."[177] In other words, he presented the calf as the representation of Jehovah God. He, in a sense, was saying, "This is what Jehovah, the God of Israel, looks like!" It was Aaron's attempt, and the people's attempt, *to make God in their image.*

People do this with Jesus all the time in the modern church, fashioning Him into their own image, and saying, "This is Jesus!" when, in fact, it is not Jesus at all, but what Paul the Apostle calls *another Jesus.* These deceivers paint Jesus in dark colors, looking on with disapproval from shadows, His harsh countenance barely visible to the soul that tries to find Him. Others paint Jesus the big sitcom buddy, winking at mischief, drawing laughter from the watching crowds.

Charles Spurgeon said, "Never make a Christ out of your faith."[178]

There are ways of thinking that create these false versions of Jesus. They are often reinforced by false teaching, doctrines made by demons—teachings that come in the name of Jesus, but have nothing to do with Him. The two most common, and perhaps the most ancient, are *legalism* and *license.* These two present Jesus in completely opposite lights, though neither of them is Christ at all, and they are both an abuse of the doctrine of God's grace. In

---

[177] Exodus 32:4
[178] Charles Spurgeon, *All of Grace.* © 2008 Biblio Bazaar: pg. 36

understanding discipleship by grace, we have to be aware of these two ditches. This chapter is dedicated to investigating legalism.

LEGALISM

Legalism is a teaching, belief system, or fundamental culture that bases your relationship with God strictly on your performance, and not on the shed blood of Jesus Christ. It makes the object of your faith your own works, and not the cross of Christ. To the legalist, God is a harsh slave driver. He is impossible to please, and rarely affectionate and tender. Legalism says:

"If I can just obey all the rules, then God would accept me."

"If I work hard enough, I'll be holy."

"If I can become a disciplined person, I'll prove that I'm a whole-hearted Christian."

"God will pour out His Spirit on me if I just try harder."

In his book *The Cross Centered Life*, author and pastor C.J. Mahaney writes that "legalism is seeking to achieve forgiveness from God and acceptance by God through obedience to God."[179]

"Huh?" you might react. "Doesn't obedience please God? I've been taught that all my life!"

Obedience pleases God, but *trusting in our obedience for our righteousness* does not. If you are among those who believe that your "forgiveness from God and acceptance by God [come] through obedience to God," then what or *who* is your object of faith? *You* are! And if *you* are the object of your faith, then Christ ceases to be, and you've emptied your faith of power. You believe in *another Jesus*.

Again, God is the Jealous One, and will not share His glory with another—and especially not with you! *He* must be the object of your faith, though not in a sentimental, God-loves-me-because-He's-nice kind of a way—you must believe and trust in the work of the cross. Christ and Him crucified must be the object of your faith. The cross is your access and right to stand before Him as a child of God.

---

[179] Mahaney, C.J., *The Cross Centered Life* (Sisters, Oregon: Multnomah Publishers, Inc., © 2002 by Sovereign Grace Ministries), p. 25

On the topic of legalism, Mahaney also writes, "Justification is being *declared* righteous. Sanctification is being *made* righteous — being conformed to the image of Christ. Justification is our *position* before God. Sanctification is our practice. You don't *practice* justification. It happens once for all, upon conversion."[180] He later adds, "[The legalist] confuses his own ongoing participation in the process of sanctification with God's finished work in justification."[181]

For a more in-depth look at leaving legalism and walking in grace, read my book *Enoch Walked With God.*[182]

DIOTREPHES

Legalistic environments usually have a powerful, controlling and domineering leader who sets himself up as the lawgiver, the standard, and the mediator between his followers and God. He turns conscience issues into laws, and sets up the priesthood all over again, keeping the inferior sinners outside, and his superiority supreme. If his followers fail to keep the standard (say, miss a meeting), their commitment to Christ is seriously questioned. I've been under this type of leadership, and its fruit is devastating in the lives of people.

Paul wrote, "I wrote something to the church; but Diotrephes, who loves to be first among them, does not accept what we say. For this reason, if I come, I will call attention to his deeds which he does, unjustly accusing us with wicked words; and not satisfied with this, he himself does not receive the brethren, either, and he forbids those who desire to do so and puts them out of the church" (3 John 9-10, NASB).

He loves to be first. It is precisely this kind of spirit that consumes the legalistic leader. *He forbids those who desire to do so and puts them out of the church.* Legalism creates precisely this kind

---

[180] Mahaney, C.J., *The Cross Centered Life* (Sisters, Oregon: Multnomah Publishers, Inc., © 2002 by Sovereign Grace Ministries), p. 32

[181] Ibid, p. 33

[182] Published by Five Stones Publishing: Potter, Kansas. This book can be ordered at www.isaiahsix.com.

of environment. Performing for men becomes the goal; the praise of man the coveted prize.

I was in a small local church in Texas at one time in my life with a strong leader. Of course, strong leadership is not a crime, but this man was given to legalism. After attending the Pensacola revival,[183] he was so taken with the revival that he wanted to duplicate it in his church. Returning from Florida, he cancelled all church programs and extra activities and called the church to prayer. Every night, he expected his people to be at the church praying. This sounds wonderful, but eventually, he created a politically charged environment where attendance at the prayer meetings had everything to do with whether or not, in his mind, you were committed to the church, a committed Christian, or interested in revival. If you were at the meetings, you were looked on with approval. If you missed them, you were marked as a half-hearted person.

I attended some of these meetings, and the longer they went on, the more mechanical they became. There was no life in them. It was the last place I wanted to be. People started acting strangely. One woman walked around for months, jerking her body every few seconds, calling it the "trevail" of intercession. Divisions erupted. *"The works of the flesh are obvious" (Galatians 5:19, ISV).* Eventually, I was kicked out of the church for not submitting to some of the legalistic demands placed on my family and me.

In this lifeless environment, the church attendance diminished quickly from 600 to 60, and eventually the senior pastor forged the name of his assistant pastor on a credit card application just to try to pay church debt. Neither is on staff at that church anymore. The one-time senior pastor doesn't even live in this country.

In another season of my life, my wife and I were part of a para-church ministry, where a similar kind of leader directed an evangelistic ministry. We moved to work with this ministry because we saw God using this man in a powerful way. We would

---

[183] The Brownsville Assembly of God Church in Pensacola, Florida experienced a great move of God from 1996-2003, where over 400,000 repented of their sins and gave their lives to Christ.

soon learn that anointing doesn't equal character, or even good doctrine!

Shortly after we arrived, we realized that this man was not attending any church in the area, and had no sincere intention of doing so. He saw himself as self-sustaining in the Lord, and told us that the churches in the area were led by blind Pharisees. He wanted everyone in the ministry to get their spiritual sustenance from him.

We were expected to be at a 6:30am prayer meeting seven days a week, and if we were not shouting during the prayer and worship times, it was seen as spiritual apathy. After a season, my wife and I grew weary of the grind. Besides the fact that we were physically and spiritually tired, we also weren't getting the time together to relax and enjoy one another as husband and wife. We were a young couple, and longed for a day when we could just sleep in and have fun together. Finally, one Friday night, I told Heidi Jo, "You know what? We're going to sleep in tomorrow. Who cares what people think!"

Late morning the next day, I got a call from my friend Phil, who also worked for the ministry, "Derek," he said, "he was all over you guys this morning, and said that you have fallen prey to laziness and compromise."

Soon after, the ministry leader forbade all staff members and interns from attending the local church that my wife and I had been attending. He proclaimed himself our pastor, and insisted that all staffers attend his meetings on the ministry property on Sundays.

Eventually, we left this ministry after the leader had an affair with his secretary.

Part of standing firm in grace is being careful not to submit to the legalistic teaching of a false teacher. Galatians 5:1 says, "It was for freedom that Christ set us free; therefore keep standing firm and do not be subject again to a yoke of slavery."[184] 99.9% of the time, when I've heard this Scripture referenced, the freedom spoken of is deliverance from sin, fear, sickness or some other

---

[184] NASB

malady. But in context that is not what this freedom is referring to. What Paul the Apostle is referring to here is *freedom from living under law*. He's encouraging the Galatians to not submit to slavery by accepting legalism. No one has the power to take away your liberty!

THE SYMPTOMS OF LEGALISM

There are some telltale signs of legalism. Galatians 5:25-26 puts it best: "If we live by the Spirit, let us also walk by the Spirit. Let us not become boastful, challenging one another, envying one another."[185]

Here, right after a long discussion about living and walking in grace, Paul finishes with this strange admonition about not boasting, challenging, or envying. What exactly is Paul getting at here?

I believe that Paul is simply revealing the symptoms of *not* walking in grace. *Boasting, challenging, and envying.* Here we have the poles of legalism, boasting in the far north, envying in the far south.

Boasting speaks of the religious self-righteous pride owned in the heart of the one that thinks he's gotten over the bar of works. He is under law, supposing himself, at least for a moment, to be worthy of admiration, so he boasts. "Look how spiritual I am!" he says, putting his deeds on display for all to see, and patting himself on the back.

Envying is the opposite. This poor soul sees that he has *not* gotten over the bar, and he looks on others with envy, wishing he were more like the boaster, perhaps. The condemned one is, in a sense, envious of another's righteousness or position. Even though the symptom is different, it is exactly the same disease—legalism. Both the boaster and the envious one are under law; both are measuring themselves by their ability to meet the Law's demands. One made it, one didn't.

Challenging lies in the middle of the two, and is the cause of the boasting and the envy! Challenging speaks of competing

---

[185] NASB

against another. Legalism creates competition, and when one challenges another in the game of law, one will boast the win and one will envy after the loss.

During one season of our ministry, we had an "intern house" where young men lived while being trained in our internship program. It didn't take long for the competition to begin. One would get up at 6:00am, and then tattle on the others who slept in. Boasting and envy were rampant among our interns, as some tried to assert their spiritual dominance over others, while some resigned to being "unspiritual," allowing the spiritual Alpha Dogs to reign supreme.

I don't mean to use only others in my examples of legalism. I'm a pretty good bungler myself. Let me tell you about my first argument with my wife. The two extremes of pride and condemnation existed in my own home before my grace conversion. I was the "spiritual one" that could get over the bar, and Heidi Jo was the "unspiritual one" who couldn't. Early on in our marriage, I wanted to set the tone that we would be radical intercessors, storming the gates of hell together every day in prayer. I told my wife that we'd get up at 6:00am to pray. She consented, and at 6 o'clock, we rose up to set the world straight with our mighty intercession. I began to pray, stirring myself into a frenzied state. My wife sat quietly against the wall, nodding off. The longer I prayed and she didn't, the more annoyed I got. Finally, I asked her, "Are you going to join me or not?"

Tears welled up in her eyes as she said, "I can't just flip on the switch like you!" Then she ran back to bed, thus ending our first and final early morning prayer meeting together. What an idiot I was.

Isaiah 40:4 says, "Every valley shall be exalted, and every mountain and hill brought low…"[186] This means that the gospel of grace will bring the haughty and prideful ones *down*, and the condemned and broken ones *up*. Grace will put everyone on the same level in the eyes of God. No one wins the competition! There is no competition! Jesus gets *all* the glory.

---

[186] NKJV

143

You either live under law or under grace. There is no middle ground. These may be likened to two different countries on different sides of an ocean. You cannot live in both simultaneously, nor can you straddle the borders. You must live in one or the other. So it is with living under grace or under law.

Jesus said to "beware the leaven of the Pharisees" (Matthew 16:6, KJV), for "a little leaven leavens the whole lump of dough" (Galatians 5:9, NASB). In other words, a little bit of legalism will eventually destroy all spiritual life. If you've embraced *some* legalism, you are now *under law*. You serve *another Jesus*.

So how do I know if I'm living under law or under grace? Check your symptoms.

Under Law	Under Grace
Discouraged	Encouraged
Love the praise of men	Love to give God praise
Competing with others	Serving others
Motivated by fear	Motivated by love
Self-loathing	Seeing the worth Christ sees
Condemnation	Free
Many laws	One law: Love
Complexity	Simplicity
Insecure	Confident

PHARISAICAL COMPLEXITY

Remember that Second Corinthians 11:3 says that the "other Jesus" will cause us to be "*led astray from the simplicity and purity that is found in Christ.*"

Simplicity.

When we walk in grace, the Christian life is simple. We only have to focus on the law of love, and in doing so, we fulfill all other laws. If I love you, I won't kill you, steal from you, covet your goods, etc. But in legalism, things get complicated. We begin to stack law on law, work on work, until we are driven mad by the sheer complexity of it all!

Remember, God did not make it complicated. The devil did. Then you did.

The Pharisees were mired deep into complexity, and not only were they trapped, they brought others down with them. The Pharisees were glory-stealers. They were expert boasters and legalists. They were celebrities, governors, and policemen in the country we're calling Under Law. To understand the self-righteousness that Jesus confronted in His day, here's a quick look at the different kinds of Pharisees:

Seven Pharisees

1) Shechemite Pharisees: circumcised as Shechem for their own glory

2) The Dashing Pharisee: walked around gently, heel to toe, heel to toe, barely lifting up his feet (and so "dashing them against the stones"), so he would appear to be in deep meditation

3) The Pharisee Letting Blood: pretended to close his eyes as he walked, so as not to look lustfully upon women, faking collisions with walls so that blood would run down his face

4) The Depressed Pharisee: went doubled over so he could not look upward, nor to either side, only downward or right forward

5) The Pharisee that said, "What is my duty and I will do it?": An expert in the intricate details of the Law, and always searching for new laws to obey, so as to outdo other law-keepers.

6) The Pharisee of Fear: who does what he does from fear of punishment

7) The Pharisee of Love: who does what he does for the love of the reward of the commandment, and not the love of the commandment itself

Jesus said of them, "For they loved the praise of men more than the praise of God."[187] Jesus said to them, "How can you believe, who receive honor from one another, and do not seek the honor that comes from the only God?"[188]

Here we have one of the greatest signs of legalism: *We love the praise of men.* It's impossible to receive grace from God *that we don't deserve* when we're seeking praise *that we think we do deserve from men.* This thinking is based in the idea that we have performed well and deserve applause from God and man. It's legalism again.

MORE ON CONDEMNATION

Condemnation is an awful and potentially spiritually debilitating symptom of legalism. If you experience condemnation and discouragement as a frequent part of your Christian life, you are living under law. Do you experience condemnation when the Bible says, "Now therefore there is no condemnation to those who are in Christ Jesus" (Romans 8:1)?

Do you feel *encouraged*? Let me give you an acid test.

Have you ever been pulled over by a cop? When he walked up to your window, what did he say? Did he commend you for driving the speed limit or praise you for your textbook left turn? Probably not. I'm sure he told you what you did wrong. Why? Because he represents the *law*. His job is not to encourage you, but to point out your infractions. This is what it's like for the person living under condemnation. The condemned person never feels *encouraged*. For the person living under law, that cop is always in his window. Discouragement is a constant companion. If that cop is in your window, you are living under condemnation. You are living under law.

Condemnation is a deadly killer that has driven scores from the faith. There are several poisonous fruits that grow on this branch. Among them are:

---

[187] John 12:43, KJV
[188] John 5:44, NKJV

146

Asceticism

Asceticism is self-denial, self-punishment, and abstinence from worldly pleasures for the sake of achieving greater spirituality, and it is often marked by the severe mistreatment of the body. Ascetics mistakenly believe that by punishing themselves, they will gain a greater status with God. An ascetic also believes that purifying the body helps to purify the soul, again a perceived step toward gaining God's favor.

Martin Luther struggled with asceticism before his grace conversion. After making a fearful vow to God in the midst of a thunderstorm that he would become a monk if God saved him from death, he joined a German monastery to fulfill his pledge. Terribly afraid of the wrath of God, Luther strove for personal holiness through the rituals of the Catholic church. In spite of his best efforts, he found himself tormented by his own sins and the terrors of God's judgment. He lived beneath the crushing weight of condemnation. On one occasion, he whipped himself until he lost so much blood that he passed out. On another occasion, monks found Luther lying naked in a snow bank. Thanks be to God, mercy found Luther.

Resignation

Condemnation can also bring its victim to *resignation*. Resignation basically says, "This is the way I am, and I cannot change." The poor soul will see himself as an outcast in the kingdom, a second-rate citizen of heaven, sentenced to the outer courts of defeat. Resignation is half right—we cannot change ourselves. But God can! Resignation sees the problem, but not the cure, so the poor soul remains in defeat.

Exaltation of Man

Legalism ultimately restores the priesthood, setting up those who achieve the standard as superior, and those who don't as inferior. "Don't touch the Lord's anointed" is the mantra of the ego-driven leader, as he exalts himself as God's friend, leaving his followers in a state of lowly condemnation.

147

I have an acquaintance who used to work for a famous pastor, and he told me that his boss had constructed his office to keep himself in ultra-isolation from "the common people." He had several security doors complete with codes as if he worked in Langley instead of a church. When you finally reached his office, it was like entering the Holy of Holies.

In a culture of legalism, there are "less thans" and "more thans." If condemnation is your symptom, then you see yourself as a "less than" and the exaltation of man begins. James felt to warn the church about this trap when he said of Elijah in James 5:17, "Elijah was a man just like us."

LEGALISM CREATES FEAR

John says, "There is no fear in love, but perfect love casts out fear, because fear involves torment. But he who fears has not been made perfect in love."[189] This verse is often referred to as a fear-stopping verse for whatever threatens us. *Don't be afraid of the dark! Perfect love casts out fear! Don't be afraid of your financial trouble! Perfect love casts out fear! Et cetera.*

But really, this verse speaks of the fear of *torment,* or as another translation puts it, the fear of *punishment.* In other words, the believer who does not understand that grace has saved us fully from the punishment for our sins will be trapped in the fear of that punishment, and will never grow in God. He'll always be working and striving to offset the wrath of God with his efforts, but of course will never achieve it, and therefore will be frozen in time, unable to grow in God.

It is the believer who understands the cross and the grace given to us that will grow.

I have some friends that adopted some children from Kazakhstan. One child was eighteen months, and the other was eight months. Before they left the orphanage, they were told, "Do not be surprised at how much the children grow during the first year. This will be the result of parental stimulus as they have

---

[189] 1 John 4:18, NKJV

148

lacked such interaction up to this point in their lives. The absence of parental love stunts human growth."

Many babies in orphanages have actually died because they cried with no one to hold them. Parental love not only keeps a child alive, but makes the child grow.

It's the same way in the kingdom of God. If you will not understand the Father heart of God, you will never grow in your faith. When the pure water of God's grace cleans out the heart contaminated with sin, fear, and insecurity, only love remains. And love will not make you cower in fear and die in legalism. It will give you confidence to stand before a holy God in white robes of righteousness, and walk in joy and peace. *Perfect love casts out fear.*

Tim Keller, author of *Prodigal God,* said, "Religion says, 'I obey, therefore, I'm accepted. The gospel says, 'I'm accepted, therefore, I obey.'"[190]

Such is the peace in the heart of the child of God that realizes that the Father has accepted him in Christ.

---

[190] Tim Keller, pastor of New York's Redeemer Presbyterian Church in Manhattan said this in a sermon on renewal at *The Leadership Summit 2009.*

CHAPTER 11
Another Jesus, Part 2: License

"He who has love is far from all sin."
— Polycarp,[191] disciple of the Apostle John

"Why don't you love me?" she said to her friend. "Stop judging me!"

Kelly had made some bad choices that Beth considered self-destructive. She decided to have an affair with a married man, and when Beth confronted her, she got defensive.

Kelly made the mistake of thinking that Beth's decision to confront her was *not* loving, but in Beth's heart, she knew that she was confronting Kelly *because* she loved her.

"God's grace is bigger than you think," Kelly argued.

"But God's grace doesn't give you permission to sin," Beth explained.

"God knows my heart," Kelly concluded, "and I don't need you to tell me what to do."

License.

License turns God into a big Santa Claus that caters to our every command and winks at sin. He just loves, loves, loves. This deception makes people believe (or act as if they believe) that grace gives them a license to sin, or at least that God overlooks their sins in light of the sacrifice of Christ. This, however, is an abuse of the gospel, and is not the gospel at all. Let me say it plainly: Sin is not the gospel. God's grace is not permission to sin, *it's a way out of sin.* If you believe in a gospel that gives you permission to sin, then you have not believed the gospel. You believe in *another Jesus.*

"My God loves me, and is okay with what I'm doing!" they say, and they are correct—their god does love them and is okay with what they're doing. The only problem is that their god is not the God of the Bible. It's another Jesus.

---

[191] The Epistle of Polycarp to the Philippians.

John wrote, "Whoever claims to be in Him, and continues to sin, is a liar, and the truth is not in him" (1 John 2:4). Licentious people turn God's laws into conscience issues, and have no passion for holiness. They do not believe in a Jesus who drives money-changers out of temples; who says to Peter, "Get behind me, Satan," or calls His followers to deny themselves—or a God who kills Ananias and Sapphira. They do not believe that the Father disciplines those He loves. They want nothing to do with it.

Titus 2:11-12 says, "For the grace of God has appeared to all men. It teaches us to say 'No' to ungodliness and worldly passions."[192] According to this verse, grace is a *teacher*. It teaches us to deny sin, not embrace it. Anyone that claims to believe in the gospel and also claims that it's okay to sin is not listening to the right teacher. They are not walking in true grace. They are listening to demons.

BY NO MEANS!

This is not a new problem. Paul asked the Romans, "Shall we continue in sin that grace may abound?" Then he answered the question by saying emphatically, "By no means!"[193]

How can we choose to sin if we love God?

Seeing God's grace causes an abundant love for God to fill the heart; it purifies the motive of the heart until we cry, "All for Jesus!" How can love hurt its lover?

I know my wife loves me dearly, and will love me "until death do we part." How could I respond to this love by looking at pornography or pursuing other lovers? Would my wife still love me? She would be hurt, but she would still love me. Should my knowledge that she'll still love me give me permission to be unfaithful? I'll echo Paul the Apostle. *By no means!*

A few years ago, when the movie *The Passion of the Christ* was in theatres, it was amazing to see the emotional responses that saved and unsaved people would have to the movie. If you saw the movie and you responded like I did, you left the experience asking, "How can I thank the Lord for what He's done? How can I

---

[192] NIV
[193] Romans 6:1

152

live for Him now?" I didn't see one Christian respond by saying, "You know, I'm so thankful for the cross that I'm going to go get wasted tonight!"

The only appropriate response to love seemed to be love.

The very phrase "I love you" evokes only one response: *"I love you, too."*

It is the same with the cross. The cross is the ultimate demonstration of God's love. It is God saying to the world, "I love you!" Our *only* response is to love Him back with our lives.

Over and over, this is actually the main argument the Bible makes for why you should worship God and honor Him with your life—God loved us first.

> *"We love Him because He first loved us."* *(1 John 4:19, NKJV)*

> *"I beseech you therefore, brethren, by the mercies of God, that you present your bodies a living sacrifice, holy, acceptable to God, which is your reasonable service."* *(Romans 12:1, NKJV)*

The message of the Scriptures is that after seeing the love of God demonstrated in the cross, it's reasonable to live a holy life of worship. It's not an outrageous request. It makes sense. You'll *want* to live a holy life. That's why anyone who lives in sin and claims to be in Him leaves me to wonder if he has ever heard, understood, or believed the true gospel. How can he live in sin if he's tasted the goodness of God?

He is following *another Jesus.*

GOD HURTS

King David committed adultery. Then he had the husband of his mistress killed. No one knew. For over a year, David hid this wickedness in his heart until Nathan the prophet confronted him. When David finally confessed his sin and poured out his soul to God, he said these words: "Against You, You only, have I sinned" (Psalm 51:4, NKJV).

It is possible to hurt God.

This was one of the things that grieved David most. In the natural, David's kingdom went on as it had been. Not many were affected by his secret sin. So what's the big deal? *Against You, You only, have I sinned.*

He hurt God.

License hurts God.

True love would not dream of hurting its object, but that is exactly what license does.

"It's my choice!" they say. "You don't know my heart, so don't judge me, and besides, God will forgive me."

Against You, You only, have I sinned.

How can true love do such a thing to the one it loves? My only conclusion is that *it's not true love.*

Love is the only motive of true faith. If this is biblical faith, then true faith is marked by a passion to love God, honor Him, and worship in all things, at all times. Any other kind of "faith" is a product of worshiping a golden calf, and following another Jesus. Any other kind of "faith" is not faith at all. It's not the gospel at all. It's not Jesus at all.

SYMPTOMS OF LICENSE

License can be difficult to read at first, as many who end up in licentiousness begin the journey sounding like believers in grace. But it is counterfeit grace. Ultimately, "you will know them by their fruits" (Matthew 7:16, NKJV). The following are some of the fruits of license:

A mistrust or hatred for authority
People trapped in licentiousness do not want anyone telling them what to do or what to believe. Wishing to follow the desires of their flesh, they justify their ways, and it will not do to have anyone make an objection.

A lack of conviction
I've heard it said that tolerance is the virtue of a man with no convictions. With license, morality is very subjective, and can be

flexible between situations and people. That said, conviction in absolutes is seen as naïve or arrogant.

Insincerity in fellowship
There is a relational shallowness within the heart of licentious people because fellowship cannot be authentic. Healthy Christian fellowship happens around the topics of Scripture, the cross, the work of the Church, and the ongoing work in the heart of becoming like Jesus. These topics are awkward for licentious people because they do not share the same views about these things as a healthy believer. Discussions on sin are absolutely off limits. A licentious person can come across as "nice" but leave you with the feeling that you did not connect with him in real fellowship. Sometimes licentious people are downright bitter at the Church and don't come across as nice at all.

Bitterness toward the Church
You often hear those deceived by license teaching slamming the church for being full of Pharisees, judgmental, critical, and unloving. There is an incredible mistrust for the organized church and anything that comes from it. They claim to love God, but hate their brothers.

Questioning of Scripture
Licentious people find ways to play with the words of Scripture, twisting them to their own pursuits, or rejecting the infallibility of Scripture altogether for any number of reasons.

Sin is a dirty word
Licentious people usually avoid the word sin. Those who preach license won't mention it, and those who believe it won't discuss it. But as the old hymn *Amazing Grace* teaches us, the grace isn't amazing if the wretch isn't a wretch!

A BAD DAY FOR A DUDE

A friend of mine named Chris grew up in a Christian home, but wandered from the faith, and ended up involved in a drug ring in Tyler, Texas. He has since come to Christ. Even when he was wayward, he knew that to live for Christ meant that he must give up everything and live a life of purity. That's why he was a bit alarmed when some license evangelists approached him one day on the streets. They handed him a "Sinner's Prayer" on a card and said, "Hey man, if you just say this prayer, you'll go to heaven."

"I ain't saved," Chris said, "but if you believe saying this prayer makes you saved, then you ain't saved either."

"Who told you that?" asked one of the deceivers.

"My dad."

"Well, your dad's full of garbage."

Chris, a stocky athlete, handily slammed this guy on his car, and pummeled him with fists.

Beware the other gospels. Beware of "another Jesus." Beware the golden calves. They are all around us today. Unfortunately, I have seen people with whom I've walked closely in the Lord drift to these golden calves. Some have drifted to legalism and some to license. The results have been painful to watch.

As we've noted in another chapter, Paul said, "For in Christ Jesus, neither circumcision nor uncircumcision means anything, but faith working through love" (Galatians 5:6, NASB). *Faith working through love.* Here Paul strikes down legalism and license in one fell swoop. Neither circumcision (representing legalism) nor uncircumcision (representing license) means *anything.* The only thing that matters is *faith working through love.* We're going to take a look at that in the next chapter.

CHAPTER 12
What Grace Looks Like

"Do not work so that you may be saved, but serve Him because you are saved." —Charles Spurgeon, *Grace*[194]

Grace is not just something we believe, it's something we *experience*. It's not just a theological concept, but is a tree of life growing in the heart. Like a seed planted in a field, grace grows up and bears fruit in our lives. Therefore, grace is measurable. It is quantifiable. It has fruit. It has evidence. *It looks like something.*

Lima bean seeds grow lima beans; corn seed grows corn, and grace grows into holiness. So how do we know if someone has believed true grace or counterfeit grace? *Look at its fruit.* Throughout the New Testament, we are encouraged to do this.

> *"You will know them by their fruits. Grapes are not gathered from thorn bushes nor figs from thistles, are they? So every good tree bears good fruit, but the bad tree bears bad fruit. A good tree cannot produce bad fruit, nor can a bad tree produce good fruit."* (Matthew 7:16-18, NASB)

> *"The acts of the sinful nature are obvious: sexual immorality, impurity and debauchery; idolatry and witchcraft; hatred, discord, jealousy, fits of rage, selfish ambition, dissensions, factions and envy; drunkenness, orgies, and the like. I warn you, as I did before, that those who live like this will not inherit the kingdom of God. But the fruit of the Spirit is love, joy, peace, patience, kindness, goodness, faithfulness, gentleness and self control. Against such things there is no law."* (Galatians 5:19-23, NIV)

Paul is basically teaching us how to identify what's real and what's fake. In essence, he's saying, "I don't care what someone tells you he believes, if you see this fruit, you'll know whether it's

---

[194] Charles Spurgeon, *Grace*. © 2003 Whitaker House.

authentic or not." Grace is not a subjective feeling, only known between the believer and God. Eventually, grace will prove itself true or false in a way that is visible to others. Others can see if the person's faith was legitimate and if he believed in true grace or counterfeit grace. John had no problem giving us such an acid test when he said, "The one who says, 'I have come to know Him,' and does not keep His commandments, is a liar, and the truth is not in him" (1 John 2:4, NASB). He also added, "This is how we know we are in Him: Whoever claims to live in Him must walk as Jesus did" (1 John 2:6, NASB).

This is exactly why the Reformers used to say, *"We are saved by faith alone, but we are not saved by faith that is alone."* In other words, true faith is marked by the fruit of the Spirit. The fruit will show us if a person has really received a revelation of the gospel of Jesus, or if he is following *another Jesus.*

GRACE IS AN INSTRUCTOR

"For the grace of God has appeared to all men. It teaches us to say 'No' to ungodliness and worldly passions" (Titus 2:11-12, NIV).

Those who object to grace teaching as "dangerous" don't understand the power of grace. As I mentioned previously, grace is an *instructor.* It teaches followers of Jesus to deny ungodliness. It puts us on the path to holiness because our hearts overflow with gratitude and a zeal to please the Lord.

I spent the previous two chapters talking about what the fruit of grace *isn't.* It is not legalism and it is not license. So what is it?

Love.

Grace teaches us to love God with all our heart, soul, mind, and strength; not in word only, but in deed.

If I love God, I will not sin against Him.

If I love people, I will not sin against them.

Love fulfills the Law. Love is holy. Holiness equals love.

If I love you, I'm not going to steal from you, bear false testimony against you, covet your goods, or kill you. By loving you, I will *accidentally* fulfill the Laws of God. That's why Paul's comments on the fruit of the Spirit in Galatians 5:22-23 ends with,

"Against such things there is no Law." As we love, we will do the things the Law requires. Grace teaches us how to live like that.

That's why it bothers me when I hear people say, "We need to balance grace and Law. Then people won't drift into error." You mean mix grace and legalism? Remember, "A little leaven leavens the whole lump of dough" (Galatians 5:9, NASB). A little legalism will eventually destroy all spiritual life.

Grace balances itself.

Built into grace is the instruction for holiness because grace alters our desires and purifies our motives. Grace actually *causes us* to choose what is good and right.

An example of this may be in my parenting. I love my children very much. Because I love them, I do everything I can to serve them and bless them. Now, down in the county courthouse, there are probably scores of laws in the lawbooks about what I can't do to my children. Even so, not once have I had to go down to the courthouse to study the laws so I can figure out how to properly parent my children. Love has already taught me that. Because I love my children, I fulfill *all* the laws written in the lawbooks at the county courthouse. I am not *under law.* I am *under grace.*

In John 14:21, Jesus says, "Whoever has my commands and obeys them, he is the one who loves me."[195] I used to read that verse in fear and say, "Whoa. I better obey Him to prove that I love Him!" Instead, I now see that Jesus was not teaching obedience as a *condition* of our love, but as a *result* of our love. He is teaching His followers that if we love Him, the fruit will be obedience and character.

GRACE IS HOLY

There is no such thing as a Christian gospel that gives us permission to sin, and there is no God that winks at sin. Holiness is the only fruit of a true believer. Throughout the Scriptures, we see that grace converts the heart to obedience.

---

[195] NIV

"The Law of the Lord is perfect, converting the soul." (Psalm 19:7, KJV)

"By this we know that we have come to know Him, if we keep His commandments." (1 John 2:3, NASB)

"The one who keeps His commandments abides in Him, and He in him. We know by this that He abides in us, by the Spirit whom He has given us." (1 John 3:24, NASB)

I've heard it said that, "Only God produces God." I'd like to alter that slightly by saying, "God produces only God." In other words, God will only reproduce in us what He is in essence. God is a holy God who lives in the absence of sin, and He will lead our lives toward its absence in us as well.

Grace is holy.

What a stark contrast to what we often hear of grace today! Today, grace is often associated more with sin than with holiness, as if it's only for those who need forgiveness; or it's a buzzword for wishy-washy teachers that don't want to talk about sin. *Grace is holy.* It's a way out of sin.

Author Jerry Bridges wrote, "We abuse grace when, after sinning, we dwell on the compassion and mercy of God to the exclusion of His holiness and hatred of sin."[196]

GRACE WORKS

When I preach grace, I do want to be careful not to suggest a gospel of laziness. I do believe in a gospel of works! I just don't put the cart before the horse. For us to work, grace acts first.

"For by grace you have been saved through faith; and that not of yourselves, it is the gift of God; not as a result of works, so that no one may boast. For we are His workmanship, created in Christ Jesus for good works, which God prepared beforehand so that we would walk in them." (Ephesians 2:8-10, NASB)

---

[196] Copied from The Pursuit of Holiness by Jerry Bridges, © 1996, p. 65. Used by permission of NavPress – www.navpress.com. All rights reserved.

I love the paradox of this passage in Ephesians. Within two verses, Paul tells us that the gospel is "not of works...for good works." Make up your mind, Paul! Which is it? Brothers and sisters, it's both. The revelation of "the gospel of done" will produce in us "the do." Understanding grace will produce good works in us.

I've taken a great effort in this book to convince you that everything depends on God. Now, I want to give you my best counsel on how to apply grace. *Believe that everything depends on God, and act like everything depends on you.*

Take a moment with me and consider the words of 18th Century preacher, Jonathan Edwards: "In efficacious grace we are not merely passive, nor yet does God do some and we do the rest. But God does all, and we do all. God produces all, we act all. For that is what produces, viz. our own acts. God is the only proper author and fountain; we only are the proper actors. We are in different respects, wholly passive and wholly active."[197]

Grace works. Grace produces works. The Holy Spirit guides us into them as we commune with the presence of God.

GRACE HONORS OTHERS

The work of grace in the heart always makes you more loving of others, more considerate of others, and more humble toward others.

You *honor* others because grace puts everyone on the same playing field before God. No more can I exalt myself over you, or think myself more loved by God because I have pleased Him more than you. Instead, grace causes us to value all men as God did when He sent Christ to the cross. If it was grace that saved you, and not personal merit, how shall you not honor your brother? Slavery cannot exist where grace is believed. Abuse cannot persist when the eyes of the heart are opened to grace. Why do you think slave ship captain John Newton had to recant his lifestyle when he saw God's grace? Grace taught him to honor all men. Such a revelation is where the great song came from that was penned by

---

[197] Jonathan Edwards (1703–1758), "Efficacious Grace," WC, 2: 580

his hand: *Amazing grace, how sweet the sound that saved a wretch like me…*

Humility moves into the heart when grace arrives. Your poverty qualified you for grace, not your success, so how can you look with haughtiness on another? A beggar has his problems, but usually haughtiness is not one of them. The lowly heart will look on one's self with self-depreciating perspectives. After all, didn't Jesus tell us that He "is gentle and humble in heart" (Matthew 11:29, NASB)? If God has a humble heart, how severe will your judgment be if you have exalted your own!

When grace comes in, you begin to *esteem others over yourself.* In light of the revelation of his own sin and God's grace, Paul's self-evaluation was that he was "the chief of sinners,"[198] so I'm sure that he saw all others with greater esteem than he saw himself. And if this was how Paul the apostle described himself, how dare we lay claim to a higher rank than he! Grace honors others; it does not parade itself.

GRACE LOVES

God is love. We love Him because He first loved us. Therefore, the fruit of grace is love for Him and for others. When we love Him, we will love what He loves.

I used to get so concerned about whether or not I loved souls. I would beg and pray and plead, and ask for a greater burden. But now I realize that a lack-of-love-for-souls-problem is actually a lack-of-love-for-God-problem.   And a   lack-of-love-for-God-problem is a lack-of-revelation-of-God's love-problem.

I remember leading worship at a missions conference in Omaha, Nebraska, and watching someone burst through the front door into the foyer of the church and give a message to an usher. I could see the whole thing happening. The usher walked down the aisle toward me, and put a note on my music stand. It said, "A man two blocks from here just shot himself in the head. Please pray."

---

[198] 1 Timothy 1:15

I remember feeling not compassion, but inconvenienced. I was annoyed and thinking, "So how am I going to fit this into my setlist?"

That's when the Lord convicted my heart for being so cold.

I stopped the music, and we prayed for the man. When we were finished, I confessed to the congregation, "I'm afraid that when I read this, it didn't bother me, and for that I'm sorry. But I want to know—how many of you also felt no compassion for this man?"

Hands went up all over the room.

"God forgive us," we prayed.

I wondered how I, and so many others attending a *missions* conference, could be so unmoved by such a real need. That was when I realized that my love for God was equally as cold. Soon after, the Lord would take me on a journey to show me that His grace is the source of all Love. Without Him, I could never talk myself in to loving anyone the way He does.

GRACE IS POWER

Grace is not permission to sin, it's a way *out* of sin. Grace is power. George Whitefield put it this way: "It is sweet to know and preach that Christ justifies the ungodly, and that all truly good works are not so much as partly the cause, but the *effect* of our justification before God."[199]

Consider this profound verse in Ezekiel:

> *"Moreover, I will give you a new heart and put a new spirit within you; and I will remove the heart of stone from your flesh and give you a heart of flesh. I will put My Spirit within you and cause you to walk in My statutes, and you will be careful to observe My ordinances." (Ezekiel 36:26-27, NASB)*

Grace *causes us* to choose godliness and to find victory over sin and the weaknesses of our flesh. Church planter Bob Weiner

---

[199] *George Whitefield* by Arnold Dallimore: The Banner of Truth Trust, Carlisle, PA. pg. 406.

used to say that every time you see the word grace in Scripture, you should insert the phrase "power beyond my ability." So, for example, when Paul said, "To me, the very least of all saints, this grace was given, to preach to the Gentiles the unfathomable riches of Christ," you would say instead, "To me, the very least of all saints, *power beyond my ability* was given, to preach to the Gentiles the unfathomable riches of Christ."

Seeing grace as empowerment will place grace in its proper role in our lives.

ZOE AND DUNAMIS

I think it would be helpful to take a few moments to discuss a few words that have strong bearing on this topic—the Greek words *zoe* and *dunamis*. *Zoe* is the Greek word for "life" and *dunamis* the Greek word for "power." As we look deeper into the definitions, however, I believe that we should biblically define them as "God-life" and "God-power." The words appear in verses such as these:

> "*The thief comes only to steal and kill and destroy; I have come that they may have life [zoe], and have it to the full.*" (John 10:10, NIV)

> "*That he would grant you, according to the riches of his glory, to be strengthened with might [dunamis] by his Spirit in the inner man.*" (Ephesians 3:16, KJV)

Zoe and dunamis are not just a little help from God, or a little caffeine-like bump in energy. This is God-DNA working inside the heart of the believer! Peter said, "For by these He has granted to us His precious and magnificent promises, so that by them you may become partakers of the divine nature..."[200]

Through grace, we become partakers in the divine nature. Faith gives us access to divine DNA! This is the new birth, the new creation, the new man—wired with the nature of the divine, we

---

[200] 2 Peter 1:4, NASB

become more like Jesus by the power of God. Zoe and dunamis come and work in the heart, and the God-life and God-power produce godliness. O what a promise!

This should help shed some light on the phrasing in Galatians 5:22, "But the fruit of the spirit is love, joy, peace, patience..."

Of the spirit.

If the fruits mentioned here are fruits *of the Spirit*, then they are miracles of God! Yet how often do we try to *do* love or *do* patience? You cannot, in your own strength, *do* the fruits of the Spirit. They are *of the Spirit!*

To be loving is as much a miracle of God as is parting the Red Sea!

To be joyful is as supernatural as opening blind eyes!

To have peace is no different than raising Lazarus from the grave!

Patience is like turning water into wine!

Kindness is like the feeding of the 5000!

Zoe and dunamis.

The fruits *of the Spirit.*

A.W. Tozer said, "The man who has struggled to purify himself and has had nothing but repeated failures will experience real relief when he stops tinkering with his own soul and looks away to the perfect One. When he looks at Christ, the very things he has so long been trying to do will be getting done within him. It will be God working in him..." [201]

We may seek these things in our flesh, but we will never find them there. As C.S. Lewis once said, "God cannot give us happiness and peace apart from Himself, because it is not there. There is no such thing."[202]

Augustine said, "Grant what Thou commandest, and command what Thou dost desire."[203] He understood something, that if God would command us, then He would also work in us the strength to be able to carry out that command.

---

[201] A.W. Tozer, *The Pursuit of God,* Christian Publications; Christian Publications edition (June 1982).

[202] C.S. Lewis, *Mere Christianity.* HarperOne; 3rd edition (February 6, 2001).

[203] R.C. Sproul, "Augustine and Pelagius." © 1995-2009 Leadership U

John Piper said, "Grace is not simply leniency when we have sinned. Grace is the enabling gift of God not to sin. Grace is power, not just pardon."[204]

His grace is enough to transform us. Grace is holy. Grace works. Grace looks like Jesus.

"You can give without loving, but you cannot love without giving."
— Amy Carmichael

---

[204] John Piper, from a sermon at Bethlehem Baptist Church in Minneapolis, Minnesota.

CHAPTER 13
True Revival

"Authentic Christianity never destroys what is good. It makes it grow, transfigures it, and enriches itself from it." – Anonymous

I used to be a revival preacher. Revival preaching introduces behaviors, suggesting that if you will do these behaviors long enough, you will see revival. Before my grace conversion, this was my message. When I ended up farther away from revival at the end of my journey than when I began, I realized that something was terribly wrong. Not one "revival message" that I heard or preached in all my years ever had the power to change my heart! Only the Word of grace could do that.

You see, I eventually did experience a revival when I had a grace conversion, but it did not come in the way that I thought it would, or that I'd once promised others it would. Revival finally came when I realized not what I needed to do, but what had already been done in Christ's sacrifice. When I stopped looking forward to what I must do, and looked at what was already done, I experienced true revival! Through God's Word, the Holy Spirit breathed new life into me, in fact a kind of life that I had never known.

The whole experience made me wonder, "When a follower of Jesus sees the truth of the Word, and experiences the life of God as a result of it, is that really revival or is it just *normal?"*

I don't think there's anything abnormal about what some might call revival. The regenerating, rejuvenating, effervescent presence of God should be normal in the life of every believer that hears the truth, believes it, and applies it to his life.

At the risk of being misunderstood, I want to tell you that I'm not interested in "revival" – at least the way I once perceived it to be. I just want every follower of Jesus to have an authentic Christian experience. If Christians everywhere would have an authentic Christian experience, we'd call probably call it revival.

THE SONG OF THE SIRENS

In Homer's *The Odyssey*, the main hero, Ulysses, passes by an island inhabited by singing Sirens, whose beautiful song lures many mariners away to their death. Ulysses has to stop his ears in order to avoid the temptation.[205]

In some ways, I believe that an obsession with revival (and the performance needed to acquire it) can be like that. It sounds wonderful, but it *distracts* us. It *misleads* us. It takes us off the journey of grace. It can steal away the simplicity of our faith. An obsession with revival preaching actually replaces the preaching and teaching that will ultimately bring it!

Where you see an obsession with revival, you often see a famine of the teaching of God's grace, the message of the cross, and justification by faith. Why is that? Revival preaching has replaced such truths. Some churches have given years to such an emphasis.

If the devil can distract us from grace, and make us obsessed with the fruit of it instead of the root of it, he has won a great battle. Talking about the fruit will never change the root.

Where you see an obsession with revival, you often see people being driven into a frenzy, where they will finally commit themselves to a series of behaviors with a promised happy ending. But it never comes. My whole Christian life, I have heard message after message, and prophecy after prophecy about revival coming, as if it's right around the corner, and it never seems to come to those who are obsessed with it. Some loud meetings may come, some outrageous manifestations may come, but what they are looking for does not come.

What if true revival is already here?

We've become a people that talk about what God used to do a long time ago, or what God might do in the future, but Jesus said, "Do you not say, 'There are yet four months, and then comes the harvest '? Behold, I say to you, lift up your eyes and look on the fields, that they are white for harvest" (John 4:35, NASB). Paul wrote, "For he says, 'In the time of my favor I heard you, and in

---

[205] Homer, 1 Odyssey, 12.

the day of salvation I helped you.' I tell you, now is the time of God's favor, now is the day of salvation" (2 Corinthians 6:2, NIV).

The harvest is right now. His grace is available right now to change lives.

CHASING GOD?

One of the popular ideas by "revivalists" in recent years is the idea that we need to be "God chasers." My honest opinion is that this kind of teaching is damaging and is religious nonsense. God doesn't need to be found. I'll tell you right where He is. He is enthroned in the heavens, and His Holy Spirit is in your heart if you believe in the work of the cross.

This kind of teaching sells books and platforms the fantastic, but it leads God's children into a hopeless and exhausting "chase" for something they already have. It is a Siren song.

Only those who are in the Word can withstand such dynamic drivel, and recognize it to be what it is: a trumpet blast for a subtle form of legalism. Don't be drawn away by such teachers, because they will never let you rest, and will never teach you to "cease striving and know that He is God."[206]

This is not to undermine a healthy pursuit of a deeper relationship with God, but that is not the fruit of most "God-Chaser" teaching. Most teachers who beat this drum do not understand grace themselves and confuse their hearers with a man-centered gospel.

THE GOAL OF PREACHING

I hear so many preachers and evangelists and I wonder: What is the goal of their teaching? What are they after? What do they want the finished product of their hearers to be? Here's what Paul the Apostle said his was: "But the goal of our instruction is love from a pure heart and a good conscience and a sincere faith" (1 Timothy 1:5, NASB).

Compare these goals with what we hear so often from so many preachers who work themselves into a froth and scream

---

[206] Psalm 46:10, NASB

that "revival is born after midnight!" Of course I have no problem with praying after midnight, but somehow in the midst of such militant preaching, the goal of preaching seems to be skewed toward radical discipline instead of a sincere faith. If radical discipline equals revival, then we should examine radical Islam (minus the violence) and imitate it: praying five times a day, generous giving of alms, strict submission to their leaders, radical memorization of their holy books, etc.

As a matter of fact, when I was being trained to do ministry in Turkey, and learned about the radical disciplines of Islam, I said to myself, "Man! If the Muslims pray five times a day, Christians should be praying *six* times a day!"

Then I sensed the Holy Spirit speaking something profound to my heart: "Shut up, Derek."

And so I did. (This would be the place I would put a smiley face if I was sending an email.)

"All those works were never enough for man to make it to Me," the small still voice said. "That's what I came to set you free *from!*""

What is the goal of the true gospel?
Love from a pure heart.
A good conscience.
A sincere faith.

Love from a pure heart.
"Love from a pure heart" speaks of our love not being contaminated by sin. There are five Greek words for love. Among them are *eros* and *agape. Eros* is a sensual, self-seeking love. *Agape* is selfless love. First John 4:16 actually says that God is *agape.* This phrase "love from a pure heart" means that the goal of the teacher of God's Word should be to remove *eros* from a person's heart and replace it with the *agape* love of God. The goal should be to purify a person's heart so that he serves others without being contaminated by competition, ambition, or sexual desire.

This phrase also speaks of purifying the hearer's love for God. It means that we should no longer approach God on the basis of fear of punishment, but on the basis of grace, just as John wrote,

"There is no fear in love [agape]; but perfect love [agape] casts out fear, because fear involves punishment, and the one who fears is not perfected in love [agape]" (1 John 4:18, NASB).

When a believer begins to understand "love from a pure heart," his heart will indeed be revived, he will grow in his faith, and find the springs of true worship flowing inside.

A good conscience

Paul the Apostle wrote, *"Everything is permissible, but not everything is helpful. Everything is permissible, but not everything builds up"* (1 Corinthians 10:23, ISV). In other words, through the liberty we have in Christ, there are certain things that are not specifically forbidden by Scripture: drinking alcohol, tattoos, listening to secular music, watching movies, eating certain kinds of food, etc. In grace, a believer may choose to engage in these things as long as it's accompanied by a good conscience. It is dangerous to engage in certain activities with an uneasy conscience. Yes, we have liberty, but we can still hinder our effectiveness.

For example, it's not illegal to run the Boston Marathon with a ball and chain, but will that really help you to win the race? Yes, you have *liberty* to do this, but why do it? We can harm our ability to make a greater impact if we allow our liberty to eclipse wisdom. I remember the old story about "The Prince of Preachers," Charles Spurgeon, who insisted that he had the liberty in Christ to smoke cigars, though many criticized him for this. Finally, a Chicago paper printed an ad that said, "Smoke the same cigars that Charles Spurgeon smokes!" It was then that Spurgeon realized that he should probably stop smoking cigars for the sake of his witness.[207]

Other times, we can grieve the Holy Spirit, who may, in a sense, be speaking to us that what might be okay for others is not okay for you. The man who was saved from alcoholism might blow his witness with recovering alcoholics and also fall into temptation if he drinks alcohol. The one struggling with a porn

---

[207] Trevin Wax, "Spurgeon the Drinker: The Rest of the Story": December 6, 2006, www.trevinwax.com.

addiction might be putting himself in harm's way by working online after midnight.

Paul puts it this way, "So whatever you believe about these things keep between yourself and God. Blessed is the man who does not condemn himself by what he approves" (Romans 14:22, NIV). He also admonishes us to "live a life worthy of the calling you have received" (Ephesians 4:1, NIV).

"So what parts of the Old Testament do we obey and what parts do we not need to obey?" one might ask. We've all had an immature Christian or legalist point out that we should not eat pork (Deuteronomy 14:8), seafood (Leviticus 11:10), or trim the corners of our hair around the temples (Leviticus 19:27).

In the Old Testament, the Law of Moses may be broken up into three parts: the ceremonial Law, the judicial Law, and the moral Law. The ceremonial Law was for the operation of Judaism and was only a type of Christ. Jesus fulfilled this in Himself and abolished the ceremonial system.[208] The judicial Law was for the governing of the nation of Israel. The moral Law is eternal and still is fulfilled today through believers who walk in the Spirit.[209]

A believer who has "a good conscience" will experience the fullness of the joy of the Lord, and also maximize his or her witness for Christ. Doesn't this sound like revival?

A sincere faith

What is "a sincere faith"? Like my wife says, "I know it when I see it."

An insincere faith is that which is temporary and worked up by the preacher or hearer.

We've all known the one that gets excited in church on Sunday and then falls on Monday. This is not sincere faith. This is sensuality. It is being driven by feelings and not by true faith, which often operates independent of the soul.

An insincere faith can be conjured up by the emotional tweaking of a good speaker who excites the soul but does not impart truth to the mind and spirit. Such a "faith" can only be

---

[208] Matthew 23:38
[209] Galatians 5:16, Romans 3:31

maintained by attending the next exciting event or listening to the next sensational preacher. Those who live on such a path will not endure the dry seasons or the hard times. Only a "sincere faith" will make this journey.

WHAT'S SO BAD ABOUT THE GOSPEL?

All this begs the question: What's so bad about just preaching the gospel? Why have we replaced this wonderful message with so many tangents? Is it too boring? Too old-fashioned? Is it not sexy enough or relevant enough?

What I'm suggesting here is that the preaching and teaching of the gospel of God's grace is enough to give us everything we truly need *and want* in Christ.

In spite of all the revival preaching, why are so many Christians living defeated lives? I had a visiting friend tell me just a few days ago, "There are more Christians I know that are struggling than are doing well."

Could it be that we have turned off the valve through which true revival flows? The preaching of the gospel of Jesus Christ! "Whoever believes in me, as the Scripture has said, streams of living water will flow from within him" (John 7:38, NIV).

TRUE REVIVAL IS ALWAYS TRUTH REVIVAL

Today's "revivals" are too often associated with manifestations and not truth. Modern revivals are often associated with gold dust, gold fillings, glory clouds, and being "slain in the Spirit," but these kinds of revivals won't bring enduring change in the church, in society, or ultimately in a person unless truth accompanies the movement. Historically, revival has been associated with the powerful preaching of age-old tried and true doctrines. Whether it's the restoration of truth or a fresh experience in what we already know, true revival always has been and always will be about truth. As a matter of fact, revival cannot last or be passed on to another generation unless there is some teachable doctrine to impart. Manifestations alone cannot sustain a move of God. This is not to say that signs and wonders don't follow God's Word. They do! But too often signs and wonders are pursued and truth is neglected.

On October 31, 1517, Martin Luther nailed *The Ninety-Five Theses* to the door of the Catholic church in Wittenburg, Germany. This set off a series of events that changed the world, sparking the Reformation. This movement has affected millions of people. What was in those ninety-five theses that ignited a move of God? It was a trumpet blast of the doctrine of justification by faith. It was a truth revival. Such is an example of Martin Luther's preaching at that time: "The true change of heart that brings true forgiveness and salvation can come only through contemplation of the wounds of Christ, through true remorse, and through the grace that God freely gives to the believer."[210]

In the 18th century, there was a great revival that swept across the western world as John Wesley preached in England and George Whitefield preached in America. As I've mentioned before, John Wesley's message was "the witness of the Spirit": the doctrine[211] that teaches that salvation is not cold theology, but an experience that is accompanied by the witness of the Holy Spirit in the heart of the believer. He described his own experience as "a heart strangely warmed." Wesley's preaching of this truth set a nation ablaze with revival fire. I don't believe Wesley would have counted himself a "revivalist" as so many preachers do today (who have yet to bring a "revival"), but simply preached the gospel truths that affected his own experience.

Meanwhile, in the United States, Whitefield set cities ablaze by preaching "the new birth," a doctrine that teaches the regenerating power of the gospel and the indwelling Holy Spirit working in us. Again, it was truth preached surgically and powerfully from the mouth of a profoundly gifted messenger. An eyewitness anonymous writer who published a letter about Whitefield in the *New England Journal* said of him, "…He speaks much of the language of the New Testament; and has an admirable faculty in explaining the Scriptures. He strikes out of

---

[210] *Martin Luther* by Mike Fearon: Bethany House Publishers: Minneapolis, Minnesota. pg. 79
[211] Romans 8:16

them such lights, and unveils those excellencies which surprise his hearers...He declares that his whole view in preaching is to bring men to Christ, to deliver them from their false confidences, to raise them from their dead formalities, to revive primitive Christianity among them; and if he can obtain this end he will leave them to their liberty..."[212]

I'd like to make an appeal to all readers who preach God's Word to carefully examine what you are preaching and what are the goals of your preaching. I know many people who are praying for revival and perhaps God's answer lies with you. Let's open the valves of the water of life by teaching and preaching the truths of God's grace.

Will we see whole cities transformed? I hope so, but remember that revival happens one person at a time. God counts by ones and so should we. We cannot get so concerned about the masses that we fail to see the sparrow.

If we will preach the gospel of God's grace, we will see inward transformation one soul at a time. We will see true revival. His Spirit will honor His Word, and all the fun stuff will accompany truth, but if we make the fun stuff the goal, we will never see true revival, and we will never transform ourselves or society.

May God give us grace, and grace to teach grace. May true revival come through the channel God has already cut through Immanuel's veins.

---

[212] *George Whitefield* by Arnold Dallimore: The Banner of Truth Trust: Carlisle, Pennsylvania. pg. 435-436

Discipleship by Grace

CHAPTER 14
Liars Among Us

"Whosoever does not confess the testimony of the Cross is of the devil."
— Polycarp,[213] disciple of the Apostle John

Before we dig for too long into this topic, let's remember that without Christ, we're all false teachers. Without grace, our flesh is does just fine leading us astray from the truth of the gospel. We were born with a built-in liar. We can blame the devil and false teachers, but we did just fine perverting God's truth ourselves!

That said, the Scriptures have quite a bit to say about false prophets rising up in the last days.

> *"But the Spirit saith expressly, that in later times, some shall fall away from the faith, giving heed to seducing spirits and doctrines of demons." (1 Timothy 4:1, ASV)*

> *"But there arose false prophets also among the people, as among you also there shall be false teachers, who shall privily bring in destructive heresies..." (2 Peter 2:1, KJV)*

The Bible is very clear about the fact that false teachers, and even the antichrist, will arise *from among us.*[214] False prophets will not come in red tights with a pitchfork and devil horns and say, "Hey, I'm here to deceive you!" Instead, they will move to and fro *among us,* teaching and preaching, selling books and teaching CDs, hosting radio programs and television shows. People will clamor to attend their meetings, and will be impressed with their messages.

The question is, will the false teachers know they are false teachers? I think not. They will be deceivers because they are

---

[213] The Epistle of Polycarp to the Philippians
[214] 1 John 2:19

deceived, and the nature of deception is that the one who is deceived doesn't know it.

False prophets will preach many false doctrines, and some of them will be obvious — universalism (the teaching that all faiths are the same), challenging the infallibility of Scripture, questioning the deity of Christ, etc. — but some will not be obvious. Some will preach a disguised Pharisaism that will not center on the cross, but on works. They will not preach a gospel in which the object of faith is Christ and Him crucified, but man and him striving. They will not preach the all-sufficiency of the Savior, but the self-sufficiency of man.

These liars will impress with grand stories of their own exploits, their own accomplishments, their long fasts and nights of prayer, and their intolerance for sins. But subtly, quietly, unbeknownst to scores of hearers, a small viper will slither through the grass. Do not think that a hard word against sin is always indicative of a biblical teacher. The Pharisees and the Muslims preach against sin, too. Like them, these false teachers will introduce behaviors, disciplines, rituals, and man-made religions that will heap burden upon burden upon little lambs, leaven upon leaven into the mixture. Soon the hearers will no longer see grace; they will forget who they are in Christ and will be far from the cross. Those who ran well at the beginning will be seduced into striving and flesh. The cross will become about self-denial alone and will not be about resting in the finished work of Christ. The message will glorify man and not God — a man-centered religion that will be based on Christianity, but will not be Christianity at all.

Liars tell us that, like them, we can *achieve* holiness. How ridiculous! What an impossibility! If "no good thing dwells in me" (Romans 7:18) then what hope do I have to produce my own righteousness? Telling flesh to destroy flesh is like dumping gasoline on a fire to try to put it out!

The liars will turn all into laws, rules, and commands until prayer is a burdensome task, and evangelism becomes a duty driven by guilt and not by love. The One who looked with compassion upon the multitudes will look with compassion on

His own people, crushed under the weight of the Law, just as such concerns once grieved Him on a hill in Israel. Oh, the saints will try their best, searching for the reward of revival promised by the preacher, but will find only death, walking in condemnation, exalting those who "can" and pitying those who "can't."

Those who "can" will expect to be followed, pampered, respected, admired, and even worshiped by those who can't. The pedestals will be raised high; men will be exalted, esteemed and idolized for their anointings, their disciplines, their deeds, and their gifts. The liars will unknowingly restore the priesthood, shutting out the lowly, the weak, and the sinner, exalting those who have attained personal holiness.

Many in the church will be impressed with their passionate preaching, their flamboyant personalities and bombastic preaching. Scores of Christians will buy their books, teaching CDs, handkerchiefs, and miracle spring water. They'll hurry to watch their TV shows and listen to their radio programs. They'll send large amounts of money to support the dubious work of the liars.

Since the message of the cross will almost disappear entirely, new "revelations" will be introduced. These tangents will become the replacement passions of Christians far and wide, since the cross is no longer in view. For some it will be revival, others prophecy, for others end-time theology, still others Israel, and on the list goes: prayer, fasting, worship, spiritual warfare, prosperity—anything but Christ and Him crucified.

Liars would have us to believe that our righteousness is conditional upon our performance; that it comes from man and not God. Liars would tell us that though grace saved us, it is now upon us to keep ourselves, and to become like Jesus. They turn grace into a dirty word, looking at the abuses of grace as evidence that we dare not tread too far into that realm. Grace will be treated like a cheap piece of candy after dinner. The implication is that it is unnecessary (though if you need a little feel-good, then enjoy the candy). Liars think grace is dangerous, hesitantly consenting that it's part of the Bible after they heap commandment after commandment on the poor, thinking these commandments to be "the meat of the word."

One day, as prophesied by Jesus Christ Himself, one of the liars will perform amazing signs and wonders, at the same time deceiving with doctrines of demons that eclipse the cross. Scores of Christians will say, "How can one do such signs if he were not from God?" And the antichrist will arise.

Other false teachers will present a counterfeit grace, claiming to give "liberty" to their hearers, but this will not be liberty from bondage or liberty to walk in a good conscience before the Lord, but liberty to sin.

And away they'll go: hordes of apostates following an antichrist, marching like a blind parade into the terrible fires of God's wrath. They'll cry, "Lord, Lord!" He'll answer, "I never knew you, depart from me you who practice lawlessness." All because they preach not the cross. All because there are liars among us.

Beware these false teachings, as these seducers are now among us, peddling their books, magazines, and television shows daily. These are days when we must pay attention carefully to what we hear and teach, remembering Paul's admonishment to Timothy to "watch your doctrine closely" (1 Timothy 4:16). We must, as my dear friend and author Mike Chorey[215] says, be "cross-eyed." If we will not keep the cross and its doctrines near, we may not be far from the golden calf.[216]

Let me repeat something I said earlier. When I'm listening to a teacher, I'm always asking myself the question: What is the object of faith that this person is trying to get me to put my trust in? If it's anything other than the cross of Christ, I'm very careful with what I receive from the teacher.

I do not mean to imply that all are false teachers who struggle to include grace in their messages, as there is a difference between false *teachers* and false *teaching*. Someone may be growing in grace, and may not yet be able to adequately express the grace of God in his messages. The Holy Spirit is perfecting all of us, and none are a

---

[215] Mike Chorey is the director of *Joshua Revolution,* a powerful conference ministry based in Niagara Falls, NY, dedicated to teaching young people the message of the cross. (www.joshuarevolution.org)
[216] Exodus 32:1-4

perfect replica of Christ or His message. That's why we must be "Berean" and "search the Scriptures" to make sure that everything we hear is truth.

Most of the time, I'm concerned not about what the teacher says, but what the teacher *doesn't* say. For example, I have no problem with someone saying, "Thou shalt not kill!" I believe that and can say a hearty amen. However, as a believer in grace, how can I truly obey this command in my heart unless my heart is transformed by the spirit of God? For even Jesus taught that we are guilty of murder in our hearts whether or not we ever commit the act outwardly. He also taught that without Him we can do nothing. So how can I hear a command like that and apply it without God's grace? The teaching is "false" not because "Thou shalt not kill" is false, but because the teaching was absent of the gospel truths that set a man free from his inability to keep such a command in his heart.

I would not think someone a false teacher until he has demonstrated a lack of grace as a matter of course. I may, however, question a *teaching* without labeling someone a false *teacher*. For example, a few years ago, I was at a youth conference and one of the guest speakers said to the crowd, "I'm going to tell you how to attract the fire of God." I turned to my friend who was with me and said, "There's only one thing that attracts the fire of God — the blood of Jesus."

This speaker went on to say that if you dress a certain way or listen to a certain kind of music, that you're "spiritual," attaching love for God to items of clothes and certain kinds of music. I objected to the teaching, pleading with the conference leaders that it was unhealthy to suggest that access to God is based on performance and not the cross.

I don't know the man well enough to call him a false *teacher*, but I do believe that much of his message was false *teaching*.

False teachers generally have a following or movement around themselves — a youth group, a church, a TV program, a para-church ministry, etc. Besides their words, there are other ways to recognize them.

BY THEIR FRUITS

Sometimes I'm truly amazed by the power of seduction these preachers have over their admirers. They can do no wrong. No one tests the spirits (1 John 4:1) or considers the fruits of their ministry. It's like a spell is cast upon them so that they cannot see or hear.

> *"By their fruits you will recognize them."* *(Matthew 7:16, NIV)*

To ascertain whether or not you're dealing with a false teacher, you must only look at the fruit of the ministry. Paul makes it pretty clear when he writes to the Galatians:

> *"The acts of the sinful nature are obvious: sexual immorality, impurity and debauchery; idolatry and witchcraft; hatred, discord, jealousy, fits of rage, selfish ambition, dissensions, factions and envy; drunkenness, orgies, and the like."* *(Galatians 5:19-20, NIV)*

This doesn't necessarily mean that the false teacher will be committing these acts (though it could), but that the fruit of the teacher's doctrines *in others* will be these deeds.

I know of one church that cut itself off from other churches because "they had the truth" which of course was nothing more than leaven of the Pharisees, teaching a strict adherence to certain dress, abstinence from culture, and a buy-in to questionable theology. One of the things they taught was that you had to speak in tongues to be saved, undermining the sufficiency of the cross and proving themselves to be heretics. My wife and I had some dear friends that were involved. Though we were concerned, our friends weren't even remotely interested in listening to us, perhaps counting us among the hyprocrites. We decided to just wait, knowing that its fruit would reveal its true spirit. Eventually, sharp divisions developed in the church, some once loyal began to defect until the whole community of believers began to crumble.

Our friends left in the midst of this, and are still rebuilding healthy fellowship with a much more stable church.

Dissensions, factions and envy.

As ridiculous as this sounds, I heard of one local "worship leader" who claimed he had a deep revelation of God's grace, but was known for swearing during the worship services he led. This, he felt, exposed the "religious spirits" that were in the room.

Impurity.

Another old friend did his best to obey the revival preachers with whom he surrounded himself, but grew exhausted in attempting to get over the bar. Meanwhile, he struggled with homosexuality and could never gain the mastery no matter how much he prayed and fasted. This, of course, was because he never heard the gospel of grace. Eventually, he caved in, and is now a stripper in a gay bar.

Sexual immorality.

I have another old acquaintance who went to a church and "learned what grace really meant." He began drinking heavily and ostracized himself from those he'd grown up with in the Lord.

Debauchery.

The fruit of false teaching and teachers will eventually show itself. It's like a bad harvest. You can't plant bad seed and expect a good harvest. Jesus Himself said that a bad tree cannot bear good fruit.[217]

BEWITCHED

When the Judaizers brought their false teaching to the church in Galatia, Paul asked the Galatians, "Who has *bewitched* you?" (Galatians 3:1, emphasis added).

Remember, the Judaizers were presenting themselves as insiders on Paul's teachings, sent by God to correct the poor ignorant Galatians' understanding of the gospel. What Paul really meant, they taught, was that we are to embrace the cross *plus*

---

[217] Matthew 7:18

circumcision. When Paul heard about this, he said that the Galatians were "bewitched."

That's right, their work was equated by the Apostle Paul with witchcraft. The Greek word for bewitched is *baskaino* meaning "to charm." Just imagine the snake-charmer in India, hypnotizing its reptile with a melody. That's what we have here in Galatians. And that's what we have in the modern church when false teachers arise.

There is a movement in the church today to bring Christians back to keeping some of the ceremonial Law of Israel. "Now that we have the Spirit," they say, "we *can* keep the Law. And now we understand the Jewish feasts because they were just types of Christ!"

I've seen this bewitching especially among the pro-Israel movement led by Gentile Christians. One man told one of my staff members, "Your salvation is directly tied to your position on Israel."

I was in another meeting where a Canadian pastor and his wife "testified" about how they were transformed by a trip to Israel. They said that now they give 90% of their church offerings to Israel, "and it doesn't even have to be a Christian organization! You can give to the Israeli army or whatever because Israel itself is a sacred altar!"

The pastor said that when couples come into his office with a struggling marriage, he reminds them that the Scriptures say to pray for the peace of Jerusalem. "So let's get on our knees and pray for Jerusalem," he tells them, "and God will bless your marriage." This, he proudly explained, is the extent of his counseling.

They finished their "testimony" by challenging the hearers, "We need to begin to pray to the east again! We need to keep the Jewish feasts and holidays! This is what God is doing in our day!"

Actually, God has nothing to do with this movement. The Liar himself started it to get the eyes of believers from the finished work of Christ. (Following their presentation, they were commended from the pulpit by a nationally known leader.)

FUNDAMENTALISM

When I say *fundamentalism,* I mean "Word without Spirit"; teaching without experience. The Bible says of itself that "the letter kills but the Spirit gives life." Doctrine is supposed to be accompanied by an experience. It is not simply cold creed. Charismatic evangelist Randy Clark made the excellent point, "Right doctrine without the experience of the Spirit has never advanced Christianity."[218]

Fundamentalists are some of the liars among us. Why? Because some of them have the right doctrine without the life or love of God within them. They have the creed without the experience. *They are hypocrites because their fruit does not match what they say they believe.* I would rather walk any day with believers who have an immature view of grace and yet are experiencing the Spirit of God than those who have correct doctrine and are not experiencing it.

These people are some of the greatest enemies of evangelism today. They may have the right view but do not have the love of God in their hearts. What is a lost world to think of us if fundamentalism represents us? Think of the one holding a sign at the funeral of a gay murder victim that says, "God hates homosexuality." Or the one shouting on a box on a street corner, "You're all sinners going to hell!"

What is the problem? They are correct in their moral view and their regurgitation of God's laws, but the Spirit of God has not filled their hearts with love. So they are so right and so wrong. They are misrepresenting Christ, and are liars among us.

GRACE HERETICS

Of course, I cannot write this chapter without mentioning what I call "grace heretics." These are those who come in the name of grace, and yet preach a counterfeit version of grace or encourage an incorrect response to it.

Grace heretics preach *license,* the perversion of grace we've already discussed, whose hearers believe grace gives them a

---

[218] Randy Clark said this in a message spoken at the Elim Fellowship Leaders' Conference in May of 2007.

license to sin. There are others who refuse to preach the Doctrine of Sin, believing grace eliminates their need to do so. There are some who simply preach a man-centered version of grace, not a Christ-centered grace.

In spite of my own reformed leanings, I'm well aware that there are some in the "hyper-Calvinist" camp that have done damage to the reputation of healthy Calvinists, abusing the doctrines of grace that are meant to encourage believers. Drawing outrageous assumptions from meditating on the doctrine of election, these teachers have resolved to eliminate human will and involvement in leading the lost to Christ. "When God wants to reach the heathen," they'll say, "He'll do it without using you and me."

They're half right. God isn't going to use them.

Others resolve to believing and teaching a form of Christian fatalism. In view of God's sovereignty, they resign to an attitude that "whatever happens happens." Faith is eliminated under the conclusion that we are unable to alter the course of God's predetermined will, so resignation to whatever suffering may come is the sad response.

Grace heretics are dangerous because they pervert the understanding of the truths that will truly save us, and through misguided teaching, mislead God's people into acting in a way unbecoming to the gospel of Jesus, and in contradiction to the teachings of Scripture that teach us to respond to grace properly. Grace heretics, like all heretics, turn a blind eye to whole passages of Scripture and cite only passages that reinforce their dubious positions.

The only way to recognize the liars among us is to be people of the Word of God. We must hold to the whole counsel of Scripture, remembering that to truly know what the Bible says, we must "know what the Bible also says." I'm not merely speaking about reading the Bible, but studying the Scriptures. Further, we must surround ourselves with good teaching, and be careful to stay near the message of the cross. This can be done through good books, downloading podcasts, and sitting at the feet of godly teachers. Things will only get worse in the end of days, and so we must stay close to Jesus to navigate these waters.

Discipleship by Grace

Section 2

GRACE AND WORSHIP

CHAPTER 15
It's All About God's Glory

"Love means doing all we can, at whatever cost to ourselves, to help people be enthralled with the glory of God. When they are, they are satisfied and God is glorified." —John Piper[219]

The first question in the Reformed Catechism is:

Q. What is the chief end of man?
A. Man's chief end is to glorify God, and to enjoy him forever.[220]

Our whole lives are about the glory of God. Grace is about God's glory. The moment we have a grace conversion is the moment that we see that *all* praise, *all* honor, *all* glory be unto the Lamb who sits on the throne. A revelation of our depravity shows us that anything good we *have* or that anything good that we *are* is due to the power and love of God. We find no good reason in ourselves for why He chose us and why He redeemed us, and our sole recourse becomes glorifying His name.

Failing to see this creates confusion in trials and a man-centered approach to Christianity that clogs up the springs of worship in our hearts.

GOD'S GLORY IN OUR TRIALS

If we fail to see God's glory as the chief aim of our lives, then confusion reigns every trial that comes along. We say, "Why is this happening?" and "Why is God doing this to me?"

God does bless us abundantly, but this is the result of God being glorified in our lives. If we make our aim our happiness and not the glory of God, every trial will bring with it a theological conundrum. We will fail to harmonize what we believe ("God

---

[219] John Piper, *God is the Gospel: Meditations on God's Love as the Gift of Himself.* Crossway Books: Wheaton, Illinois. © 2005 Desiring God Foundation.
[220] Westminster Shorter Catechism

wants me happy") and what is happening ("This hurts"). Many exit the faith right here on this part of the path.

However, when we see that the goal of God's work in our lives is His glory, our entire perspective changes. "God, I don't understand this, but I know that this is for Your glory, and I will trust that You're working out a plan to accomplish that."

Anyone who focuses on their own happiness will fail to sustain it once the winds blow, because sometimes your happiness and God's glory stand in opposition. Please understand, I am not saying that God wants us miserable, or that somehow He is glorified in our being miserable. He is glorified in us when we have joy, but the source of that joy cannot be our circumstances. It must be our faith.

Believing that it's all about God's glory will rescue us from seeking happiness in our circumstances, and make us "content in whatever the circumstances" because God is always working out a plan that will glorify His name.

A few years ago, our ministry put together an event called *Beyond the Song* in New York. It was a worship festival with a missions theme that featured some of the top worship artists in the country and some gifted speakers. We did it three years in a row, and our budgets were typically over $50,000. In our final year, it became obvious as the event neared that we were going to lose money, and though I hoped for the best, I sensed it might be a financial disaster. I shared my concerns with my pastor and friend, Michael Cavanaugh, and he told me about a similar situation he faced when he was younger in ministry. "I finally had a breakthrough," Mike explained, "when I told the Lord, 'If you'll be more glorified in my failure than in my success, then not my will but Thine be done.'"

When Mike finally saw that it was all about God's glory and not about what the world would call success, his heart was free like a bird in the wind.

REDEFINE SUCCESS

I believe that we need to consider a radical revision of our definition of success. We are so often affected by the world's standards that we fail to see God's definition. Success in the kingdom of God is doing the will of God and God's glory shining through our lives.

When we define success the world's way, by how popular we are, how much money we make, how many people are involved, how many awards we've won, or how much we sell, we are in great danger of missing God's plan entirely.

It's all about God's glory.

Anyone who has walked with the Lord for any length of time has at some point heard the nonsense that goes something like this: "Your mansion in heaven will be as big as the number of souls you've won on earth."

That's completely ridiculous.

What about the one who God calls to work in an obscure city with a name you can't pronounce in a nation with a name you can't pronounce? What about the one who is called to close her door and intercede in secret, affecting outcomes of situations in ways no one will ever know? What about the one who is called to suffer for Christ in a foreign prison cell where everyone but God has forgotten them?

A few years ago, I did a music tour with my band, Isaiah Six, in Turkey with a ministry under the auspices of Operation Mobilization. At the time, Turkey was a nation of 65 million people and only 2000 believers. We entered one city called Konya (once the biblical city Iconium), where there was one sole Christian worker in a city of 800,000 people. Our host arranged a lunch with him. He'd been there for several years, and no one had come to Christ yet. It was overwhelming to think of the multitudes walking by outside the restaurant, whose sole spiritual hope was this man sitting across the table from me. "How do you continue in this environment?" I asked him. "How do you avoid discouragement?"

He smiled a smile of grace, and said, "I just keep telling truth."

If Jesus returned today, should that man be ashamed at the judgment seat of Christ because he'd won no souls? Yet, he was doing the will of God for his life, suffering in a Muslim nation, being a witness for his Savior. He knew that it was all about God's glory. All that mattered in his life was that God would be glorified through his obedience, and he could be content in that environment. This man was indeed *successful*.

GOD CHOSE THE WEAK

Hudson Taylor said, "God is not looking for men of great faith, only common souls that will believe in God's great faithfulness." He also said, "All God's giants are weak men." Why? Because God is most glorified not in our perceived greatness, but in our weakness. Sorry if you thought God chose you because of your intellectual prowess or your outstanding charisma. He chose you because you were weak.

> *"God chose the foolish things in the world to confound the wise, the weak things of the world to confound the strong."* (1 Corinthians 1:27, NKJV)

Because God chose the weak things, He gets all the glory.

God gets all the glory when we trust not in ourselves, but *despair* in our flesh, and *give up* on any hope of accomplishing anything of eternal value without Him. Just when we're about to quit and think ourselves disqualified, the small still voice whispers to our souls, "It's all about God's glory." Then we see that God was never looking for our ability, but only our *availability*. We see that our failure, weakness, or trial is not the end, but simply a vehicle God is using to glorify His name.

Ask Moses at the burning bush.

Ask Moses at the Red Sea.

Ask Gideon at the threshing floor.

Ask Joseph in prison.

Ask Deborah when handed a sword.

Ask Peter when Jesus said, "Feed my sheep."

Ask Paul when he lay blind on the road to Damascus.

It's all about God's glory.

THEN WORSHIP!

When we're around the throne, no one will be taking any credit for anything he did on earth. We will throw our crowns down and cry, "Glory to the Lamb!" We'll see clearly that *it's all about God's glory*. Nor will anyone question God as to why this happened or why that happened. We will say, "Just and true are *all* your ways, O Lord!" It will be obvious that *it's all about God's glory*.

So why wait until then to be convinced of it when the Scriptures clearly say that you will be convinced of it later? Why wait until then to lay down your pride and worship with total abandonment? Go ahead and worship Him now! Exalt His great name today. Great things He has done, and He is worthy of *all* praise now and forevermore.

CHAPTER 16
Worship With Your Life

"The greatest single cause of atheism in the world today...is Christians who acknowledge Jesus with their lips and walk out the door and deny Him by their lifestyle. That is simply what an unbelieving world finds unbelievable. " —Brennan Manning[221]

IN SPIRIT AND TRUTH

In John 4, Jesus has an encounter with a Samaritan woman at a well. While speaking to her, He exposes her adultery with a word of knowledge. As a defense mechanism, she attempts to bring up a doctrinal dispute that Samaritans had with Jews. She says, "Our fathers worshiped in this mountain, and you people say that in Jerusalem is the place where men ought to worship" (John 4:20, NASB). Jesus answers:

> *"But an hour is coming, and now is, when the true worshipers will worship the Father in spirit and truth; for such people the Father seeks to be His worshipers. God is spirit, and those who worship Him must worship in spirit and truth."* (*John 4:23-24, NASB*)

Here, in one fell swoop, Jesus redefines worship as it will exist in the new covenant with two words: *spirit* and *truth*. True worshipers will worship "in spirit and truth." To paraphrase, I believe Jesus is saying, "Look lady, there's a time that's coming (and it's already here) that worship will come from the heart, 'cuz if it ain't coming from the heart, I don't care if it's the mountain or Jerusalem—it ain't worship."

Worship in truth

I believe this means that we worship with *sincerity*. Costa Deir once said, "Christians don't tell lies, they just sing them." You

---

[221] This quote appeared in the prelude to dc Talk's song "What if I Stumble?" from the album *Jesus Freak*.

know what he means. We sing the songs in church on Sunday morning, but our heart is somewhere else. By introducing the concept of *true worshipers* we must assume that there are also *false worshipers*. False worshipers are those who do not worship "in spirit and truth." It is a form of worship that is only religious or ritualistic in nature and not relational.

Worshiping in truth also speaks of approaching God in the way that He designed in the Word—through Christ's sacrifice.

Worship in spirit

Remember, the dispute that the Jews and Samaritans had was about the *geography* of worship. Jesus presents a new geography of worship: *Spirit.*

Huh?

Wherever your spirit is, you can now worship!

In the days of the Old Testament, the high priest would go into the Holy of Holies and sprinkle the blood of a lamb on the ark of the covenant. There, Jehovah God would see the blood, and His spirit would be drawn to the sacrifice; His shekinah presence would fill the room and the priest would interact with Almighty God.

When Christ died, the temple veil separating the Holy of Holies from the rest of the temple, and in fact, the world, was torn into two, signifying that the presence of God has gone out from that place and now dwells in the hearts of those who live by faith. If you're a believer, the blood of "the Lamb of God who takes away the sins of the world" was sprinkled on your heart, and the presence of God is once again drawn to the sacrifice. That's why the spirit of God dwells inside of you!

> *"Do you not know that you are a temple of God and that the Spirit of God dwells in you?"* (1 Corinthians 3:16, NASB)

As I understand it, that word "temple" is based on the same word that was used for "the Holy of Holies" in the Old Testament. In other words, if you believe on Christ Jesus *you are the Holy of Holies of the Holy Spirit.*

198

In the new covenant of grace, God's presence is no longer tied to a building, an object, a person, an artifact, or a certain time of the day or year. God's presence is now wherever the people of God are. Therefore, whatever you are saying and doing is *worship*.

All things are worship.

Worship with your life.

> *"Whatever you do in word or deed, do all in the name of the Lord Jesus, giving thanks through Him to God the Father." (Colossians 3:17, NASB)*

As we disciple young believers, we need to tell them that worship is no longer a 30-minute song service. Worship is about the way we live—what kind of a student or teacher you are, what kind of a classmate or teammate, what kind of an employee or boss, what kind of husband, father, mother, wife, daughter, son, sister, brother, etc. Since grace gives us full and constant access to the Father, worship should be taught as a lifestyle.

In John 4, when Jesus responded to the Samaritan woman who'd been living in adultery, His message to her was basically, "Hey, lady, if you're so concerned about true worship, I'll tell you what it is. Your life must worship the Father, and since you're living in adultery, your ritual of worship has become unacceptable."

Her life did not worship the Lord, so her ritual became meaningless.

SACRED OR SECULAR?

What we're talking about here, once again, is communion—living in the presence of God. Communion should be the goal of our discipleship. Without a revelation of grace, we have a dualistic approach to God, compartmentalizing our "sacred" lives from our "secular" lives. On the "sacred" side of the partition wall we create, we go to church, pray in the morning, maybe sing on the worship team, or join a small group. When we leave the "sacred" part of our lives, so we think, we walk into our "secular" lives, working our job, going to school, or playing on a sports team. But this is living in a New Testament world with an Old Testament mentality! The reason is that in the reality of grace, the partition between sacred and secular has been removed. Everything is spiritual!

Martin Luther said of those who taught dualism, "If you ask further, whether they count it also a good work when they work at their trade, walk, stand, eat, drink, sleep, and do all kinds of works for the nourishment of the body or for the common welfare, and whether they believe that God takes pleasure in them because of such works, you will find that they say, 'No'; and they define good works so narrowly that they are made to consist only of praying in church, fasting, and almsgiving. Other works they consider to be in vain, and think that God cares nothing for them. So through their damnable unbelief they curtail and lessen the service of God, Who is served by all things whatsoever that are done, spoken or thought in faith."[222]

The great healing evangelist Smith Wigglesworth was once asked by a young believer, "How often do you pray?" He answered, "I never pray more than fifteen minutes, but fifteen minutes never go by without me praying."[223]

The ritualist says, "If I want to be like Wigglesworth, I must discipline myself to pray every fifteen minutes!"

Wigglesworth wasn't describing discipline, though. He was describing *communion*. He was describing *walking in the Spirit*. As discussed in an earlier chapter, when Paul said "Pray without ceasing"[224] he was either instructing us to do something impossible, or he was describing living in the presence of God. This doesn't mean that we have to be praying a long list of prayers all day long, but that we are living our lives in His presence and constantly seeking ways to glorify the Lord.

I can ride in a car for hours with my wife without saying anything to her. Neither she nor I feel a need to validate our

---

[222] Martin Luther, "A Treatise on Good Works": Published in 1520 in: Works of Martin Luther. Adolph Spaeth, L.D. Reed, Henry Eyster Jacobs, et Al., Trans. & Eds. (Philadelphia: A. J. Holman Company, 1915), Vol. 1, pp. 173-285.
[223] Smith Wigglesworth, *Smith Wigglesworth: Ever-Increasing Faith.* © June 1971 Gospel Publishing House; Revised Edition.
[224] I Thessalonians 5:17

relationship by talking the whole time. I'm just aware of her presence and enjoy the fact that she's right there beside me.

It's the same way with God. Because of grace, we can live with God and develop an awareness of His presence, constantly knowing He's there. Jesus did say, "Surely I am with you always..."[225] We don't need to prove He's there by talking to Him all day, but we can live our lives *unto Him*.

The idea that God is "over there" or "up there" while I am "down here" is not consistent with the teachings of the New Testament. To the believer, God is *right here*.

FALSE WORSHIPERS,
THE ULTIMATE ANTI-EVANGELISM

False worshipers ultimately become a stumbling block to evangelism.

The true worshiper who is worshiping with his life has a big neon arrow on his life pointing to God. His life says, *Hey, I love God! He's worthy of all praise! He's worthy of me doing everything with all my heart!* It's as St. Francis of Assisi once said, "Preach the gospel at all times, and when necessary use words." Evangelism, like worship, becomes a lifestyle.

False worshipers, those who are driven by performance and ritual and not love, ultimately shame the Lord. Because of their dualistic thinking, when they "exit" the presence of the Lord, worship ceases.

There was once a young man in the mid-1900s who spent his days working for circuses and carnivals. He was also a talented organist and would be hired by tent evangelists to play hymns. A biographer later tells of his experiences:

> *While he was playing ``Bringing in the Sheaves,'' he would look out at the audience clamoring to be saved. ``I'd see the same @#!%&$@!# faces that had been ogling the half-naked girls at the carnival the night before.'' It was, he has said many times before, a revelation: ``I knew then that the Christian church thrives on hypocrisy and that man's carnal nature will out no*

---

[225] Matthew 28:20

matter how much it is purged or scourged by any white-light religion.''[226]

Seeing the hypocrisy, his young heart was filled with cynicism and bitterness. That little boy's name was Anton. Anton LaVey published *The Satanic Bible* in 1969.

If only little Anton had seen true worshipers instead of false ones.

A few years ago, I went to watch a young man that I was mentoring play basketball in a local high school game. When I arrived, I found that a local pastor's son was on the other team. I thought I'd watch to see how each young man represented the Lord.

The guy I was mentoring played hard with a good attitude and I was proud of him. During the game, the other kid showed a different spirit. He played dirty; he mouthed off to his coach. When a referee called a foul on him, he cursed him with a litany of profanities. I was so sad. I was sad for him and I was so sad that he had misrepresented Christ in public when he had a chance to make a difference. Was basketball that important? In the scheme of eternity, was it more important to win a silly game where you throw a ball through a hoop or to show the world the excellence of Christ?

THE GET BACK GUY

The Holy Spirit wants to lead us on an adventurous life in the Spirit, but too often we've reduced His role to slapping our wrists.

I'm a big football fan, and I was watching a program recently and found out that every NFL team has what's called a "Get Back Guy." Apparently, a common problem on every sideline is keeping players and coaches from going over the line and onto the field of play. It's such a big problem that teams actually need a guy dedicated to keep players and coaches from crossing the line. He's called the "Get Back Guy." All he does all day is yell "get back!" at people who cross the line.

[226] "Sympathy For the Devil" by Lawrence Wright in a series on religious leaders entitled "True Believers" for the magazine *Rolling Stone. Rolling Stone* is the property of Straight Arrow Publishers, Inc.

Sometimes, I think we've reduced the Holy Spirit to being a Get Back Guy — He wants to send us on the field of play, but we're so given to the pleasures of sin that we've been benched, and all He does is tell us to stay away from sin. "Get back!" He says.

"Get back from pornography!"

"Get back from drinking and drugs!"

"Get back from losing your temper!

"Get back from the wrong crowd!"

And you've become bored with your faith and the Holy Spirit has become bored with you! The Holy Spirit doesn't want to be your Get Back Guy, He wants to be your coach, calling plays for you to take the ball down the field and to win the game!

What a joy that we get to live in the presence of God and demonstrate to the world that He is worthy of living our lives unto Him! This is not a duty, but a privilege! We don't *have* to do it, we *get* to. That is the heartbeat of a lifestyle worshiper.

CHAPTER 17
The Role of Discipline

*"Spiritual exercises do not transform you, but position you for
transformation." —* Michael Cavanaugh

As I made clear in the chapter "What Grace Looks Like," I
always want to be careful when I'm presenting the grace of God to
not suggest a gospel of laziness. Discipline has its place in the
Christian life, but too often is seen as the cause of God's love
toward us, not the effect of it. Now that we've spent so much time
in this book establishing grace and not our performance as the
object of our faith, let's discuss spiritual disciplines. To disciple by
grace (or be a disciple by grace), we must understand the role of
discipline in our faith.

> *"I am writing to you, fathers, because you know Him who
> has been from the beginning. I am writing to you, young men,
> because you have overcome the evil one. I have written to you,
> children, because you know the Father." (1 John 2:13, NASB)*

What's interesting about this Scripture is how John chooses to
speak to each demographic. To fathers, he speaks to their
knowledge of God's sovereignty. *You have known Him who has been
from the beginning.* To children, he speaks tenderly to them about
their heavenly Father. *You know the Father.* When he speaks to
young men, however, he does not take the sword out of their
hand. *You have overcome the evil one.* Somehow, as we teach grace,
we do not want to take action away, but only put it in the right
place in the Christian life.

Cavanaugh also said, "Obedience is the love language of
God." We all have our love languages. For some it's gifts, for some
it's time, for some it's touch. God's love language is obedience. As
true worshipers, we begin to see that obedience and discipline are
the fruit of our love and passion for God.

THE DISCIPLINE OF BELIEVING

Before we talk about any other discipline, we must speak of the most important one. *Believing.* Believing is the most important discipline of the New Testament. Perpetual believing in the cross keeps us connected to the power source of the Holy Spirit. Thus we "fight the good fight of *faith*" (2 Timothy 4:7). A.W. Tozer wrote about this when he said, "[In Scripture] faith is defined functionally, not philosophically; that is, it is a statement of what faith is in operation, not what it is in essence...faith is the gaze of a soul upon a saving God...faith is not a once-done act, but a continuous gaze of the heart at the Triune God."[227]

Martin Luther wrote, "The first and highest, the most precious of all good works is faith in Christ, as He says in John 6 when the Jews asked Him: 'What shall we do that we may work the works of God?' He answered: 'This is the work of God, that ye believe on Him Whom He hath sent.' When we hear or preach this word, we hasten over it and deem it a very little thing and easy to do, whereas we ought here to pause a long time and to ponder it well. For in this work all good works must be done and receive from it the inflow of their goodness, like a loan. This we must put bluntly, that men may understand it."[228]

Consider these verses:

> "...the Son of Man must be lifted up that whoever believes in Him should not perish..." (John 3:14-15)

> "This is the work of God, that you believe in Him whom He has sent." (John 6:28-29)

> "Whoever believes in me...out of his heart will flows streams of living water." (John 7:37,38)

> "If you continue in my word...then you shall know the truth, and the truth shall make you free." (John 8:31,32)

---

[227] A.W. Tozer, *The Pursuit of God*, Christian Publications; Christian Publications edition (June 1982).
[228] Martin Luther, "A Treatise on Good Works": Published in 1520 in: Works of Martin Luther. Adolph Spaeth, L.D. Reed, Henry Eyster Jacobs, et Al., Trans. & Eds. (Philadelphia: A. J. Holman Company, 1915), Vol. 1, pp. 173-285.

As we think about discipline, we must make the goal of our discipline a deeper *believing* in the grace and love of God. If your disciplines do not accomplish this, they are useless dead works. Grace is really "the alpha and omega" of discipline, as discipline begins as a fruit of grace, and ends at greater discoveries of grace. Discipline should deepen our faith, and teach us how to walk in grace.

The Pharisees admired themselves for their deep study of the Scriptures, but failed to see that the end of their study should have led them to Christ instead of self-righteousness. Jesus told them, "You examine the Scriptures carefully because you suppose that in them you have eternal life. Yet they testify about me" (John 5:39, ISV). The entirety of our devotion and discipline is to come to a greater *believing* in Christ Jesus our Lord.

SELF-GOVERNMENT

Discipline should lead us, and those to whom we are ministering, to a place of self-government. Those who are not disciplined need others to constantly take care of them; to feed them; to monitor them; to explain everything to them. But those who are disciplined have matured and need not the heavy hand of big government.

Consider what John wrote: "As for you, the anointing which you received from Him abides in you, and you have no need for anyone to teach you; but as His anointing teaches you about all things, and is true and is not a lie, and just as it has taught you, you abide in Him" (1 John 2:27, NASB).

You don't need anyone to teach you.

Self-governed believers understand that we all have access to God through His grace, and that a mature believer need not have a co-dependent relationship with someone else to access God. First Peter 2:9 tells us that "you are a chosen people, a royal priesthood." We are all priests through Christ, and all have access to the Father! This is the essence of self-government: We have confidence that we can walk with God. Others may help us and encourage us, but we can access God ourselves.

Self-governed people are people of character. They are people of integrity. They still obey when there is no one else around because they have learned to hear the voice of God, and live according to His Word.

Please don't confuse self-government with rebellion. A rebellious person is someone who has not learned self-government. In extreme cases, rebellious people end up requiring the *most* government—just go visit a prison. What do you call someone who needs lots of government? *A child.*

This is where Law and discipline can assist us when dealing with those spiritually or naturally young. Until children are mature, Law is helpful to keep them steady until a revelation of grace arrives.

> *"Now I say, as long as the heir is a child, he does not differ at all from a slave although he is owner of everything, but he is under guardians and managers until the date set by the father. So also we, while we were children, were held in bondage under the elemental things of the world." (Galatians 4:3, NASB)*

This passage paints grace to be as a father, waiting until the child is trained by the Law before revealing himself in a more intimate relationship. It is drawing from a picture from Roman culture, where sons would be kept under guardians and tutors until the age of 14, when they would officially be declared as sons in a formal ceremony. Until that time, they were seen as similar to slaves, and kept under the care of the master servant. In the same way, the Law is a guardian until we see grace. Once grace comes, self-government begins. Why? Because we are confident before the Father, careful to love Him with our lives, and our consciences are trained by God's Word. This is where we can live as Jesus did when He said, "I tell you the truth, the Son can do nothing by himself; he can do only what he sees his Father doing, because whatever the Father does the Son also does" (John 5:19, NIV).

DISCIPLINE PREPARES US FOR SERVICE

Discipline should be an enthusiastic choice to forego some comforts and conveniences to reach for greater goals within our callings.

What Olympian isn't willing to give up fast food to win the gold? His vision to win the prize disciplines him and keeps him from making unhealthy choices. And what soldier that's getting ready to go off to war isn't willing to discipline himself to be in the best shape for the fighting days ahead? To fight for freedom, and to preserve his or her own life, the soldier will gladly give in to discipline for preparation.

My wife and I run 5K's to stay in shape. When I was in junior high school, I was on the cross-country team and hated it. As an adult, I find much more joy in it because my heart is in it. I want to compete and place well in races, and I want to stay in shape! Therefore, I cheerfully discipline myself by running 3-4 miles every other day. Vision gives me the willingness to discipline myself. Our vision as believers is to serve the Lord with all our heart and bring glory to His worthy name.

Something I tell my children all the time is, "People who are willing to consistently do the things in this world that no one else wants to do generally achieve the most." I'm trying to give my children a vision of what they can become, and what kind of relationship they can have with God. This will take the sting out of their discipline, giving them reason to rise above the pain, hard work, and sometimes boredom to prepare themselves for the will of God.

COMPELLED BY LOVE

This is a good place to say again that discipline should have the motive of love.

"For in Christ Jesus neither circumcision nor uncircumcision means anything, but faith working through love." (Galatians 5:6, NASB)

Faith can work through fear, pride, tradition, or pain. The only kind that is commendable is faith that works through love. God is remarkably interested in the motive of our hearts. He is not merely interested in the act alone, but in the intention of the heart behind it. Jesus said to His disciples of the Pharisees, "And when you pray, you shall not be like the hypocrites..." (Matthew 6:5a, NKJV).

Jesus was not really that interested in the scientific fact regarding whether or not the Pharisees were praying. He was looking for sincere love.

Even evangelism can be motivated by religious motives. In Matthew 23:15, Jesus told the Pharisees, "Woe to you, teachers of the Law and Pharisees, you hypocrites! You travel over land and sea to win a single convert, and when he becomes one, you make him twice as much a son of hell as you are."[229] Again, Jesus is not merely interested in whether or not these men were doing evangelism. The real question He had was: *What is the condition of the person doing the evangelism?* If self-righteousness was the motive and not love, his mission trips were useless.

Paul the Apostle, when considering why he preached to the Gentiles, said, "For Christ's love compels us, because we are convinced that one died for all, and therefore all died" (2 Corinthians 5:14, NIV).

Love was the driving force that sent Paul to the Gentile nations. May the love of Christ compel us also. May our disciplines and devotions be driven by true worship! Not only is this liberating, but creates a sustainable heart. You cannot sustain action done by fear or pride, because the fruit of it is exhaustion; but you can sustain love. It is a difficult road to be motivated by fear or pride because there is always a bar to get over. When motivated by love, we believe that Jesus got over the bar for us and that the only motive left to drive the soul is love.

---

[229] NIV

DISCIPLINE SHOULD BE DELIGHT-DRIVEN

Psalm 37:4 says, "Delight yourself in the Lord and he will give you the desires of your heart."[230] This Scripture speaks of finding our delight in the Lord, and the Lord conforming our desires to His; that He will place His own desires in our hearts. This being the case, for a disciple of Christ to know what the will of God is, he must only look into the deepest depths of his own heart and see what God put in there. This is true when determining what the will of God is for life choices, and also for determining how to approach Bible study and prayer. Let me explain what I mean.

For years, I was "under law" in my spiritual disciplines, always trying to meet the letter of the Law, and trying to do the least to get the most. Though I would read the Bible every day, I often wouldn't get much out of it. My prayer times seemed to be daily repetitions of boring laundry lists.

When grace came, everything changed.

Instead of daily rituals, I began to ask the Lord to help me to be more Spirit-led in my devotions. That was when I began to realize that He was placing desires in my heart that He wanted me to follow. Instead of *reading* the Bible and checking off a box on a reading plan, I began to *study* the Bible on topics that I was passionate to learn more about.

I was (and am) obsessed with grace, so I began to study Galatians 5 and Romans 8. Word by word I would go, verse by verse, line by line, not moving on to the next until I had a firm grasp on what I was studying. For the first time in my life, it was *exhilarating!* David experienced this when he said to the Lord, "O how I love Your Law! It is my meditation all the day" (Psalm 119:97, NASB).

I applied the same concept to prayer. I began to pray my desires instead of obligating myself to a daily laundry list. What joy, passion, and tears began to flow for the burdens of my heart! Neither did I feel obligated to have long, early prayer sessions every day. I simply prayed as the Spirit led me. Some days I would just study. Other days I would just worship. Some days I

---

[230] NASB

would only pray. Still others would be a combination of the three. The point is that I was not confined to a law, but to the desires of my heart. This takes faith, my brothers and sisters! You must delight in the Lord, and believe that you are close enough to His heart that it has become yours! Then the way that you discover God's will is to find out what moves your heart when you pray.

Jesus said, "If you abide in me, and my words abide in you, you will ask what you desire, and it shall be done for you" (John 15:7, NKJV). Notice He doesn't say, "Ask what you think you should ask for" — He says, "Ask what you *desire*."

DELIGHT-DRIVEN BIBLE STUDIES

A "delight-driven Bible study" is a wonderful blessing to the true worshiper. The following are some steps that I've developed for such a venture.

Steps to "Delight-Driven" Bible Study

1. Choose a verse or passage that interests you.
2. Get a notebook and designate it for Bible Study.
3. Write the passage reference on the top of the first page.
4. Pray David's Prayer in Psalm 119:18: "Open my eyes that I may see wonderful things in your Law."[231]
5. Write the first verse on the top of the page.
6. Read enough of the passage to gain the context.
7. Make your personal observations. Let the Holy Spirit speak to *you*.
8. Study words or phrases that raise questions or interest.
9. Read some commentaries and write anything down that speaks to you.
10. Discuss the passage with your close friends or family. You will naturally begin to meditate on the verse if you study it and it will naturally become a topic of your conversations.
11. Do not move on until you fully understand the entire verse. This may take days or weeks. Don't feel pressure to move on.

---

[231] NIV

One of the nice fruits of delight-driven Bible study is that you "accidentally" begin to memorize Scripture. As you become consumed with a verse or passage, you begin to internalize it and will surprise yourself at how it comes to memory.

CHAPTER 18
The Role of Suffering

"The object of your greatest pain can become the object of your greatest blessing if you're willing to offer it to God."
—Elizabeth Elliot, wife of martyr, Jim Elliot

Suffering is a fiercely debated topic in Christendom and has been since the early church. No one enjoys suffering, but to the one who understands grace, suffering comes with meaning and comfort as long as God allows it to remain. It's a tool to make us more like Jesus. To grow in grace, we must see the role of suffering in the life of a believer.

Jesus promised much trouble in this world,[232] though His promise was accompanied with the greater promise that He had overcome the world. The apostles spoke often about suffering and its role in our lives. Peter reminded us, "Beloved, do not be surprised at the fiery ordeal among you, which comes upon you for your testing, as though some strange thing were happening to you" (1 Peter 4:12, NASB).

Suffering should not be strange to a believer or even frightening. Paul actually *longed* for it when he said, "that I may know Him and the power of His resurrection and the fellowship of His sufferings, being conformed to His death" (Philippians 3:10, NASB). I'm not sure I fully understand Paul's perspective yet, as I'm not as welcoming to the idea as he was! However, I understand the fruit of it because I've seen it in my own life and in the lives of those I'm investing in.

Paul lets us in to some of the fruit of suffering as he shares the story of a terrible ordeal he endured in Asia on one of his missionary journeys:

---

[232] John 16:33

"We do not want you to be uninformed, brothers, about the hardships we suffered in the province of Asia. We were under great pressure, far beyond our ability to endure, so that we despaired even of life. Indeed, in our hearts we felt the sentence of death. But this happened that we might not rely on ourselves but on God, who raises the dead. He has delivered us from such a deadly peril, and he will deliver us. On him we have set our hope that he will continue to deliver us, as you help us by your prayers. Then many will give thanks on our behalf for the gracious favor granted us in answer to the prayers of many." (2 Corinthians 1:8-11, NIV)

Here we see a glimpse into how God uses suffering:

Suffering is an opportunity for God to glorify His name.
He has delivered us...many will give thanks.

Paul's trial became an opportunity for God to show off; to flex His strong arm and glorify Himself. How can God do this unless we have our backs against the wall from time to time so He can bail us out? Rees Howells, the great Welsh intercessor, said, "Man's extremity is God's opportunity."[233]

Consider the Red Sea miracle. Did you know that God actually *set that up?* The Lord told Israel to go to Pi Hahiroth where the Red Sea miracle happened. It was a setup for God's glory!

"Now the Lord spoke to Moses, saying, 'Tell the sons of Israel to turn back and camp before Pi-hahiroth, between Migdol and the sea; you shall camp in front of Baal-zephon, opposite it, by the sea. For Pharaoh will say of the sons of Israel, "They are wandering aimlessly in the land; the wilderness has shut them in." Thus I will harden Pharaoh's heart, and he will chase after them; and I will be honored through Pharaoh and all his army, and the Egyptians will know that I am the LORD.' And they did so." (Exodus 14:1-4, NASB)

---

[233] From the book *Rees Howells, Intercessor* by Norman Grubb

God led Israel into a place where they would be cornered. This was the only way to show His people His strength and grace, and to crush their enemies!

Consider Lazarus. When Jesus was first told about the fact that Lazarus was on his deathbed, He went the opposite direction. When he finally did arrive at Lazarus' tomb, Lazarus was four days dead! Jesus told Martha, "I am the resurrection and the life; he who believes in Me will live even if he dies, and everyone who lives and believes in Me will never die" (John 11:26, NASB). Then he raised Lazarus up from the grave. Dear friend and psalmist, Andrew Eastmond, said of this, "If Jesus had come when Lazarus was only sick, they would have known Jesus only as the healer. Since He waited, they knew Him as the resurrection and the life!"

God uses our suffering to glorify Himself.

Listen to what John Piper had to say about the role of suffering in the context of some comments about "the prosperity gospel":

> "*I don't know what you feel about the prosperity gospel; the health, wealth, and prosperity gospel, but I'll tell you what I feel about it — hatred. It is not the gospel. And it is being exported from this country to Africa and Asia, selling a bill of goods to the poorest of the poor: 'Believe this message and your pigs won't die, and your wife won't have miscarriages, and you'll have rings on your fingers and coats on your back.' That's coming out of America! The people that ought to be giving our money and our time and our lives, instead selling a bunch of crap called gospel. Here's the reason it is so horrible: When was the last time that any American, African, Asian, ever said, 'Jesus is all satisfying because you drove a BMW'? Never! They'll say, 'Did Jesus give you that? Well I'll take Jesus!' That's idolatry! That's not the gospel. That's elevating gifts above the Giver.*
>
> "*I'll tell you what makes Jesus look beautiful. It's when you smash your car and your little girl goes flying through the windshield and lands dead on the street, and you say, 'Through the deepest possible pain, God is enough. God is enough. He is*

good. He will take care of us, He will satisfy us. He will get us through this. He is our treasure. Whom have I in heaven but you? And on earth there is nothing I desire besides you. My flesh and my heart and my little girl may fail, but you are the strength of my heart and my portion forever.' That makes God look glorious — as God, not as giver of cars or safety or health.

"Oh, how I pray that America would be purged of the health, wealth, and prosperity gospel, and that the Christian church would be marked by suffering for Christ! God is most glorified in you when you are most satisfied in Him — in the midst of loss, not prosperity."[234]

Such a man who has glorified God in the midst of his suffering is personal friend, Darrell Scott. In 1999, Darrell's daughter Rachel was shot and killed in the Columbine school shootings in Littleton, Colorado. His son Craig was also at the end of a gun in the library just before the fire sprinkler system went off, sparing Craig's life though his friends were shot and killed on his right and left.

After Rachel's death, Darrell began a ministry reaching high school students across the country. He shares his daughter's story and presents what he calls "Rachel's Challenge" — a challenge to imitate Rachel's example of loving God, and reaching out to the world with kindness and compassion. At the time I write this, Darrell has the #1 high school assembly program in the country.

"For years I wondered what God's purpose was for my life," Darrell testifies, "but if God told me it was this, I never would have agreed. Now, however, I see that God works all things for the good for them that love Him."

Suffering teaches us to persevere.

James 1:2-3 says, "Consider it all joy, my brethren, when you encounter various trials, knowing that the testing of your faith produces endurance."[235]

---

[234] A preaching excerpt from Birmingham, Alabama.
[235] NASB

Where is grace when I'm hurting? Where is God when I feel pain? These were questions I asked myself 100 times in the wilderness. My soul seemed bankrupt of any positive emotion. It seemed that grace was nowhere near me. How could I reconcile God's promise to never leave me and still acknowledge the reality of my own condition?

Then I realized that when grace seems absent in the soul, it appears in other ways. Sometimes grace manifests in your ability to *endure*. In the dark times, it seems He gives you just enough strength for the day. Lamentations 3:22-23 says, "It is of the Lord's mercies that we are not consumed, because his compassions fail not. They are new every morning: great is thy faithfulness."[236]

When you have the strength to run, then run, but don't feel condemned if all you can do is walk or crawl. Make no mistake about it, endurance is a gift of grace just like anything else we receive from God.

I used to be so annoyed at cheery Christians who would smile at me as I was suffering, and saying to me, "The joy of the Lord is your strength!" I would end up feeling condemned because I had missed the joy of the Lord somewhere.

As I meditated on that verse, I began to understand what it really means. I've heard it said that God dwells in a perpetual state of enthusiasm. If God is the giver of joy, then He is full of joy. He is perfectly happy right now. God is joyful! That said, when I look at Him and see His joy, it gives me courage and becomes my strength. Not my joy, but *the joy of the Lord* – the joy that God has.

It's like the story of the passengers huddled below deck in the middle of a terrible storm on the sea. They were convinced that their time had come. One of the passengers ventured above to see the ferocity of the storm that was about to take their lives. When he returned below, he said, "We're going to live!"

"What?" said the fearful passengers. "How can you say that?"

He answered, "Because I saw the captain up there, and he smiled at me."

---

[236] KJV

Somehow seeing the captain smile gives us courage and strength. *The joy of the Lord is my strength.*

When you are wondering where are the joy and peace promised in God's Word, know that His grace is manifesting in a different way. He is giving you *endurance*. Let the joy of the Lord be your strength when you have none.

It would be easy if God always fixed our problems quickly, but somehow the lengthening out of a trial exposes our weaknesses and gives God a chance to work there. It's just like Peter when he walked on the water. If Jesus came quickly, he never would have fallen in! But Peter had to go on longer than he expected. Looking at the wind and waves, he fell in. That's when Jesus pulled him up from the waters.

We can persevere in trials with the knowledge that God is working on our weaknesses, and that God is sustaining us by His grace.

Suffering is used to enlarge your influence.

When you endure a trial, your testimony becomes a witness to the power and grace of God. What you are willing to suffer and endure for Christ becomes part of your gift to the world.

After the Lord delivered me from depression, burnout, and irrational fear, I began to share my story everywhere I went. Over and over again, people would come up to me after a concert or a service and tell me how they were suffering the same thing, and how my testimony encouraged their faith.

One young girl named Rachel approached me at a conference after I shared my testimony, and told me how she'd been suffering in depression for so long. I prayed for her and she thanked me. Months later, her mother contacted me and told me the story of how she had a dream right before the conference. In the dream, her depressed daughter met a man named Derek and talked to him. After her daughter spoke to this man in the dream, she was set free. So her mother told her daughter before she attended the conference, "If you see a man named Derek at the conference, you need to talk to him!" That's exactly what happened. In the months following the conference, the girl came out of her depression and was completely set free!

God is looking for "broken heroes" and "wounded healers" — people who have walked in sorrow and can reach into the same pit of sorrow to pull out others who now suffer in the same area of pain. These will have compassion and because they walk with a limp, will encourage those who are limping.

Suffering is an opportunity for God to teach us that it's still grace.

But this happened that we might not rely on ourselves but on God, who raises the dead.

God used this trial in Asia to show Paul that he still needed to trust God like a nursing child. He would never graduate from dependence upon God's graces and strength.

In the old days, shepherds would break the legs of little lambs that would wander from the flock, and then carry the little lamb on their shoulders while they healed to teach the little ones not to wander.

Corrie Ten Boom, who suffered so much in a Nazi concentration camp in World War II, once said, "Sometimes you don't know that Jesus is all you need until Jesus is all you have."

One day, when I lived on the banks of the St. Lawrence River in northern New York, I took my my children fishing. We caught some perch, along with a few crayfish that we snagged from the rocks below.

As we were gathering our things to go back to the car, I went to grab the large bucket of fish and crayfish. My four-year-old daughter Grace stopped me. "I'm going to carry it, Dad," she said. When I tried to reason with her that it was far too large for her to handle, she stubbornly insisted that she could carry it. Now, I knew she couldn't, but *she* didn't know that she couldn't. So I let her take a crack at it.

My daughter Joye and I began to walk back toward the parking lots, arms loaded with fishing poles and tackle boxes, and I heard Gracie begin to struggle with the fish bucket. She grunted and yanked, and made little progress.

Joye and I continued back toward the car.

Gracie grunted some more, and jerked and yanked, and grunted some more.

Joye and I continued toward the car.

Finally, I heard what I thought I'd hear. Gracie called out, "Daddy! I can't do it!"

I turned back toward the docks, and saw her forlorn face. "I thought you could carry it!" I hollered.

"Daddy," she repeated. "I can't do it! Can you help me?"

I strutted back and helped my little girl.

You know, sometimes God lets us carry the bucket.

We think we can do it, so we strive and work and yank and push, but we make so little progress. Then we call out to our Father, "Daddy, I can't do it!" And He comes, and once again, we see that it's still His grace.

Suffering helps us to see the value of the Body of Christ.

... you help us by your prayers. Then many will give thanks on our behalf for the gracious favor granted us in answer to the prayers of many.

Suffering drives us toward our brothers and sisters in Christ. Paul the Apostle, who saw the third heaven, and wrote half the New Testament, still needed Brother Boring and Sister Ordinary.

We all need people around us who are not impressed with us. When I walked through the darkest season of my life in 2001-2003, my dear brothers and sisters in Christ carried me and encouraged me when all seemed so bleak. Like the friends of the paralytic who carried him to Jesus in Luke 5, so my brothers and sisters carried me.

Again, in 2008, I was diagnosed with a ruptured left vocal cord. I was told to be silent for six weeks and hope that my vocal cord healed properly and would not require surgery. It was again a difficult time. After three weeks, I was far worse, not better. My specialist was concerned. I honestly did not have the faith that I would be healed. It's not that I had an inferiority complex, but I trusted enough in the sovereignty of God that His will would be good no matter what it was. The people of God, however, had a slightly different attitude. They would not take no for an answer! I began receiving dozens of emails and letters from individuals, families, and even whole churches that were praying for me to be healed. My own pastor and church surrounded me with encouragement and prayer. By the time six weeks came around, I was completely healed! My suffering brought me to a greater gratitude and love for my brothers and sisters in Christ.

Suffering is an opportunity to turn pain to praise.

John Piper once said, "Nothing is useless." God uses everything we suffer to make us like Jesus, and everything we suffer can be turned into praise. Consider for a moment the four kinds of suffering we endure: 1) Persecutions, 2) Inconveniences, 3) Sorrows, and 4) Frustrations. All of these are part of "the sufferings of Christ."[237]

Persecutions are the things we endure because we belong to Jesus. People mock us, harass us, mistreat us, and the like. When Peter and the apostles were flogged by the Sanhedrin in Jerusalem, they "left the Sanhedrin, rejoicing because they had been counted worthy of suffering disgrace for the Name" (Acts 5:41, NIV). They turned their pain to praise.

Inconveniences are those things that we suffer because we obey the Lord's Great Commission, like living in a mud hut, having to boil water because there is no clean water available, or living without electricity, and other sacrifices. The great missionary, David Livingstone, after he'd suffered so much for Christ, and lived so long without the amenities of the western world, said at the end of his life, "I never made a sacrifice." He turned his pain into praise.

Sorrows are the things that happen that tear the soul—such events as the loss of a loved one, financial ruin, or the loss of a friendship. Ruth Ruibal is a dear woman that I met only once. Her husband was killed in Columbia a few years ago, shot dead on the streets. As she knelt down next to his body and realized he was gone, she said, "It is well with my soul." She turned her pain into praise.

---

[237] 2 Corinthians 1:5

Frustrations are the petty little things that happen every day that can drive a man mad—losing car keys, a flat tire, a broken refrigerator, etc. What do these things have to do with the sufferings of Christ? You and I have every right through Christ to stand in heaven the moment we put our faith in the cross. So why are we still here? *To carry out the mission of our Lord Jesus!* Therefore, because you are still on your earthly mission, anything that happens on that mission happens as an extension of the sufferings of Christ.[238] You wouldn't lose your car keys if you were in heaven! You wouldn't pop a tire, lose your purse, or drop your cell phone. Recognizing that the only reason you are here is to carry out Christ's mission will help you, even in the smallest frustrations, to turn them into praise. You say, "Lord, I'm so frustrated right now, but I offer this to You as praise because I'm here on this earth for You!"

Suffering is an opportunity for God to teach us His sovereignty.

God's sovereignty encompasses his omnipotence, omnipresence, and His omniscience. It baffles everyone that tries to figure it out, and it should. If God is sovereign, we reason, then does that mean we don't have free will? Mysteriously, both are true at the same time. God is sovereign and man has the ability to choose. Wayne Grudem said, "God has predestined us to voluntarily choose Him."[239]

Hasn't God given us other mysteries in the natural and spiritual to teach us how to rest in faith and not intellect? Can anyone understand the mysteries of time and space? We know they both exist, and yet we cannot fathom no beginning and no end. We embrace the fact that they exist and at the same time embrace the reality that we'll never be able to fully comprehend them. How about the Trinity or the incarnation of Christ? Jesus was 100% man and 100% God at the same time. How can this be? We must have a box for mystery and trust God in faith. We must accept that certain things are true, but will always have mystery

---

[238] I first heard this concept taught by Pastor Steve Estes.
[239] Wayne Grudem, *Systematic Theology:* Zondervan Publishing (Grand Rapids, MI).

surrounding them: time, space, the Trinity, the incarnation, *the sovereignty of God.*

> *"And we know that God causes **all things** to work together for good to those who love God..." (Romans 8:28, NASB, emphasis added)*

> *"...also we have obtained an inheritance, having been predestined according to His purpose who works **all things** after the counsel of His will." (Ephesians 1:11, NASB, emphasis added)*

The phrase "all things" tells us all things. God is absolutely, unequivocally, unapologetically in control. Which of the circumstances of your life is not included in the phrase "all things"? The point of this is not a theological debate, but a comfort in your sufferings.

When we don't understand and feel hopeless, and it seems that darkness has won, we can remember these amazing promises; that God is in control of *all things*. That He's working *all things for the good.*

God will not waste your trials and God will not waste your pain! Trust Him that all things are in His hand and you will find rest. You will know that God is working on something *behind the veil* where you can't see, and you may never see until eternity, but rest will come to your soul when you place your faith in God's promise, not when you understand everything.

One of the things that greatly encouraged me when I was walking through my wilderness was when I found the Scripture that says, "Then Jesus was led up by the Spirit into the wilderness to be tempted by the devil" (Matthew 4:1, NASB). Yes, the devil was in the wilderness, but he was not in charge of the wilderness. God was!

So often, when people encounter Satan in a wilderness season, they kick and scream and shout, and yet the whole time *the spirit led Jesus into the wilderness.* God is the Lord of your wilderness, not Satan.

I remember, during some of my worst days back in 2001, my wife and I had a miscarriage. Darkness was all around us. A well-meaning woman came up to my wife at church and said, "If only the Lord would have told me that Satan was going to take that baby out of your womb, I would have prayed to stop him!"

I was dumbfounded by this woman's perspective. *"Is Satan really that powerful?"* I wondered. As I studied the word, I only saw a sovereign God who has relinquished none of His authority to the devil. My wife and I decided that we did not believe in the sovereignty of Satan, but only the sovereignty of God. Satan could not just come in and rip that baby out of my wife's womb at will. It was *allowed* by the Lord for a sovereign purpose. True rest came to our souls when we realized that.

God is in complete control. A.W. Tozer wrote:

> *"God's sovereignty is the attribute by which He rules His entire creation, and to be sovereign God must be all-knowing, all-powerful, and absolutely free. The reasons are these: Were there even one datum of knowledge, however small, unknown to God, His rule would break down at that point. To be Lord over all the creation, He must possess all knowledge. And were God lacking one infinitesimal modicum of power, that lack would end His reign and undo His kingdom; that one stray atom of power would belong to someone else and God would be a limited ruler and hence not sovereign.*
>
> *"Furthermore, His sovereignty requires that He be absolutely free, which means simply that He must be free to do whatever He wills to do anywhere at any time to carry out His eternal purpose in every single detail without interference. Were He less than free He must be less than sovereign."*[240]

Perhaps you've heard of the influential hymn, "It Is Well with My Soul"? It was written by Horatio Spafford and composed by Philip Bliss. The following is a brief summary of the story of how the hymn came to be:

---

[240] A.W. Tozer, *The Knowledge of the Holy*, HarperOne (November 15, 1978).

This hymn was written after several traumatic events in Spafford's life. The first was the death of his only son in 1871, shortly followed by the great Chicago Fire which ruined him financially (he had been a successful lawyer). Then in 1873, he had planned to travel to Europe with his family on the S.S. Ville Du Havre, but sent the family ahead while he was delayed on business. While crossing the Atlantic, the ship sank rapidly after a collision with another ship, and all four of Spafford's daughters died. His wife Anna survived and sent him the now famous telegram, "Saved alone." Shortly afterwards, as Spafford traveled to meet his grieving wife, he was inspired to write these words as his ship passed near where his daughters had died.[241]

It Is Well With My Soul
When peace like a river, attendeth my way
When sorrows like sea billows roll
Whatever my lot, Thou hast taught me to say
It is well, it is well, with my soul

Refrain:
It is well, with my soul
It is well, with my soul
It is well, it is well, with my soul

Though Satan should buffet, though trials should come
Let this blest assurance control
That Christ has regarded my helpless estate
And hath shed His own blood for my soul

My sin, oh, the bliss of this glorious thought!
My sin, not in part but the whole
Is nailed to the cross, and I bear it no more
Praise the Lord, praise the Lord, O my soul!

And Lord, haste the day when my faith shall be sight
The clouds be rolled back as a scroll
The trump shall resound, and the Lord shall descend
Even so, it is well with my soul

Horatio Spafford

---

[241] Wikipedia

Suffering is one of God's tools to conform us to the image of Christ.

Jonathan Edwards said, "Grace is but glory begun, and glory is but grace perfected."[242]

A few years ago, I heard a man named Graham Cooke speak. Graham is a very respected Bible teacher from California who originally hails from England. He told a story about two men in England who were convinced he was a heretic. They harassed him; they'd publicly tell those attending his event not to listen to him; they mocked him; they were the first to sign up for every conference, where they'd sit in protest in the front row. Graham Cooke was being tormented by them.

One night, he said, he had a dream that God was chiseling a beautiful statue in his likeness. "That's beautiful, Lord!" he said.

Then the Lord asked him, "Do you want to see the tools I used to make this beautiful image of you?"

"Yes, Lord!" Cooke answered.

Then the two men that were harassing him stepped out from behind the statue.

"And I learned," said Cooke, "that these men were *grace growers.*"

I know that you have a vision for your life. It might be to do this great thing or that great thing, but God also has a vision for your life.

> *"And we know that God causes all things to work together for good to those who love God, to those who are called according to His purpose. For those whom He foreknew, He also predestined to become conformed to the image of His Son..."* (Romans 8:28-29, NASB)

God's vision is that we would be *conformed to the image of Christ.* If we don't understand this, trials can be extremely disorienting. We may think that God is solely concerned about

---

[242] Warren W. Wiersbe, *The Bible Exposition Commentary: Old Testament: The Prophets, Volume 3.* © 2002 David C. Cook, pg. 67.

"my" successful career, business or ministry, and then these fail or struggle. "What are you doing, God?" we cry. He is fulfilling His vision for our lives. He is making us like Jesus!

All that we suffer is used by the Lord to this end. Knowing this will help us understand our suffering.

Suffering is an opportunity to become eternity-focused.

I mentioned earlier that my wife and I have been running 5K races. It's amazing how seeing the finish line can affect a runner. Knowing that the pain is almost over gives new courage and strength to run well and finish the race. That's why the middle part of races can be so difficult.

As followers of Jesus Christ, the powerful thing about our journey is that we can fix our eyes on the finish line from the beginning until the end of the race! God wants us to be eternity-focused. To be "in this world, but not of it."[243]

This life is just a dressing room for eternity. Without grace, however, it is impossible to see beyond this life, and so we live for the temporary. Jesus said in Luke 9:58, "Foxes have holes and birds of the air have nests, but the Son of Man has no place to lay his head."[244] In other words, though foxes and birds have found their home here, if we will follow Christ, our home will not be here. Our afflictions and sufferings somehow remind us of that.

> "For momentary, light affliction is producing for us an eternal weight of glory far beyond all comparison." (2 Corinthians 4:17, NASB)

How encouraging are these words. *Light and momentary.* On my worst day, reflecting on that has brought great comfort. In comparison to eternity, anything that I endure in this life is *light and momentary.*

Dear friend and one-time pastor, Rick Sinclair, once likened the trials of this life to a picture frame. "No one looks at a picture

---

[243] John 17:16
[244] NIV

and remarks how beautiful the frame is. Often it is harsh and far less attractive than the picture it borders. The frame is meant to draw your eye away from itself and toward the picture. So it is with this life. We are not meant to admire this life, but the next." This world and its sufferings become the harsh frame for the beauty of the next world.

Consider Job and the lesson he learned with the loss of his children. In Job 1:2, we learn that Job had seven sons and three daughters. When he was afflicted by Satan, he lost all of them. At the end of the story, the Lord restores Job's fortunes:

> "*And the Lord restored the fortunes of Job, when he had prayed for his friends. And the Lord gave Job twice as much as he had before...And the LORD blessed the latter days of Job more than his beginning. And he had 14,000 sheep, 6,000 camels, 1,000 yoke of oxen, and 1,000 female donkeys. He had also seven sons and three daughters." (Job 42:10,12-13, ESV)*

It doesn't take a rocket scientist to figure out that seven sons and three daughters is not *double*. It would seem that Job could ask God, "Why have you given me double of everything back from what I lost except for the children?"

God would answer, "Because you didn't lose the first ten."

We are eternal beings. We must live in this world for the next. Our afflictions bring us back to that endearing eternal perspective, where our affections are on things above, and not the things of this world.

IN THE SUFFERING

Both my wife and I have written a lot of music about suffering.[245] One song that means a lot to me is a song I wrote as the Lord was bringing me out of the wilderness of 2001-2003 and teaching me grace. It's called "In the Suffering":

---

[245] Our music can be found on I-tunes, Rhapsody, and albums can be ordered at www.amanirecords.com.

The Role of Suffering

When I was a little child
I reasoned like a little child
I thought your plan was my happiness
But your desire is to know me

In the suffering
There is something that You're teaching me
I could never
Know much better
That You're my hope and my God
Than in my suffering

When I went to the altar
I said, "Lord, make me like Christ"
Then the knife of the Gardener cut me deep
And my silly soul asks, "Why?"

In the suffering
There is something that You're teaching me
I could never
Know much better
That You're my hope and my God
Than in my suffering

You said, "I am the true vine,
You are the branches,
Abide in me"
You prune me and drive me toward the vine
So I could find true life in you
And bear good fruit[246]

I'll finish this chapter with an amazing story of God's grace, His love, and His sovereignty in the midst of suffering. I read this a few years ago and was deeply moved. It's a fitting end to this chapter.

---

[246] words and music by Derek Joseph Levendusky, © 2007 Prophet Hall Music

Aggie Hurst: A Story of Eternal Perspective[247]

Back in 1921, a missionary couple named David and Svea Flood went with their two-year-old son from Sweden to the heart of Africa to what was then called the Belgian Congo. They met up with another young Scandinavian couple, the Ericksons, and the four of them sought God for direction.

In those days of much tenderness and devotion and sacrifice, they felt led of the Lord to set out from the main mission station and take the gospel to a remote area. This was a huge step of faith. At the village of N'dolera they were rebuffed by the chief, who would not let them enter his town for fear of alienating the local gods. The two couples opted to go half a mile up the slope and build their own mud huts. They prayed for a spiritual breakthrough, but there was none.

The only contact with the villagers was a young boy, who was allowed to sell them chickens and eggs twice a week. Svea Flood — a tiny woman only four feet, eight inches tall — decided that if this was the only African she could talk to, she would try to lead the boy to Jesus. And in fact, she succeeded. But there were no other encouragements. Meanwhile, malaria continued to strike one member of the little band after another. In time the Ericksons decided they had had enough suffering and left to return to the central mission station. David and Svea Flood remained near N'dolera to go on alone. Then, of all things, Svea found herself pregnant in the middle of the primitive wilderness. When the time came for her to give birth, the village chief softened enough to allow a midwife to help her. A little girl was born, whom they named Aina. The delivery, however, was exhausting, and Svea Flood was already weak from bouts of malaria. The birth process was a heavy blow to her stamina. She lasted only another seventeen days.

Inside David Flood, something snapped in that moment. He dug a crude grave, buried his twenty-seven-year-old wife, and then took his children back down the mountain to the mission

---

[247] An excerpt from *Aggie Hurst, Aggie: The Inspiring Story of A Girl Without A Country* [Springfield, MO: Gospel Publishing House, 1986]. ARR. UBP.

232

station. *Giving his newborn daughter to the Ericksons, he snarled, "I'm going back to Sweden. I've lost my wife, and I obviously can't take care of this baby. God has ruined my life." With that, he headed for the port, rejecting not only his calling, but God Himself.*

Within eight months both the Ericksons were stricken with a mysterious malady and died within days of each other. The baby was then turned over to some American missionaries, who adjusted her Swedish name to "Aggie" and eventually brought her back to the United States at age three. This family loved the little girl and were afraid that if they tried to return to Africa, some legal obstacle might separate her from them. So they decided to stay in their home country and switch from missionary work to pastoral ministry. And that is how Aggie grew up in South Dakota. As a young woman, she attended North Central Bible College in Minneapolis. There she met and married a young man named Dewey Hurst. Years passed. The Hursts enjoyed a fruitful ministry. Aggie gave birth first to a daughter, then a son. In time her husband became president of a Christian college in the Seattle area, and Aggie was intrigued to find so much Scandinavian heritage there.

One day a Swedish religious magazine appeared in her mailbox. She had no idea who had sent it, and of course she couldn't read the words. But as she turned the pages, all of a sudden a photo stopped her cold. There in a primitive setting was a grave with a white cross and on the cross were the words SVEA FLOOD.

Aggie jumped in her car and went straight for a college faculty member who, she knew, could translate the article. "What does this say?" she demanded. The instructor summarized the story: It was about missionaries who had come to N'dolera long ago ... the birth of a white baby ... the death of the young mother ... the one little African boy who had been led to Christ ... and how, after the whites had all left, the boy had grown up and finally persuaded the chief to let him build a school in the village. The article said that gradually he won all his students to Christ ... the children led their parents to Christ

... even the chief had become a Christian. Today there were six hundred Christian believers in that one village ... All because of the sacrifice of David and Svea Flood.

For the Hursts' twenty-fifth wedding anniversary, the college presented them with the gift of a vacation to Sweden. There Aggie sought to find her real father. An old man now, David Flood had remarried, fathered four more children, and generally dissipated his life with alcohol. He had recently suffered a stroke. Still bitter, he had one rule in his family: "Never mention the name of God because God took everything from me."

After an emotional reunion with her half brothers and half sister, Aggie brought up the subject of seeing her father. The others hesitated. "You can talk to him," they replied, "even though he's very ill now. But you need to know that whenever he hears the name of God, he flies into a rage."

Aggie was not to be deterred. She walked into the squalid apartment, with liquor bottles everywhere, and approached the seventy-three-year-old man lying in a rumpled bed. "Papa," she said tentatively. He turned and began to cry. "Aina," he said. "I never meant to give you away."

"It's all right, Papa," she replied, taking him gently in her arms. "God took care of me."

The man instantly stiffened. The tears stopped. "God forgot all of us. Our lives have been like this because of Him." He turned his face back to the wall. Aggie stroked his face and then continued, undaunted. "Papa, I've got a little story to tell you, and it's a true one. You didn't go to Africa in vain. Mama didn't die in vain. The little boy you won to the Lord grew up to win that whole village to Jesus Christ. The one seed you planted just kept growing and growing. Today there are six hundred African people serving the Lord because you were faithful to the call of God in your life. Papa, Jesus loves you. He has never hated you."

The old man turned back to look into his daughter's eyes. His body relaxed. He began to talk. And by the end of the afternoon, *he had come back to the God he had resented for so many decades. Over the next few days, father and daughter enjoyed warm moments together. Aggie and her husband soon had to return to America and within a few weeks, David Flood had gone into eternity.*

A few years later, the Hursts were attending a high-level evangelism conference in London, England, when a report was given from the nation of Zaire (the former Belgian Congo). The superintendent of the national church, representing some 110,000 baptized believers, spoke eloquently of the gospel's spread in his nation. Aggie could not help going to ask him afterward if he had ever heard of David and Svea Flood. "Yes, madam," the man replied in French, his words then being translated into English. "It was Svea Flood who led me to Jesus Christ. I was the boy who brought food to your parents before you were born. In fact, to this day your mother's grave and her memory are honored by all of us." He embraced her in a long, sobbing hug. Then he continued, "You must come to Africa to see, because your mother is the most famous person in our history."

In time that is exactly what Aggie Hurst and her husband did. They were welcomed by cheering throngs of villagers. She even met the man who had been hired by her father many years before to carry her back down the mountain in a hammock-cradle. The most dramatic moment, of course, was when the pastor escorted Aggie to see her mother's white cross for herself. She knelt in the soil to pray and give thanks. Later that day, in the church, the pastor read from John 12:24: "I tell you the truth, unless a kernel of wheat falls to the ground and dies, it remains only a single seed. But if it dies, it produces many seeds." He then followed with Psalm 126:5: "Those who sow in tears will reap with songs of joy."

235

CHAPTER 19
Blessed Contentment

"I have learned to be content whatever the circumstances."
—Paul the Apostle (Philippians 4:11, NIV)

Grace makes you finally all right with who you are in Christ, what you are called to do, and into whatever circumstances the Lord may lead you. Grace makes you realize that you are what you are *by the grace of God*; you have what you have *by the grace of God*; you don't have what you don't have *by the grace of God*. If all good comes by His power and provision and not our striving, then why should we be anxious for anything? Like David, we can say, "The Lord is my shepherd, I shall not want" (Psalm 23:1, NASB).

The blessing of contentment is that I'm only called to be what I am. God made me, gave me my strengths and weaknesses, and "by the grace of God I am what I am" (1 Corinthians 15:10, NASB).

My pastor friend Pierre DuPlessis told me, "Part of maturity in Christ is when you're finally okay with who you are not." I also like the proverb I heard along the way, "Blessed is the man who wants what he has."

A number of years ago, when my wife and I were young in ministry, we were constantly obsessed with what we didn't have. When you're in music ministry, people are constantly putting pressure on you to be more popular with comments like, "I hope you make it big one day!" or "One day, when you're famous..." We were always looking outward for our contentment, that somehow we needed more connections, more influence, or more money.

That's when the Lord led us to Psalm 34:10, which says, "The young lions do lack and suffer hunger, but they who seek the Lord shall not be in want of any good thing."[248] If Heidi Jo and I were people that sought the Lord (and we were), then we would never

---

[248] NASB

lack any good thing. Therefore, the provision and platform we had at the time were considered by the Lord to be "good." On the reverse, we also realized that if we didn't have it, *then the Lord didn't think it was good for us to have it!*

What a place of contentment this is when you can shake off your flesh and live there.

Please don't think that I'm suggesting a form of Christian fatalism. Fatalism is a fruit of hopelessness. Contentment is a fruit of faith. Contentment says, "I believe that God's will is the best place for me to be." There are many voices in culture and in the church today that would lead us away from contentment.

Never before has there been a more addicted society than the United States of America. The idea that happiness is always in the next toy, the next dollar, or the next high is drilled down our throats through secular media. God calls us to come away from such a mess.

In the church, some teachers would have us to believe that lack of faith is the cause of all our want. Surely we all need to grow in our faith, but don't the Scriptures tell us to, ""Be still, and know that I am God" (Psalm 46:10)? Churches today are often driven to programs and so much activity that we can scarcely hear the small still voice of God telling us to sit at His feet.

A.W. Tozer was right when he wrote, "Every age has its own characteristics. Right now we are in an age of religious complexity. The simplicity which is found in Christ is rarely found among us. In its stead are programs, methods, organizations and a world of nervous activities which occupy time and attention but can never satisfy the longing of the heart. The shallowness of our inner experience, the hollowness of our worship and that servile imitation of the world which marks our promotional methods all testify that we, in this day, know God only imperfectly, and the peace of God scarcely at all."[249]

Things and ungodly ambitions call us away from contentment until we forget what the Christian faith is even about. Is it about

---

[249] A.W. Tozer, *The Pursuit of God* (Christian Publications: Camp Hill, PA), © 1982, 1993 by Christian Publications, Inc., pg. 17.

my successes or my work? My personal blessing or my positions? Come away from this mess!

Tozer also said of Abraham in a chapter titled "The Blessedness of Possessing Nothing": "I have said that Abraham possessed nothing. Yet was not this poor man rich? Everything he had owned before was his still to enjoy: sheep, camels, herds, and goods of every sort. He had also his wife and his friends, and best of all he had his son Isaac safe by his side. He had everything, but he possessed nothing. There is the spiritual secret. There is the sweet theology of the heart which can be learned only in the school of renunciation. The books on systematic theology overlook this, but the wise will understand."[250]

THE PRAISE OF MAN

The Proverbs say, "The fear of man brings a snare, but he who trusts in the Lord will be exalted" (Proverbs 29:25, NIV). The fear of man is a trap that will destroy all spiritual life. Desiring the approval of man will never lead us to a good place. Grace destroys that instinct of the flesh.

Grace teaches us that our performance is insufficient and unnecessary to gain God's approval. It teaches us that we don't need man's approval. Grace teaches us that, "The One who knows you the best loves you the most."

Like it has been said of Paul: "Paul is like the musician who doesn't need the approval of the masses, but is satisfied with the approving glance of his master."[251]

Jesus said, "I do not accept praise from men."[252]

The Pharisees did accept praise from men. They were legalists. The logic is simple. If you seek to attain your righteousness by keeping the Laws of God, then you will take credit for it when you perceive that you've done it. Man's praise would seem to validate your performance.

Grace says, "God's love is enough for me."

---

[250] Ibid, "The Blessedness of Possessing Nothing."
[251] Anonymous
[252] John 5:41, NIV

Great missionary Jack Schisler said, "If you want to gain something with God, you need to lose something with men." That's exactly what happened to me when I walked into the Dark Night of the Soul. When I was in the wilderness, out of ministry for six months, the Lord led me to a simple Scripture in Genesis 5:24: "Enoch walked with God; then he was no more."[253] And I sensed the Lord asked me a question: "Derek, do you think Enoch was a failure?"

"How could he be, Lord?" I answered. "You commend him among the greats listed in 'The Hall of Faith' in Hebrews 11!"

The conversation with Abba continued. "But all he did was 'walk with God.' He had no other great exploits that so many today would typically consider to be the mark of a true greatness. You still don't think he was a failure?"

That's when I realized how backwards my thinking had been. I used to think that "walking with God" was a consolation prize for those who didn't have a clear direction in life. You know what I mean—"You dunno what God has called you to do? He'll tell you one day! For now, just *walk with God.*"

But God was showing me that knowing God and walking with Him was the pinnacle achievement of Enoch's life. It wasn't *part* of his calling—it *was* his calling! Everything else flowed out of that. Enoch was content with the simplicity of his relationship with God.[254]

I began to examine my life and was embarrassed at how much I'd sought the approval of men. One day, while I was still out of ministry, the Lord asked me, "Derek, if you never ministered again, is that okay?"

"Well what about my ministry?" I objected.

"What if your ministry was just to bless Me in seclusion with your worship and to minister to others in intercession, though they would never know it? Are you okay with that?"

I realized that until I could honestly answer that question *yes*, I would live my life for the praise of man. The Lord would hold me

---

[253] NIV
[254] I wrote a book that has blessed many people titled *Enoch Walked With God.* It can be ordered at www.amanirecords.com or other public book-selling sites.

down until He convinced my heart. I pray He convinces yours as well.

GOD'S PICTURE OF YOU

Second Corinthians 3:18 says, "But we all, with unveiled face, beholding as in a mirror the glory of the Lord, are being transformed into the same image from glory to glory, just as from the Lord, the Spirit."[255]

The good news in this Scripture is that you do not have to change yourself. God does it for you. But how are you transformed?

When the starting point of your love for God is His love for you, as you love God in return, you begin to see all things through the eyes of His love, including yourself. Your entire view of the world will change. Your entire view of yourself will change. You will see a version of you that you never dreamed existed. That's because the only place it existed is in the heart of God.

This is why I believe it's impossible to truly know who you are, and to "find yourself" without God. Only God's love has the key to the real you, and as you worship Him, you will see with His eyes.

Isn't this what happened in Isaiah Chapter 6 when Isaiah began to worship? It says that Isaiah saw angels worshiping, "And one cried unto another, and said, 'Holy, holy, holy, is the Lord of hosts: the whole earth is full of his glory'" (Isaiah 6:3, KJV).

This happened during "the year King Uzziah died"[256] and there were warring nations coming against Israel on the north, south, east, and west. Isaiah could have said, "The whole earth is full of your glory? Not from where I'm looking at it!" But somehow, as Isaiah began to worship the Lord, his very perspective of the earth changed, and he saw it with God's eyes. *The whole earth is full of His glory.*

James likens God's Word to a mirror.[257] In other words, as we study the Scriptures, it should be like looking in a spiritual mirror,

---

[255] NASB
[256] Isaiah 6:1
[257] James 1:23-24

241

finding out what we really look like and who we really are. Our response should be: "Ah, God *does* love me! I *am* a child of God!"

This is why it's so important to be "rooted and grounded in love."[258] This is God's love it's speaking of, likening it to good soil. If we are planted in it (God's love), we will grow. If not, we will not grow. First John 4:18 says, "There is no fear in love; but perfect love casts out fear, because fear involves punishment, and the one who fears is not perfected in love."[259]

This is how you can have Christians who have been in the church for fifty years still be babes in Christ. They never learned grace! They never saw themselves through God's eyes, so they still see themselves through the eyes of the one who hurt them in their childhood, or the way that others see them, or the way they see themselves—anyone but God!

Michael Cavanaugh once said, "Let your only evaluation of worth derive from the awareness of God's love for you. All other measures leave you in a state of delusion."[260]

The ones who see this amazing, transforming, perfect Love will never be the same. They will be content no matter the circumstances; they will live carefree from the opinions of others, and they will say with David, "The Lord is my shepherd, I shall not want" (Psalm 23:1, NASB).

> "*The test of Christian character should be that a man is a joy-bearing agent to the world.*"
> —Henry Ward Beecher

---

[258] Ephesians 3:17
[259] NASB
[260] Cavanaugh said this in a teaching series titled "Galatians: Is It That Easy?" at Elim Gospel Church in Lima, NY, in the fall of 2008.

CHAPTER 20
Tear Down the Idols

"Put to death, therefore, whatever belongs to your earthly nature: sexual immorality, impurity, lust, evil desires and greed, which is idolatry."
—Paul the Apostle (Colossians 3:5, NIV)

Okay, time to ask a strange question for a Christian book.
What do you worship?

I know your Sunday School answer. I don't need to hear that. Of course, you worship God. But *what else do you worship?*

Huh?

Let me define worship: You worship anything that you attach your happiness to.

By that definition, you and I worship a lot of things, don't we? It's idolatry of the heart, my brothers and sisters! Paul wrote, "Therefore consider the members of your earthly body as dead to immorality, impurity, passion, evil desire, and greed, which amounts to idolatry" (Colossians 3:5, NASB).

This started in the Garden of Eden with Adam and Eve. What happened when they took the fruit? They were seeking to satisfy themselves *outside of God.*

God said to Moses in Exodus 34:14, "Do not worship any other god, for the Lord, whose name is Jealous, is a jealous God."[261]

God called His name *Jealous?* I've seen lots of nice names for God on refrigerators—Prince of Peace, Fairest of Ten Thousand, Lamb of God—but I've never seen that one! Why would God call His name that? Here is the essence: When you and I seek to satisfy ourselves outside of God, we arouse the jealous heart of God, because He wants all of our worship and wants to be the source of all our strength! Why? Because He knows that He's the only one that can be.

---

[261] NIV

Tozer put it well: "Our woes began when God was forced out of His central shrine and 'things' were allowed to enter. Within the human heart 'things' have taken over. Men have now by nature no peace within their hearts, for God is crowned there no longer, but there in the moral dusk stubborn and aggressive usurpers fight among themselves for first place on the throne."[262]

Of course there's nothing wrong with enjoying the things God has given you, but only when you worship God do these things have the proper place in your life. You do not look to them as the source of your joy, but only as a fruit of your relationship with God.

WORSHIPING CANDY

One of the main and most frequent lessons I've had to teach my children is not to worship idols. Like their dad, their natural tendency to do so is enormous. Like their dad, they are born idolaters. They are constantly linking their happiness to objects outside of Christ.

Recently, my sweet little daughter, Esther, wanted some candy. When I declined her offer to spend my money, she had a nervous breakdown. I calmed her down and asked her, "Sweetheart, who is supposed to make you happy?"

"Jesus," she answered correctly.

"Then why are you looking for happiness in the candy?" I asked.

She puzzled for a moment, and said, "I dunno!"

"Are you worshiping the candy?"

She nodded with big tears in her eyes, for a moment incapable of answering until she finally blurted, "Yeesss!"

I held her in my arms, and said, "It's okay, let's just repent and ask Jesus to forgive you. Now just repeat after me: Dear Jesus..."

"Dear Jesus," she echoed.

"...please forgive me..." I continued.

"Please forgive me."

---

[262] A.W. Tozer, *The Pursuit of God* (Christian Publications: Camp Hill, PA), © 1982, 1993 by Christian Publications, Inc., "The Blessedness of Possessing Nothing."

"...for worshiping the candy."

"For worshiping the candy."

"All done," I told her. "All clean! Jesus has forgiven you!"

My children have learned to confess their worship of idols, and have learned to recognize its symptoms. Sometimes we'll be watching television, and a sensual commercial will come on about some beauty product. Inevitably, one of my children will analyze it, and say, "That woman is worshiping beauty." Other times, in a movie, they might say, "That movies teaches the worship of romance."

Anything can be an idol. Things, reputation, education, career, romance, beauty, fame, family, spouse, etc. For teenagers, I've often seen that *friends* can become an idol—what they think becomes more important than what God thinks.

As a mentor and father, part of my responsibility is to help those I'm discipling learn how to recognize the object of their worship. If they find their hearts drawn to idols, I must teach them to allow the Lord to uproot their idolatry through repentance and faith. The earlier any of us can come to grips with our weakness, the earlier we can gain the mastery, through God's grace, over our sinful nature. Part of discipling by grace is helping our understudies to recognize and avoid this tendency to give in to the temptations of idolatry. You'll find the searchlight turned on in your own heart as you become adept at analyzing idolatry.

Let's say to the Lord, like David, "Search me, O God, and know my heart. Try me, and know my thoughts, and see if there be any wicked way in me, and lead me in the way everlasting" (Psalm 139:23,24, NKJV). Then let's allow the Lord to tear down the idols.

Section 3

GRACE AND EVANGELISM

CHAPTER 21
The Gospel That Saves

"Hell's best kept secret is God's Law." —Ray Comfort

Understanding true grace is essential to being an effective evangelist. The gospel makes no sense without a revelation of grace, but with that truth, it becomes the most powerful message in the universe, capable of transforming nations. In this chapter, we'll revisit what the gospel is and is not, and how to effectively share it with the lost.

WHAT'S THE QUESTION?

"Jesus is the answer!" said the young Christian.

The kid dressed in black took a long draw on his cigarette and said, "Dude, what's the question?"

This is the question that humanity is asking; the question that every gospel preacher must answer, for unless our hearers see their great sin, they will not receive the great Savior.

If God's messengers today will use the Law of God as a tool to reveal sin, we can offer grace to our hearers, but if we insist on not offending them, we will never see a true harvest. Let's just settle that one right here. The gospel offends people. First Peter 2:8 calls our message, "a stone that people trip over, a large rock that people find offensive." Then it says, "The people tripped over the word because they refused to believe it."[263] If you are hoping to be liked and to win friends, this is not for you. Jesus said, "All men will hate you because of me" (Mark 13:13, NIV).

The plain fact is that people are not interested in following a Savior that they don't believe saved them. Without preaching sin and grace, the unbelievers will continue to justify themselves all the way to hell.

When it comes to my understanding of using the Law of God in preaching, I owe a great debt of gratitude to evangelist Ray

---

[263] God's Word Translation

Comfort. Fifteen years ago, someone handed me a book he authored called *Hell's Best Kept Secret*. I almost wish I could just print his entire book in this chapter. A few footnoted comments and quotes will have to do.

THE DOCTRINE OF SIN AND EVANGELISM

If modern evangelists will not show a lost world that they are lawbreakers that have fallen short of God's glory, we will never see a *true* harvest. There is no way to accurately communicate to man his need of a Savior until he first sees his sin.

The greatest preachers in church history knew this secret. From Jonathan Edwards to George Whitefield, John Wesley to Charles Finney, Billy Sunday to D.L. Moody, Charles Spurgeon to A.B. Earle, they knew that if a lost soul would ever cry out for a Savior, he must first see that he is a lawbreaker guilty of death in the eyes of God.

John Wesley said, "Before I can preach love, mercy, and grace, I must preach sin, Law, and judgment." Wesley also later instructed a young man in a letter, "Preach 90% Law and 10% grace."[264]

Revivalist Charles Finney believed that "all the sinners foundations must be torn up until there was no refuge in sight other than the atoning blood of Jesus." In his book *Revival Lectures*, Finney is not shy on the importance of using the Law in sharing the gospel:

> *"It is of great importance that the sinner should be made to feel his guilt, and not left to the impression that he is unfortunate. Do not be afraid, but show him the breadth of the Divine Law, and the exceeding strictness of its precepts. Make him see how it condemns his thoughts and life. By a convicted sinner, I mean one who feels himself condemned by the Law of God, as a guilty sinner."*[265]

---

[264] Comfort, Ray, *Hell's Best Kept Secret* (Bellflower, CA: Whitaker House, © 1989 by Ray Comfort), pg. 23
[265] Comfort, Ray, *Hell's Best Kept Secret* (Bellflower, CA: Whitaker House, © 1989 by Ray Comfort), pg. 24-25

Hymn writer and famous evangelist A.B. Earle wrote, "I have found by long experience that the severest threatenings of the Law of God have a prominent place in leading men to Christ. They must see themselves lost before they cry out for mercy. They will not escape from danger until they see it."[266]

"The Prince of Preachers," Charles Spurgeon, said, "They must be slain by the Law before they can be made alive by the gospel!"[267] The following is an example of how Spurgeon, in one of his sermons, used the Law of God to convince his hearers of their great need of a Savior:

> *"All the Ten Commandments, like ten great cannons, are pointed at thee today, for you have broken all God's statutes, and lived in daily neglect of all His commands. Soul! Thou wilt find it a hard thing to go to war with the Law...What will ye do when the Law comes in terror, when the trumpet of the archangel shall tear you from your grave, when the eyes of God shall burn way into your guilty soul, when the great books shall be opened, and all your sin and shame shall be punished?"[268]*

Read some excerpts from one of the most famous sermons ever preached, *Sinners in the Hands of an Angry God* by Jonathan Edwards:

> *"The second consideration is that sinners deserve to be cast into hell. Divine justice never stands in the way of God using His power at any moment to destroy them; it makes no objection whatsoever. Rather, justice calls aloud for an infinite punishment of their sins. Divine justice says of the tree that brings forth fruit like that of the poisonous grapes of Sodom, 'Cut it down; why cumbereth it to the ground?'"[269]*

---

[266] Ibid, pg. 25
[267] Ibid, pg. 24
[268] Ibid, pg. 23-24
[269] Edwards, Jonathan, *Sinners in the Hands of an Angry God* (New Kensington, PA: Whitaker House, © 1997 by Whitaker House), p.19

"Everyone lays out in his own mind how he will avoid damnation, and flatters himself that he contrives well for himself, and that his schemes will not fail...they trust in nothing but shadows."[270]

"Your wickedness makes you as heavy as lead; it drives you down, with great weight and pressure, toward hell...you have no more influence to uphold you and keep you out of hell, than a spider's web has to stop a falling rock."[271]

"O sinner! Consider the fearful danger you are in! It is a great furnace of wrath, a wide and bottomless pit, full of the fire of wrath, over which you are held by the hand of God."[272]

"We often read of the fury of God, as in Isaiah 59:18: 'According to their deeds, accordingly he will repay, fury to his adversaries.'...The fury of God! The fierceness of Jehovah! Oh, how dreadful that must be!"[273]

George Whitefield's voice was one of the greatest voices ever heard resounding in England and the United States during the Great Awakening of the 1800's. A contemporary of John Wesley and Jonathan Edwards, he once wrote in a letter to a friend, "...How can they possibly stand who never felt themselves condemned criminals? who were never truly burdened with a sense, not only of their actual, but original sin, especially that damning sin of unbelief? who were never brought to see and heartily confess...that it is only owing to God's sovereign love that they can have any hopes of being delivered from the wrath to come."

He also said of the contemporary preaching of Gilbert and John Tennant, "It is for preaching in this manner that I like the Tennants. They wound deep before they heal. They know that

---

[270] Ibid, p.28

[271] Edwards, Jonathan, *Sinners in the Hands of an Angry God* (New Kensington, PA: Whitaker House, © 1997 by Whitaker House), p.34

[272] Edwards, Jonathan, *Sinners in the Hands of an Angry God* (New Kensington, PA: Whitaker House, © 1997 by Whitaker House), p.41

[273] Edwards, Jonathan, *Sinners in the Hands of an Angry God* (New Kensington, PA: Whitaker House, © 1997 by Whitaker House), p.46

there is no promise made, but 'to him that believeth,' and therefore they are careful not to comfort overmuch those who are convicted. I fear I have been too incautious in this respect, and have often given comfort too soon."[274]

The difference between a fire and brimstone preacher and a true gospel preacher is that the fire and brimstone preacher condemns with the Law and the gospel preacher uses the Law to show a lost man his need of a Savior.

Evangelist Ray Comfort has done a masterful job of heralding these truths to the modern church. He teaches that much of modern evangelism has reduced the gospel to "life enhancement" — that Jesus will give us life, joy, peace, and happiness — and that many modern evangelists have ceased using the Law to convince a lost world of its need of Christ.

One of my favorite illustrations that he uses is that of contrasting two passengers on an airplane.[275] The first passenger is told that if he puts on a parachute, it will improve his flight. The passenger believes the messenger, and puts the parachute on. Hunched over in his seat because of the awkwardness of wearing a chute while sitting on a plane, passenger number one begins to get an ache in his lower back. "But," he thinks, "someone told me this chute is going to improve my flight! I'm sure things will change soon." Indeed things do change soon, as the other passengers notice the passenger wearing a chute, and begin to mock him. It doesn't take long for the passenger to take the parachute off, throw it on the floor, and say, "I'm never putting that stupid thing on again!" And frankly, he's pretty upset at the person who told him that the parachute would improve his flight.

Contrast this man with the second passenger who is told that he better put a parachute on because halfway through the flight, he'll be required to jump 35,000 feet to the ground. This passenger gladly endures the ache in his back, and the mocking and jeering of the other passengers. Later on, floating lazily toward the earth

---

[274] Whitefield's *Works*, Vol. I, pg. 190
[275] Comfort, Ray: *Hell's Best Kept Secret* cassette tape: Bellflower, CA. © 1993 Ray Comfort.

while the others around him are splatting on the ground, he is very grateful to the one that told him to put on the parachute.

"Instead of telling people that Jesus will improve their flight," Comfort explains, "we need to tell them about the jump to come!"

He writes that the Law is useful in gospel preaching in the following ways:[276]

1.   The Law shows us our guilt before God and stops us from justifying ourselves.
"Now we know that whatever the Law says, it says to those who are under the Law, that every mouth may be stopped, and all the world may become guilty before God." (Romans 3:19, NIV)

2.   The Law brings us to the knowledge of sin.
"Therefore by the deeds of the Law no flesh will be justified in his sight, for by the Law is the knowledge of sin." (Romans 3:20, NKJV)

3.   The Law defines sin.
"What shall we say then? Is the Law sin? Certainly not! On the contrary, I would not have known sin except through the Law. For I would not have known covetousness unless the Law had said, 'You shall not covet.'" (Romans 7:7, NIV)

4.   The Law was designed for the very purpose of bringing men and women to Christ.
"Therefore the Law was our tutor to bring us to Christ, that we might be justified by faith." (Galatians 3:24, NASB)

So then, the Law becomes a measuring stick, but not one that gives us confidence that we have succeeded in carrying out its demands and standards. On the contrary, it is a measuring stick that shows us that we have fallen miserably short, shaking our confidence in self until we cry out to God for mercy.

---

[276] Comfort, Ray, *Hell's Best Kept Secret* (Bellflower, CA: Whitaker House, © 1989 by Ray Comfort), pg. 20-21

Listen to what evangelist D.L. Moody, who led a million souls to Christ (that's not bad), said about using the Law of God.

> *"God, being a perfect God, had to give a perfect Law, and the Law was given not to save men, but to measure them. I want you to understand this clearly, because I believe hundreds and thousands stumble at this point. They try to save themselves by keeping the Law; but it was never meant for men to save themselves by. Ask Paul why it was given. Here is his answer, 'That every mouth may be stopped, and all the world may become guilty before God' (Romans 3:19)."* [277]

Recently, I heard about an attempt to change the words to the old hymn *Amazing Grace*. The reasoning was that calling yourself a *wretch*, as stated in verse one, is not good for self-esteem. One thing here must be obvious, however — the grace ain't amazing if the wretch ain't a wretch!

Jesus said that He did not come for the righteous, but sinners (Mark 2:17). Paul the Apostle said before Agrippa that he "was not disobedient unto the heavenly vision, but declared both to them of Damascus first and at Jerusalem, and throughout all the country of Judaea, and also to the Gentiles, that they should repent and turn to God, doing works worthy of repentance" (Acts 26:19-20, NKJV).

Therefore, "receiving Christ" (Colossians 2:6, Romans 5:17) is not merely asking Jesus to live in your heart, be your friend, or even to be your Lord and Savior. It is repenting of sin, and placing faith solely on the finished work of Christ. Then *He becomes* Lord and Savior.

How many false conversions have we had in the modern age, as evangelists offer a life enhancement gospel while seeking quick conversions for newsletters? Consider author Arnold Dallimore's thoughts on Great Awakening preacher, Jonathan Edwards:

> *"A knowledge of what Edwards meant by his words, 'the work of conversion', ought to prove highly valuable to our*

---

[277] Ibid, pg. 29

present age. He made plain that he did not (as so many do today) 'take every religious pang and enthusiastic conceit, for saving conversion.' On the contrary, he looked for evidence of a deep and abiding work of the Spirit of God in the heart—a work which, though it varied from one individual to another, necessarily included a weighty conviction of sin, an utter rejection of all trust in things human, and finally, a very definite experience—that which he referred to as 'a saving closure with Christ.'"

"In regard to conviction of sin as experienced among his hearers, he writes: 'When awakenings first begin, their consciences are commonly most exercised about their outward vicious course, or other acts of sin; but afterwards are much more burdened with a sense of heart-sins, the dreadful corruption of their nature, their enmity against God, the pride of their hearts, their unbelief, their rejection of Christ, the stubbornness and obstinancy of their wills: and the like.' Thus awakened by the Spirit of God, many suffered severe anguish of soul."

"It will have been noticed that Edwards' description of the experiences of the soul prior to conversion is very different from the common concept today. But if the sense of sin and soul distress was deep, so also was the joy that attended conversion…Edwards did not lightly come to the conclusion that a person was converted."[278]

Consider how Jesus dealt with the rich young ruler in Luke 18:18-23:

Now a certain ruler asked Him, saying, "Good Teacher, what shall I do to inherit eternal life?"

So Jesus said to him, "Why do you call Me good? No one is good, but One, that is, God. You know the commandments: 'Do

---

[278] Dallimore, Arnold, *George Whitefield* (Carlisle, PA: Banner of Truth Trust, © 1970,1971,1975,1979,1989,1995,2001 Arnold Dallimore).

not commit adultery,' 'Do not murder,' 'Do not steal,' 'Do not bear false witness,' 'Honor your father and mother.'''

And he said, "All these things I have kept from my youth."

So when Jesus heard these things, He said to him, "You still lack one thing. Sell all that you have and distribute it to the poor, and you will have treasure in heaven; and come, follow Me."

But when he heard this, he became very sorrowful, for he was very rich. (Luke 18:18-23, NKJV)

What was Jesus doing? Aren't we saved by *grace*? Why is Jesus telling this man that the way to eternal life is through obeying *commandments*? Why doesn't He just lead the man in a quick "sinner's prayer"? Let's take a closer look at the passage.

To be truthful, there are two ways to heaven, and here Jesus is presenting the one that most evangelists never offer: 1) Be perfect and obey all the commandments all the time, or 2) Receive grace and forgiveness available through the cross of Christ. Jesus is offering option #1.

Ray Comfort says of this principle, "Law to the proud and grace to the humble."[279]

This young ruler is full of pride, and Jesus sees every filthy ounce of it. So, Jesus sets up a situation to humble the man and show himself his true heart. He offers him option #1—He tells him that if he's obeyed the Ten Commandments, then he has earned eternal life.

The man arrogantly boasts that he's kept "all these" from his youth. Really?

With one request—to sell his possessions and give them to the poor—Jesus shows the young hypocrite that he had broken many of the Ten Commandments. Let's take a look and see how he might have done this:

---

[279] Comfort, Ray: *Hell's Best Kept Secret* cassette tape: Bellflower, CA. © 1993 Ray Comfort.

The First Commandment
"You shall have no other gods before Me"
(Deuteronomy 5:7, NASB)

Because this young man was not willing to obey the Lord's command, he clearly had disobeyed the First Commandment. He placed the idol of his riches before God.

The Sixth Commandment
"Honor your father and your mother"
(Deuteronomy 5:16, NASB)

Through his disobedience and idolatry, the man dishonored his parents for all the world to see through the pages of the greatest selling book of all time—the Bible.

The Seventh Commandment
"You shall not murder"
(Deuteronomy 5:17, NASB)

Am I out of bounds to say that this rich young ruler, through his indifference to the poor, had actually murdered them with his heart? They mattered so little to him that his heart could care less if they even existed.

The Eighth Commandment
"You shall not steal"
(Deuteronomy 5:19, NASB)

By disobeying Christ's command and withholding his wealth from the poor, was he not stealing from the poor? Had not God assigned his wealth for the poor?

The Tenth Commandment
"You shall not covet your neighbor's goods"
(Deuteronomy 5:21, NASB)

Since God designated this man's wealth to the poor, in the eyes of God, did not this man's wealth actually *belong* to the poor? So by hoarding his wealth, was he not coveting *their* goods?

The plain and obvious truth is that this rich young ruler had *not* kept the commandments. He had actually broken at least five of the Ten Commandments, and it only took one demand from Jesus to show him that. The conclusion the rich man must come to is that he is a sinner, just like everybody else, in desperate need of a Savior. Jesus used the Law masterfully to get to the issues of the young man's heart.

Unfortunately, modern evangelists are in a frenzy to count heads so they can report big numbers to supporters. If most modern evangelists were approached by the rich young ruler, they would quickly have him say a prayer and "get saved." Jesus was far more concerned about the actual condition of the man's heart than whether or not he filled out a commitment card.

I am praying that God would purge modern evangelism of the life enhancement gospel and that God would raise up laborers who would preach the gospel that saves.

Discipleship by Grace

CHAPTER 22
How to Share the Gospel

"How then will they call on Him in whom they have not believed? How will they believe in Him whom they have not heard? And how will they hear without a preacher?" —Paul the Apostle (Romans 10:14, NASB)

Often I have believers remark on how they enjoy hearing me preach the gospel. Recently, someone told me, "I've heard and given hundreds of gospel presentations, but the one you just gave is the most amazing presentation I've ever heard."

I know I'm risking sounding like I'm bragging here, but I'm really trying to show you the impact that the true gospel has on people. When I share, what are they hearing that is touching them so deeply? I'm no great orator. I believe that they are moved by the content in my preaching.

I've gone on three music tours to the Middle East with my band, Isaiah Six, where we've performed concerts and shared the gospel in dozens of cities. One of the things I learned in my overseas experience is that the gospel is *simple*. It's not a complex 10-point sermon that changes the nations (including our own), but the simplicity of the message of the cross. I always include three things when I preach the gospel to the lost:

1) The Doctrine of Sin
2) The Doctrine of Grace
3) A Parable or Story

Let's take a closer look at these three as they apply to sharing the gospel.

The Doctrine of Sin

The goal here is for the unbeliever to take a look inward at the miserable condition of his or her own heart apart from Christ. It's one thing to call a person a sinner—this is what the fire and brimstone preacher does well—it's another to create an opportunity for the searchlight of the Holy Spirit to search the hearts of the hearer.

When I preach, what I'll do first is choose a short passage of Scripture that will reveal the sin nature of man. I'll usually read that passage to open my gospel presentation. One of my favorites is found in Luke 5:17-26, the story of the paralytic who was lowered through the roof by his four friends. The key to this passage is Christ's response when He sees the poor man. He says in verse 23, "Friend, your sins are forgiven you."

The following is an actual quote from one of my evangelistic messages when I used this passage:

> *"I want you to notice what Jesus said to the paralytic that was laid before Him. He said, 'Friend, your sins are forgiven you.'*
>
> *"Huh? Why would Jesus say that? Everybody in the room, and everyone that's ever read the passage knew why that man had been dropped in front of Jesus—that Christ would heal the man! Did Jesus miss this fact? Why is He talking about the man's sins?*
>
> *"Here it is right here: The paralytic thought he knew what his greatest need was— 'Oh, if I would just be healed, I'd be happy!'—but Jesus knew what the greatest need of his heart was: that his sins be forgiven. Only that would give him true peace and happiness.*
>
> *"In the same way, maybe you're in here tonight, and you think you know what your greatest need is. 'Oh, if I could just get that job!' 'If I could just get married!' 'If I would just get healed!'—but Jesus knows the greatest need of your heart, too—that your sins would be forgiven. Have you ever heard Jesus say to your heart, 'Friend, your sins are forgiven you.'?"*
>
> *"Am I calling you a sinner? Well, let's take a fair look at this…"*

This is where I'll use the Law to help the hearer see his or her need of a Savior.

My goal here is to remove every prop and false confidence that unbelievers have until they despair in their own ability to save themselves. Everything must crumble before their eyes—perceived personal merit, self-righteousness, self-sufficiency, resistant fortresses of the mind, pride and ego. As someone once wrote of the great preacher George Whitefield, "He declares that his whole view in preaching is to bring men to Christ, to deliver them from false confidences..."[280]

To illustrate how to do this, I'm again indebted to the evangelist Ray Comfort. Comfort has become a master of using the Ten Commandments to show a man his need of a Savior. Consequently, he's become a master of teaching believers how to do this as well. Here's an example of how I've use the Law in a gospel presentation after applying Comfort's principles:[281]

> *"Christ's sacrifice doesn't only save us from hell, but it saves us from sin and all its effects. That's why, when a person believes in Christ, eternal life begins now. The cross is not just for the sweet by-and-by, but changes our lives here on earth. One of the consequences of sin is that without Christ we are condemned to the punishment of hell. Even so, I meet many people who tell me that they think God will accept them (into heaven) because they are 'good people.' Now, if you don't remember anything else I say tonight, remember this: There are no good people in heaven...just forgiven people."*

> *"God's definition of 'good' is 'moral perfection.' So unless you can keep the whole Law, you fall short of His standard of holiness and are a lawbreaker in His eyes, guilty of eternal death. Keep in mind the Bible says that 'if you break one commandment, you're guilty of breaking all of them.' Is that fair? Well, how many murders would I have to commit to be a*

---

[280] Dallimore, Arnold, *George Whitefield* (Carlisle, PA: Banner of Truth Trust, © 1970, 1971, 1975, 1979, 1989, 1995, 2001 Arnold Dallimore), pg. 436

[281] This presentation is a convergence of many of Comfort's principles and examples along with a few of my own personal ideas I've developed through the years.

murderer? One, right? Even I only killed one out of 1000 and was nice to 999 people, I would still be a murderer, right? In the same way, I only have to commit one sin to be a sinner, and the Bible says that the wages of sin is death."

"Let's look at just a few of the Ten Commandments to see if in fact you are a 'sinner.' One of the Ten Commandments says, 'Thou shalt not lie.' Now it's confession time. How many of you have told a lie before? The Eighth Commandment says, 'Thou shall not steal.' How many of you have ever taken something before that wasn't yours—a cookie, a pencil, or a car? Ever cheated on a test? That's stealing, too! How about illegal downloading off the internet? The Sixth Commandment says, 'Thou shall not kill.' You may feel you are innocent, but Jesus taught that if you have hatred, unforgiveness, or even unrighteous anger in your heart toward someone else, you've committed murder in the eyes of God. You've murdered them with your heart! By that definition, how many of you have murdered someone with your heart?"

"Okay, by your own admission, I'm standing in a room full of lying, murderous thieves! Listen to me—unless we've been forgiven by Jesus Christ, that is exactly what we are before God. We are lawbreakers in His eyes. What hope do you have to escape the consequences of your sin? How can God overlook your crimes? Some of you may say, 'Well, God knows my heart, and besides, it was a long time ago that I sinned and I'm doing better now.' Let me ask you a question: If someone stole your car ten years ago, would you want justice today? Of course you would, and the reason it's right is because it's just. Justice cries out for punishment, no matter how long ago the crime was committed. God must punish sin because He is holy.

"'Well,' others say, 'God is good and merciful and will overlook my mistakes.' On what basis? Your good heart? Your reformed behavior? Let's say a police officer catches you driving 100 miles an hour in a blind children's zone. What would the officer say to you if you said, 'Sir, I believe that you're a good man and because of that, you'll overlook my crimes'? He'd probably say, 'You're right about one thing—I am a good man.

And because I'm a good man, I'm going to make sure you're punished!' The very thing you depended upon—his goodness—is the very thing that will condemn you. Why? Because good men are just. They make sure justice is served. Now listen...God is good. It is His goodness that will condemn you, not free you."[282]

"The truth is, you and I have no hope except for grace, for the Bible says, 'All have sinned and have fallen short of God's glory, but the gift of God is eternal life through Christ Jesus our Lord.' What's the difference between Jesus and every other religion? First, He rose from the dead. Second, Christianity is the only religion that offers forgiveness. Grace is being in a closed room with no exit but 100 feet straight up and God lifts you out. Eternal life is not the reward of the righteous, but a gift to the guilty. Let me tell you about God's great gift."

Now we can talk about grace. Now they see they are sinners and lawbreakers, and have no hope but a Savior.

The Doctrine of Grace

As I've discussed thoroughly in this book, the cross is impossible to understand without a revelation of sin. But now that the unbeliever sees his own sin, the speaker can introduce him to the answer.

Here the evangelist should highlight the "God-side" of the gospel, that the Redeemer has paid the ransom in full that man could not pay for himself; that the gospel is not about what man can do for God, but what God has done for man. This is where the gospel becomes good news indeed.

Again, I would choose a verse or a brief passage of Scripture to describe grace. I love using the passage in Luke 4:16-21. Here's another quote from an actual message I preached:

"What we could not do, God did! It was the cross of Jesus Christ that became the instrument of both God's justice and

---

[282] Ray Comfort teaches this idea about God's goodness resulting in justice.

mercy. *Justice was satisfied when Jesus took the punishment for our sins in Himself, and mercy is given to all who would repent of their sins and believe in Christ. Christian thinker and writer R.C. Sproul said, 'The glory of the gospel is this: The one from whom we need to be saved is the one who has saved us.'*[283]

"*When Jesus was on the earth, He stood up one day in the temple, and quoted a passage from the Book of Isaiah which says, 'The Spirit of the Lord is upon me, because he hath anointed me to preach the gospel to the poor; he hath sent me to heal the brokenhearted, to preach deliverance to captives, and recovering of sight to the blind, to set at liberty them that are bruised, to preach the acceptable year of the Lord.'*

"*According to this verse, Jesus came for 'the poor,' 'the brokenhearted,' 'the captives,' 'the blind' and 'the bruised.' Now hear me well—unless you're one of those, I have no message for you tonight, and nor does Jesus Christ. But if you recognize tonight that you are lost, that you are helpless without Christ and in prison to your sins, I have good news. Jesus saves!*"

Remember what John Wesley said? 90% Law and 10% grace? It does not take long for the dying to reach for the cure once they see that they are, in fact, dying.

If I spent hours convincing you that you have all the symptoms of Watt's Syndrome, a deadly new disease that kills in days, how long would it take you to drink the cure if I offered it to you? Probably as long as it took for you to reach out and grab it, right?

At this point, I would immediately use a parable—a story that illustrates a spiritual truth—to illustrate the substitutionary death of Christ. Parables are powerful (if not necessary) tools in gospel preaching. Jesus used them, generations of great preachers have used them, and we do well to imitate their example. Let's take a good look at the use of parables.

---

[283] R.C. Sproul, *Saved From What?* Published by Crossway Books, © 2002.

Parables

Matthew 13:34 tells us that, "All these things spake Jesus in parables unto the multitudes; and without a parable spake he nothing unto them."[284]

The Greek word for parable is *parabole*, which literally means "a placing beside; a comparison." *Smith's Bible Dictionary* says "a parable is therefore literally a placing beside, a comparison, a similitude, an illustration of one subject by another."[285] *Vine's Expository Dictionary of New Testament Words* says, "It is the lesson that is of value; the hearer must catch the analogy if he is to be instructed."[286]

From the dawn of time, storytellers have gained the ear of generation after generation, and have used parables, stories, and allegories to impart truths. In my missionary journeys, I've found that storytellers are highly respected in Islamic societies, and some missionaries in rural areas strive to be known as storytellers in the villages. Likewise, my service in Africa has shown that storytelling is highly effective in preaching. People do not think in concepts. They think in pictures. I'll prove it to you.

The purple cow ate the green cheese on the moon.

Did you see a picture in your mind of the purple cow, or did the above sentence remain plain text in your mind? You saw the purple cow, the green cheese, and the moon, right?

In the same way, we do well when we leave our hearers with pictures and illustrations that will help them remember gospel truths. Besides the fact that it makes the sermon more memorable, it also keeps the message from being boring. Boring preaching may be one of the greatest enemies of evangelism today. I would that more preachers would work harder to serve the church and the lost by teaching and preaching with more parables and stories!

---

[284] NKJV

[285] William Smith, *Smith's Bible Dictionary.* © *1990* Hendrickson Publishers (Rev Sub edition).

[286] W.E. Vine and Merrill F. Unger *Vine's Expository Dictionary of New Testament Words.* © 1999 Thomas Nelson.

One of the things Michael Cavanaugh, known for being one of the best, taught me about preaching is that we need to "make the Word flesh." He is referencing, of course, the verse in John 1:14 that says, "The Word became flesh, and dwelt among us."[287]

Jesus is the Word, but we did not fully understand the ways, the mind, or the heart of God until Jesus became flesh and walked among us. Then we could *see* the Word. Jesus *is* the Word. In the same way, we need to use parables, stories, and illustrations to help our hearers *see* the Word.

The following are some of the proven parables that I've used in gospel preaching.[288] These stories assist in opening people's eyes to saving grace. Please note that I do finish every parable with a Scripture verse to drive the point home and make the parable spiritually applicable.

The Henry Tisdale Story

Again, this is based on a true story that occurred in the early 1900's in the southern United States. There are conflicting reports on what actually happened, and what the name of the man actually was. My version is probably only an embellished version paralleling the actually story, re-fashioned by evangelists over the last century for maximum effect. Regardless, this story has been a powerful tool for me personally.

What I'm about to tell you is based on a true story that happened in the early 1900s in Mississippi.

There was a man named Henry Tisdale that operated a drawbridge over a river. He had the very important job of making sure that the bridge was up when ships were passing through on the river, and the bridge was down when trains crossed over.

He had a son named William, whom we'll call Billy, who always wanted to see what his Daddy did at work, and Henry

---

[287] NASB
[288] These, and other stories like them, can be found in the "Resources" link of www.isaiahsix.com.

Tisdale told his son, "When you turn six-years-old, I'll take you to work with me."

As promised, when Billy Tisdale turned six, Daddy took him to work with him. They climbed the small tower together that overlooked the river, and Henry showed his son the big lever that operated the bridge. "When you push the lever," he told him, "the bridge goes up. When you pull the lever, the bridge goes down."

Little Billy thought his dad was the greatest thing in the world.

Around lunchtime, Henry and Billy went down by the river, and were enjoying a nice time together in the beautiful afternoon sun. That's when Henry heard a terrible sound. It was the sound of a train coming. Problem was, he wasn't expecting a train, and the bridge was up.

Not wanting to panic his son, Henry said, "Billy, stay right here. Daddy will be right back."

Henry Tisdale ran up the hill, got into the tower, and looked out at the train coming over the crest of the hill on the far side. He recognized the train. It was an early passenger train with 400 people on it. If Henry Tisdale did not get the bridge down in time, the train would crash into the river, and these 400 people would lose their lives.

As he normally did, Henry Tisdale looked down at the gears and the place where the bridge would come down to make sure it was clear. Horror of horrors, Henry Tisdale saw that in the excitement of the moment, his son Billy had come running up the hill, wanting to see his father in action, and little Billy slipped and fell into the gears! If Henry Tisdale pushed the lever, his son Billy would be killed, crushed in the powerful gears.

I know what you're thinking: Go down and save your son, Henry! Well, Henry Tisdale didn't have the time to run down the hill, save his son, run back up to the tower, throw the lever, and get the bridge down in time to save those 400 people. He had an awful, dreadful, terrible decision to make: Save Billy, or the 400 people in the train?

Now maybe you're asking yourself, "What would I have done?" Henry Tisdale didn't have as much time as you just had to think about it.

I don't know anything else about Henry Tisdale except what happened next. Henry Tisdale began to weep and he pulled the lever. Henry chose to save those 400 people over his own son. He heard Billy cry out his name for the last time, and then Billy died.

The bridge came down just in time for the train to cross over, and soon it passed right in front of Henry Tisdale, where he could see inside. You know what he saw? He saw people laughing, talking, drinking tea, reading the newspaper—they had no idea how close they were to losing their lives only moments before! And even though they couldn't hear him, he screamed at the people on the train, pointing at the blood of his son, "Look at what I've done for you! Look at what I've done for you!"

But no one noticed him.

Tonight, God sits in His heavenly tower, looking down at this world—looking at you—pointing at the blood of His Son, and saying through me, "Look at what I've done for you."

Will we notice His sacrifice? Or be like the people on that train, going on with life, never considering what He's done for us?

"For God so loved the world that He gave His only begotten Son, that whosoever believes in Him would not perish, but have everlasting life."

The Loliondo Lion

This is a true story that I heard while I was in Tanzania serving as a missionary in 1989-1990. I went to Loliondo in the middle of the Serengeti Plains, and while there, heard the story and met the woman this happened to. She was actually the wife of the pastor of a small church we worked with while in the village. So Americans wouldn't be tripped up by the lesser-known species of animals originally featured in the story, I changed the characters to a lion and a lamb instead of a leopard and an impala.

What you're about to hear is a true story.

Once, in a small African village, there was a woman cooking outside of her mud hut when suddenly she was startled by a noise in the bushes beyond her grill.

Slowly, carefully, sinisterly, like a cat trying to sneak up on a mouse, a wild lion appeared, crawling in a crouched position from underneath the thicket. The thing was hungry, and its cold-blooded eyes were locked on the helpless woman.

Not wanting to frighten the lion into a premature attack, the woman backed up slowly and carefully toward her home. But the more she looked into the lion's wild eyes, the more her heart raced, and the more the adrenaline rushed through her veins.

Her instincts took over. She turned and ran toward the house, screaming for help. When she reached the door, she began pulling on the handle. Her husband, who had heard the commotion, was pulling the handle from the other side. The panicked woman forgot that the door pushed—not pulled—open. And unfortunately, she was winning the tug-of-war.

The lion would pounce any moment, and she braced for the worst pain of her life. Turning around to venture one last glance at the predator, she cried out, "Jesus, save me!"

In that very moment, a lamb ran around the corner of the mud hut, and ran between the woman and the lion. And the lion saw the Lamb. The lion immediately chased the lamb and made its meal of the poor animal instead of the woman. The lamb saved her.

2000 years ago, a man named John the Baptist stood in the Jordan River, and pointed at a man named Jesus, saying, "Behold, the Lamb of God, who takes away the sin of the world."

Jesus is that Lamb that saved you! When death was so near, Jesus took your sins upon Himself so you might live.

Romans 10:13 says, "Whoever calls on the name of the Lord shall be saved." And you're a "whosoever," aren't you? Just like that woman in Africa, you can call on the Lord Jesus tonight, and the lion will see the Lamb. And you will be saved.

The Bee Sting

I can't remember where I heard this story, and can't attest to whether or not it's true. What I like about this story is its brevity, and I've used it in many situations when I'm trying to keep my message shorter.

Once there was a father who picked up his little daughter from elementary school, and on the way home, a bee began buzzing around the car. The little girl was hysterical because she was deathly allergic to bee stings. "Daddy," she shrieked, "there's a bee in the car!"

While driving, the father reached back and grabbed the bee, holding it in his hand. The girl calmed down until a moment later when the father let go of the bee, letting it loose in the car again.

"Daddy!" the little girl screamed. "Why'd you let go of the bee? I'm going to die!"

"No you're not, sweetheart," insisted the father, and he reached back and opened his hand so the little girl could see it. "What do you see?" he asked.

The little girl looked at her father's hand.

"A bee sting?" she asked.

"Yes, sweetheart," he said. "And how many stings do bees have?"

"One," she answered.

"That's right," said the father. "This bee can't hurt you anymore because I've taken the sting for you."

And your sins can't hurt you anymore if you believe in Jesus. The Bible says, "Oh death, where is your victory? Oh death, where is your sting? Thanks be to God, who gives us the victory through our Lord Jesus Christ."

It's stories like these that God uses to remove the blinders from an unbeliever's mind, opening his eyes to the truth of the gospel.

Discipleship by Grace

CHAPTER 23
Satisfied Customers

*"Blessed are those who hunger and thirst for righteousness,
for they shall be satisfied."* —Jesus (Matthew 5:6, NASB)

Did you know that God *wants* to satisfy you? It is His great desire to satisfy you. Now why would God want to do that? I already mentioned that everything in our lives is about His glory. If that's true, then satisfying our hearts with Himself must glorify Him the most!

John Piper, in his book *Let the Nations Be Glad,* teaches that God's chief aim in our lives is to glorify Himself. He adds, "God is most glorified in us when we are most satisfied in Him...Therefore, God's pursuit of His own glory is not at odds with my joy, and that means it is not unkind or unmerciful or unloving of Him to seek His own glory."[289]

To the thirsty soul, His grace is enough. Grace satisfies because it ushers us into intimacy and peace with God the Father.

It was enough for David when He said, "Because Your lovingkindness is better than life, my lips will praise You" (Psalm 63:3, NASB).

It was enough for Paul when he said, "More than that, I count all things to be loss in view of the surpassing value of knowing Christ Jesus my Lord, for whom I have suffered the loss of all things, and count them but rubbish so that I may gain Christ" (Philippians 3:8, NASB).

It was enough for St. Augustine of Hippo when he said, "O God, Thou hast made us for Thyself, and our hearts are restless until they find their rest in Thee."[290]

May it be enough for us. As we grow in discipleship by grace, indeed it will be.

---

[289] John Piper, *Let the Nations Be Glad* (Grand Rapids, MI: Baker Academic). © 1993, 2003 by Desiring God Foundation, p. 31
[290] St. Augustine of Hippo, *Confessions, Book 1.*

THE GREATEST ADVERTISEMENT GOD HAS

What is the greatest advertisement any business has? *Satisfied customers.* Why is God so interested in satisfying us? *It's the greatest advertisement He has to show the world that He is good.*

Would you be interested in coming to a restaurant if I told you, "The food was terrible, the people mean, the chairs uncomfortable, and the music too loud. That said, it's my duty to attend this restaurant every week. You wanna come?"

I'll pass, thanks.

Then why do we expect people to be interested in Christianity if we ourselves are not happy with our faith?

In the book *The Christian's Secret of a Happy Life,* author Hannah Whitall Smith tells the story of how she was witnessing to a friend of hers, and he said, "Why should I be interested in your religion? It seems to me that Christians are the most miserable people that I know!"

This conversation provoked her as she realized that he was right, and that there was something terribly wrong with so many Christians' experience. She ended up writing the now famous book that has blessed so many.[291]

Let me ask you a simple question. *Are you enjoying your relationship with Jesus?*

When you see the love of God and it transforms you, true joy and contentment fill your heart and your life begins to evangelize accidentally. Fruit is excess life, and when the life of God is inside of you, you will bear fruit.

Grace transforms. Legalism sucks out all spiritual life until you are dead and useless to God and the world. It's a double loss. You cannot enjoy God, nor can you enjoy the pleasures of sin. You lose twice. You have neither authentic joy nor synthetic joy!

An encouraged church is an evangelistic church. Churches that hammer Law and obedience wear people down until their joy is drained out due to spiritual exhaustion, but when you find a church that edifies and builds up and encourages believers in

---

[291] *The Christian's Secret of a Happy Life* was first published in 1875 by Fleming H. Revell Company and republished by Spire Books in 1974.

grace, you find a church full of vigor and life and reaching people everywhere.

I was at a large missions conference in Phoenix, Arizona, a few years ago, listening to some of the top missions speakers in the United States. One of them stood up and said, "I want to tell you what the greatest need is today in world evangelism. I know what you *think* I'm going to say—maybe intercession or more workers, but this is not the greatest need. The greatest need in world evangelism today is *inwardly transformed people.*"[292]

God needs people who will advertise His goodness, power, and love through the lives they live, and the joy that fills their hearts.

JUNK FOOD

All this begs the question: If God is so interested in satisfying His children, then why are so many Christians so miserable?

I guess the best way to answer that question is to look at the whole verse again. *Blessed are those who hunger and thirst for righteousness, for they shall be satisfied.*

If we will be satisfied, we must do our part and that is to "hunger and thirst." Perhaps so many Christians are not satisfied because we are not hungering and thirsting! We've sought to satisfy ourselves with things that don't satisfy. *We are eating junk food.*

> *"Woe to you who are well-fed now, for you shall be hungry."*
> *(Luke 6:25a, NASB)*

As I've mentioned, America is an addicted society, constantly tempting us to eat the apple—to satisfy ourselves outside of God. As long as we are gorging ourselves at another table, we will never be satisfied at the Lord's table.

Stop eating junk food. Stop seeking to satisfy the needs of your heart with the things of this world. Not to say that we can't enjoy the things God may have blessed us with, or be entertained by

---

[292] Spoken in a sermon by George Miley in an Antioch Churches and Ministries missions conference in Phoenix, Arizona in June of 2003.

something we like, but there is a difference between enjoying these things and allowing them to replace God in our lives.

When God stands at the door to bring peace, we numb ourselves with television or video games instead of finding life in His Word.

When God stands at the door to bring provision and deliver us, we deliver ourselves by laying down the plastic or borrowing from the bank.

When God stands at the door to satisfy us, we seek for satisfaction in another person or thing.

Stop eating junk food.

Let God satisfy us, and then we will shine like a city on a hill to our world.

THEY HAD BEEN WITH JESUS

Acts 4:13 says, "When they saw the courage of Peter and John and realized that they were unschooled, ordinary men, they were astonished and they took note that these men had been with Jesus."[293]

When we are satisfied with Christ and transformed by the gospel, the world will see that we are His. The term Christian actually means "little Christs." It is actually a man-made term that was first used in Antioch by unbelievers to identify those who followed Christ.[294] As we walk in grace, we will be true Christians; true *little Christs;* true representations of Him on the earth to a lost world.

Richard Wurmbrand was a Romanian pastor who suffered in a communist prison, separated from his family, for fourteen years. Eventually, he was ransomed out, after which he wrote the book *Tortured For Christ* and founded the ministry *The Voice of the Martyrs.* Wurmbrand once recalled an encounter he witnessed between two men in prison:[295]

---

[293] NIV
[294] Acts 11:26
[295] "Learn to Smile Like Jesus" by Richard Wurmbrand

There was among us a Jewish believer. His name was Milan Haimovitch. This man had been so beaten. He was often beaten for his own crimes but frequently, just as another prisoner was to be beaten, he would step forward and say, "I will take his place." He was a model of Christ.

Once there was a discussion between him and a great scientist who was also in jail with us. He was a member of the Academy of Science and a godless man. Milan Haimovitch was not of the same intellectual and cultural level as this professor. He had not read so many thousands of books as this professor, but he tried to tell the professor about the Messiah, about Jesus.

The professor laughed and scorned him and said, "Why do you come with such stupidities. Why do you believe in Jesus? How do you know He exists?"

Milan replied, "Well, I know by the fact that I walk with Him and talk with Him."

The professor said, "You are such a liar. How can you walk with Jesus? Jesus lived 2000 years ago, somewhere in Israel, then He died. How can you walk and talk with Him?"

Milan replied, "Yes, sir, it is true that He died 2000 years ago, but He also resurrected and is living even now."

The scientist continued: "Where is He now? In heaven? Where is heaven? Thousands of miles away beyond the sun, the moon, beyond all the stars? In another world? Can he walk and talk with you? Don't you see that you speak stupid things?"

Milan replied, "I myself have no explanation. I wonder myself, too, but the fact is that He walks and talks with me."

The professor was indignant and said, "Well, I will ask you one more question. You say that He talks with you. How does He talk with you? What is the expression of His face? Does He look angry? Wrathful? Does He look interested or disinterested? Does He look lovingly at you? Does He perhaps smile at you?" He was mocking with these questions.

Milan answered, "Sir, you have guessed. Sometimes He smiles at me."

The scientist interrupted and said, "Ha, ha, ha, such a lie, such a lie. I never met such a liar. Jesus smiles at you. When you say Jesus smiles at you, show me how He smiles."

Milan said, "I will show how Jesus smiles."

Now, you must realize how Milan looked. Like all of us, he was shorn. He was only skin and bones with dark circles around his eyes. He was without teeth. He was in the uniform of a prisoner. He looked like a scarecrow. We were all very ugly.

Yet such a beautiful smile appeared on his lips. His dirty face shone. The glory of God can shine from behind a thick crust of dirt. There was so much peace, so much contentment and so much joy on his face, in a smile that was not from this earth. This atheist, godless professor bowed his head and said, "Sir, I have seen Jesus."

I have been witness of such a thing. My aim in life has been also to bring to a world, in which there is so much suffering and so much darkness, the smile of Jesus.

Milan had been with Jesus. Even in a prison, where he was tortured, Milan was a satisfied customer.

"No man has seen God at any time. If we love one another, God dwells in us, and his love is perfected in us." (1 John 4:12, NKJV)

No man has seen God. But if we are satisfied with Christ, they will see God in us.

CHAPTER 24
Pastoring Lost Sheep

"Have you no wish for others to be saved? Then you are not saved yourself, be sure of that." — Charles Spurgeon

Since grace gives us full and confident access to the Spirit of God, evangelism ceases to be a Friday night outreach, and becomes an exhilarating lifestyle where we can *walk in the Spirit* and allow God to use us to change our world. Therefore, the equipping ministry of the evangelist is not only to equip in methods and scripts, but to alter the heart, and change the entire culture of one's life from the self-indulgent life of comfort to the selfless life of service.

In Luke 15, the Pharisees and the teachers of the Law are indignant that Jesus eats with tax collectors and sinners. So Jesus tells this story:

> *"What man among you, if he has a hundred sheep and has lost one of them, does not leave the ninety-nine in the open pasture and go after the one which is lost until he finds it? When he has found it, he lays it on his shoulders, rejoicing. And when he comes home, he calls together his friends and his neighbors, saying to them, 'Rejoice with me, for I have found my sheep which was lost!' I tell you that in the same way, there will be more joy in heaven over one sinner who repents than over ninety-nine righteous persons who need no repentance."* (Luke 15:8:4-8, NASB)

I wonder how many who read this book would be excited if 99% of their city got saved? Certainly most would! However, even if 99% of the city got saved, God's heart would still not be satisfied. God would still be thinking about the one that is lost!

Allow me to use an illustration that may make more sense of it.

Let's say you are the parent of five children and they all get lost in a storm. How many is *enough* for you to get back? *Three?* Maybe *four?* That would be 80%! Of course, until all five came home, there would be weeping in your house. God is a Father, and His human heart yearns for His children to come home just like yours would.

How will God bring them home?

In this passage in Luke, there are two kinds of sheep: lost sheep and found sheep. There are also two functions of a shepherd: to oversee the ninety-nine, and to go and search for the lost ones.

"Found sheep" are obviously God's people. Who are the *shepherds* of the "found sheep"? Those, of course, are pastors and elders who oversee the flocks of local churches. Biblically, the term "shepherd" is synonymous with the term "pastor." Who, then, are the shepherds of "lost sheep"? *Every believer in Jesus Christ!*

Let me take a moment and define the term "pastor." A pastor is someone who takes concern and responsibility for the soul of someone else. By that definition, I want to encourage you, dear reader, that you are called to be a *pastor of lost sheep!*

Every shepherd knows his sheep and every pastor knows his people. As a pastor of lost sheep, do you know who your people are? I believe that God has strategically placed lost sheep in the lives of every believer. We simply need to identify them and begin to reach out to them intentionally. I encourage you to identify your flock. Usually, I've found that every believer has between three and five people that God has placed under their spiritual care.

I'm challenging you to answer the call and say, "Here am I. Send me!"[296] God doesn't have an ace up His sleeve to reach the harvest. He needs His people to go. *I'm challenging you to begin to pastor lost sheep!*

How exactly do we do that? Let's look at how Jesus taught us to do it.

---

[296] Isaiah 6:8

AS JESUS TAUGHT IT

In Luke 10, Jesus teaches His disciples how to pastor lost sheep. I want to acknowledge Ed Silvoso here, who impacted our ministry and my thinking early on in this area.[297]

> *"After this the Lord appointed seventy-two others and sent them two by two ahead of him to every town and place where he was about to go. He told them, "The harvest is plentiful, but the workers are few. Ask the Lord of the harvest, therefore, to send out workers into his harvest field. Go! I am sending you out like lambs among wolves. Do not take a purse or bag or sandals; and do not greet anyone on the road.*
>
> *"When you enter a house, first say, 'Peace to this house.' If a man of peace is there, your peace will rest on him; if not, it will return to you. Stay in that house, eating and drinking whatever they give you, for the worker deserves his wages. Do not move around from house to house.*
>
> *"When you enter a town and are welcomed, eat what is set before you. Heal the sick who are there and tell them, 'The kingdom of God is near you.'" (Luke 10:1-9, NIV)*

Here, Jesus teaches us the components of evangelism:[298]

1) Pray (Luke 10:2)
2) Bless (Luke 10:5)
3) Fellowship (Luke 10:7-8)
4) Meet felt needs (Luke 10:9a)
5) Preach (Luke 10:9b)

This is Christ's own teaching on how to impact people. It's not a program, but a lifestyle of pastoring lost sheep and reaching

---

[297] Ed has written several books that have impacted me, including *That None Should Perish* (Gospel Light Publications, © February 1997) and *Prayer Evangelism* (Regal Books, © September 2000).

[298] Ed Silvoso taught principles 2-5 from Luke 10:1-9 at the 1998 *Antioch Churches & Ministries Men in Ministry Conference*, Orlando, Florida..

people. If we don't understand Jesus' teaching, and walk in the Spirit, evangelism becomes nothing more than, "I gotta get this message off my chest because I feel guilty!"

Historically, I think that people have associated evangelism solely with point #5—preaching. Therefore, scores of believer have dismissed or disqualified themselves from ever being used of God due to fear or a sense of inadequacy. C. Peter Wagner has found that only 10% of all Christians feel that they have the gift of evangelism.[299] That means that the church is only giving a tithe to the work of the harvest, but when we begin to understand the other components of evangelism, we begin to see that God has a place for everyone. We must remember that though preaching is the finish line, Jesus taught us many things about how to win our world. But the things He teaches must be planted deep in your heart—to love, to have compassion, to bless, to show mercy, to serve. These all spring from nothing less than a dear relationship with Christ Himself.

The order in which the components that Jesus taught appear is not essential. Sometimes they happen simultaneously, and other times they go in reverse order. What's important is the components themselves. Yes, we are called to preach, but we would be foolish to leave out the other four things Jesus taught us to do in pastoring lost sheep.

Pray: "Beseech the Lord of the Harvest" (Luke 10:2).

Honestly, I don't understand exactly how it works. Why pray if God is in control of all things? I definitely believe in election and the sovereignty of God, but simultaneously believe that our obedience to the Great Commission is part of God's predestining work.

If Jesus said to "beseech the Lord of the harvest to send out laborers into His harvest," then the laborers must have something to do with bringing it in! I don't care what you believe about Calvinism or Armenianism, or if you even have a clue what those

---

[299] C. Peter Wagner, *Your Church Can Grow* (Ventura: Regal Books, 1976) p. 39.

terms mean, God's people have a significant role in God's plan to bring people to Christ.

Prayer is the starting point.

What do these three Scriptures have in common?

> *Then he said to me, "This is the word of the LORD to Zerubbabel saying, 'Not by might nor by power, but by My Spirit,' says the LORD of hosts." (Zechariah 4:6, NASB)*

> *"No one can come to Me unless the Father who sent Me draws him; and I will raise him up on the last day." (John 6:44, NASB)*

> *"I am the vine, you are the branches; he who abides in Me and I in him, he bears much fruit, for apart from Me you can do nothing." (John 15:5, NASB)*

They all remind us to depend completely upon the Lord, and not in ourselves.

As I mentioned in the chapter "Cross-Centered Living," prayer is the first and simplest act of dependence. Why? Because the minute we pray is the minute we are admitting that we can't do it ourselves, that we need help. Jesus builds into evangelism the absolute dependency upon the Father by calling us to pray.

George Mueller, the great man of England who built orphanages in the mid to late 1800s, was a great man of prayer. Though he was responsible for 10,024 orphans during his lifetime, he asked no man for anything, but depended completely upon God to meet his needs. Describing his own remarkable life, he once said, "I was never called to build orphanages. I was called to show the world that God is worthy to be trusted, and I felt that starting orphanages was the best way to do that."

There's a story told of George Mueller choosing to pray for five of his friends. The first four received Christ over a number of years, but the fifth man was stubborn. After years had gone by, someone asked Mueller, finding out that he was still praying for the stubborn man. "Do you still believe that this man will come to Christ?"

Mueller answered, "How can he *not* come to Christ? I'm praying for him!" Such was the quality of Mueller's faith.

Many years after Mueller began to pray for the stubborn man, Mueller died, but there, by old George Mueller's grave, that fifth man knelt down and said, "I want to know the God of George Mueller!"

Bless: "First say, 'Peace to this house'" (Luke 10:5).

This has to do with our attitude toward the lost. It's about having compassion and kindness and not a holier-than-thou attitude. Somehow, prostitutes and homosexuals knew they could come to Jesus, and that He would accept them, though He didn't approve of their sin.

In Luke Chapter 7, Simon the Pharisee invites Jesus over to his house for a meal, and right in the middle of the meal, a "sinful woman" comes in and begins to weep at Jesus' feet and to wipe her tears from His feet with her hair. That's where we see the true spirit of Simon.

> *When the Pharisee who had invited him saw this, he said to himself, "If this man were a prophet, he would know who is touching him and what kind of woman she is — that she is a sinner."*
>
> *Jesus answered him, "Simon, I have something to tell you."*
>
> *"Tell me, teacher," he said.*
>
> *"Two men owed money to a certain moneylender. One owed him five hundred denarii, and the other fifty. Neither of them had the money to pay him back, so he canceled the debts of both. Now which of them will love him more?"*
>
> *Simon replied, "I suppose the one who had the bigger debt canceled."*
>
> *"You have judged correctly," Jesus said.*
>
> *Then he turned toward the woman and said to Simon, "Do you see this woman? I came into your house. You did not give me any water for my feet, but she wet my feet with her tears and*

wiped them with her hair. You did not give me a kiss, but this woman, from the time I entered, has not stopped kissing my feet. You did not put oil on my head, but she has poured perfume on my feet. Therefore, I tell you, her many sins have been forgiven — for she loved much. But he who has been forgiven little loves little." (Luke 7:39-47, NIV)

On first glance, it may appear that Jesus is unfairly giving the sinful woman more ability to love God than He'd given Simon. More sin forgiven equals more love, right? But this is not the ultimate message of this conversation. The ultimate message is that He's trying to get self-righteous Simon to see that *he's just like this woman without grace.* He's just as far away from God, but Simon doesn't realize it. He thinks he's graduated to some elite level of humanity that gives him the right to look down his nose at other people. In reality, the poor blind man is just as far away as this prostitute was — he just didn't know it.

Understanding grace saves us from being holier-than-thou. We realize that evangelism is just one beggar telling another beggar where to find bread.

We must be like Jesus was toward the lost, and not like Simon. We must look at them with compassion and mercy and not judgment. We must speak and pray blessings on them.

No one wants to be around someone who doesn't have an attitude of blessing. My wife and I often wonder why we are more drawn to cursing sinners than pious Pharisees? *Because those who are honest are closer to the kingdom than lying Pharisees.*

The bottom line is, do you want to be the farmer or the policeman? It's awfully hard to feel at ease around a policeman. Instead, God wants us to be the farmers, sowing the seeds of kindness, grace, and truth.

Fellowship: "Stay in that house, eating and drinking whatever they give you" (Luke 10:7).

As we have an accepting and peaceful attitude of blessing toward the lost, we'll be welcomed into their lives, and they into ours. This is how we become, like Jesus, "the friend of sinners"

(Matthew 11:19). Our lives are now a permanent outreach. Here a heart and lifestyle of hospitality are born as our very lives must be open to the unbeliever if we are truly friends.

As we have an attitude of blessing, people will want to be around us. They will want to be our friends. We'll get to *fellowship with them*. And as you have lunch with your unbelieving friend, don't feel like, between bites of the hot dog, that you've got to cram The Four Spiritual Laws down his throat. *Walk in the Spirit!* Download wisdom from the Lord.

In some ways, most believers have to escape the entrapments of the Christian culture. You know what I mean: We go to church on Sunday, go to a Christian restaurant with our Christian friends, listen to Christian radio, watch Christian TV and get our Christian news, go to Christian bingo nights, Christian schools and Christian jobs!

Is this our Lord's intention?

None of these things are bad in themselves, but is living in a Christian bubble the will of God for our lives? I don't think so.

> "*Let your light shine before men in such a way that they may see your good works, and glorify your Father who is in heaven.*" (Matthew 5:16, NASB)

God wants His people to be shining light! The only way this is possible is to be *among men*. We cannot hide or live in a Christian subculture and have no interaction with the real world! We must *be missionaries reaching out of the Christian culture into the real world* if we are to pastor lost sheep.

Meet Felt Needs: "Heal the sick who are there" (Luke 10:9a).

As you are now involved in the lives of unbelievers, you can be God's representative to them. Again this is where prayer and evangelism are married. God wants you to trust Him to use the crisis moments in the lives of unbelievers as opportunities for Him to glorify Christ through answered prayers.

People don't know that their greatest need is salvation, so God will often advertise Himself through the kind deeds of His people, or His supernatural acts. Consider the conversation Jesus had with Philip:

> *Jesus answered, "I am the way and the truth and the life. No one comes to the Father except through me. If you really knew me, you would know my Father as well. From now on, you do know him and have seen him."*
>
> *Philip said, "Lord, show us the Father and that will be enough for us."*
>
> *Jesus answered: "Don't you know me, Philip, even after I have been among you such a long time? Anyone who has seen me has seen the Father. How can you say, 'Show us the Father'? Don't you believe that I am in the Father, and that the Father is in me? The words I say to you are not just my own. Rather, it is the Father, living in me, who is doing his work. Believe me when I say that I am in the Father and the Father is in me; or at least believe on the evidence of the miracles themselves. I tell you the truth, anyone who has faith in me will do what I have been doing. He will do even greater things than these, because I am going to the Father. And I will do whatever you ask in my name, so that the Son may bring glory to the Father. You may ask me for anything in my name, and I will do it.* (John 14:6-13, NIV)

After Jesus explained to Philip that He is "the way, the truth, and the life," Philip requested to see the Father. In other words, Philip wanted to see God without going *through* Jesus.[300] Isn't that an accurate depiction of our world today? What was Jesus' reply? *At least believe on the miracles themselves.* In other words, "Philip, if you don't believe my words, believe my works."

Can we say that to the people in our world? Have we demonstrated God's love and power to them?

---

[300] Again, I heard this passage explained in a sermon by Ed Silvoso in a series titled "Prayer Evangelism."

At the end of the passage, Jesus made this outrageous offer: *And I will do whatever you ask in My name, so that the Son may bring glory to the Father.*

What a promise! God wants to advertise Himself in Christ Jesus by doing miracles when we pray for unbelievers!

Whoa.

Here it is right here: God wants us to see the crisis moments in the lives of the unbelievers we are "pastoring" as opportunities to advertise Jesus to them when we pray. I've seen this happen many times in my life as I've shared with others.

I was in Turkey on tour with my band Isaiah Six, and we were using our concerts as a platform to share Christ with Muslims. At a concert in the capital city of Ankara, in spite of police harassment, the concert went on. As I normally did, I let those in attendance know that the band would be available to pray with them afterward if there were any needs they'd like to lift up. At the end of the event, a Muslim woman came up and presented her sick daughter to me. She had a disease and was desperate for a miracle. So I prayed, and left the results with God.

After I returned home to the United States, I was contacted by our host in Turkey who told me that this little girl received a miracle the night I prayed for her. So profound was the impact on her mother, that she received Christ. Then her husband followed her into the kingdom.

I went back to Turkey two years later, and we did another concert in the city of Ankara. Right before the concert, the local pastor pulled me aside and pointed out into the crowd, where a whole row was filled with people young and old. "You see those people?" the pastor asked me.

"Yes," I answered.

"Those are all people in the same family and extended family that came to Christ because of that little girl's miracle."

And I will do whatever you ask in My name, so that the Son may bring glory to the Father.

On another occasion, I stopped in a local gas station run by the Miller family, a family that our church had been reaching out to. When I walked in to pay for my gas, Mrs. Miller was at the cash register with one hand in the air, swollen up like a water balloon. "Mrs. Miller," I asked, "are you okay?"

"I was stung by a bee," she told me, and I could tell she was afraid, "the swelling is moving down my arm, and I'm afraid it's going to hit my heart!"

"Don't be afraid," I said, "I know a doctor."

"Nearby?" she asked.

"*Very* close," I said.

"Who?"

"He's the greatest physician that's ever lived," I explained.

She smiled briefly and said knowingly, "Oh, *that* doctor!"

"Can I pray for you?" I asked.

"Please."

I don't even remember what I prayed. Nothing seemed to happen right away, and I paid for my gas and went on my way.

Two or three days later, I returned to the gas station. When I walked in and Mrs. Miller saw me, she beamed with an enormous smile. "How are you today, Mrs. Miller?" I asked.

"Better now!" she exclaimed, grinning at me.

"What happened?"

"I can't believe it!" she explained. "Within minutes after you left the other day, I was completely healed! I mean, God *really* healed me!"

"That's great, Mrs. Miller!"

Then Mrs. Miller stared grinning at me for another moment before she said, "You're gonna make a believer out of me!"

A miracle settled the issue. The Father had glorified Himself in the Son. She wasn't giving thanks to Buddha or contemplating Islam—she was turning her gaze to Jesus!

Such is the fruit when we are willing to pray for the felt needs of lost people.

I believe that God wants you to be known, among your unsaved friends, as, "That guy who prays for people." Or, "That woman who prays for people." Most unsaved people I know do not resist prayer in a moment of crisis, but are thankful when someone is willing to pray for them. How much more will they be thankful if God chooses to grant what you're asking for? The Father will be glorified in the Son right before their eyes!

Preach: "The kingdom of God has come near to you" (Luke 10:9b).

The finish line of evangelism is to "preach" the gospel. What Jesus taught is not a way to escape the discomfort of preaching, it's a way to prepare people to hear the truth. *No one will be in heaven that has not heard or believed the gospel.* But "How then will they call on Him in whom they have not believed? How will they believe in Him whom they have not heard? And how will they hear without a preacher?" (Romans 10:14, NASB).

As we walk in the Spirit, God will give us wisdom as to when and how to share the gospel with our friends and family. It happens very organically as we pray, bless, fellowship and meet felt needs.

I have a growing concern that too few Christians know how to even share the gospel. Most have not thought it through clearly enough to articulate it. This doesn't mean that you have to be a Bible school student. It just means that you need to be adequately trained to "always be prepared to give an answer to everyone who asks you to give the reason for the hope that you have" (1 Peter 3:15, NIV). I would encourage every believer to *become an expert in sharing the gospel.* If it is indeed the most important and powerful message in the universe, we would do well to sharpen our swords and know how to share it! There are many resources available (including this book) to train us in how to share the gospel. One of the best ways, however, remains to be outreach ministry. To borrow a baseball analogy, we need "at-bats." Nothing trains us better for future at-bats than present ones. If you have no outreach ministry available, grab another brother or sister, and you're ready to go!

HEIDI JO GOES TO THE BAR

Let me share a testimony about my wife, Heidi Jo. She learned and applied these outreach principles in the late 1990's right around the time we moved back to northern New York. We moved into a small house in a little town on the St. Lawrence

River called Waddington. Immediately, Heidi began to pray for our neighbors. Relationships began to develop, and soon our home was shining light into the community.

We moved a few times, and ended up buying a house a little outside of the Waddington village limits in 2003. Heidi was in the middle of raising our three young girls; and being solely consumed with the demands of family life, had lost a little momentum in her community outreach. That's when she prayed a bold prayer. "Lord, she said, "You know how much I love raising my children, but when it comes to evangelism, I'm bored. Would you open a door and use me?"

Shortly after, Heidi came to me with an idea. "Honey," she said, "I heard there's a competition in a local bar in Waddington called 'North Country Idol.' A lot of the people I've been praying for will be there, and I'd like to join the competition so I can have an opportunity to get to know more people. What do you think?"

When I saw her faith, I could not get in the way, and encouraged her to follow her heart. Odd as it was for me, while on the road ministering, I'd get calls from her at 1:00am while she was in the local bar performing. It was clear God was giving her favor. When the 10-week competition was over, Heidi made the finals. I watched her on the final night along with some Christian friends, my mother and father-in-law, and half the town in a packed bar. Her new found fans cheered her like she was a rock star and she won their hearts, placing second. (She was the best singer, but not the best hip-shaker which was okay with me.)

Suddenly, everyone knew Heidi as "the singer." Those who might fear her as the religious one were disarmed by her willingness to enter their world, and share her gift with them. In some ways, she was somewhat of a local celebrity.

We asked the Lord how we might make the most of this favor she had, and decided to make an evangelistic album, which we called *The Way Home*.[301] Many of the songs were written with certain people of the town in mind, almost as if we were writing

---

[301] Heidi Jo's albums are available at www.amanirecords.com.

293

the songs to them or from their perspective. Here's an example of the lyrics from one of the songs, titled "Who You Are":

How can I believe in a God that I can't see or hear?
Don't think I can, but why am I here praying once again?
And I don't understand just how to take Your hand
But lead me in Your way everlasting

I don't know who You are
I don't know where You are
But there's a hunger in my heart to know You
So lead me where You are
Show me who You are
Help these eyes to see
And I follow You

You – are You a stranger?
When You feel like my Father
You – oh, You are calling me
And I can't stay away from You[302]

After the album was released, we gave away dozens to people in the town, and then the miracles began. Within three days, a couple that we'd been reaching out to received Christ because of Heidi's album. Then a newspaper article. Then a call from a secular radio station that wanted Heidi on the air during morning rush hour. Then the concerts began, where we reversed roles, and I was her "background singer." She'd sing and testify of Christ and I would share the gospel. In the end, hundreds heard the gospel, and several dozen came to a saving knowledge of Christ! Before we left northern NY in 2005, it all culminated with a final concert attended by many unbelievers that we'd been praying for and reaching out to. God raised Heidi up as a light in northern New York.

---

[302] words and music by Derek Joseph and Heidi Jo Levendusky, © 2004 Prophet Hall Music

If you'll walk in the Spirit and apply what Christ taught us about lifestyle evangelism, He'll use you too. The plain fact is, God has always been in the business of taking ordinary people, and using them to do extraordinary things. Why not you and me? Why not now?

Discipleship by Grace

CHAPTER 25
Relevant Evangelism

"Christianity still has the most relevant message in the world because our message is love." — Anonymous

For a few years, a guy named Joe Courtney worked with our ministry. Joe was a talented guitarist and songwriter, and a good friend. When I met him, he was just coming out of a dark season of his life, where he'd known the sting of legalism, and he'd grown to detest man-made religion.

While he lived with my wife and me in Rochester, New York, he used to go downtown to weekly meetings formed by fans of *Relevant Magazine*. He'd always come back with interesting topics for conversation, as he wrestled through the desire to reach people by using culture, the frustration with the organized church, and the negative spirit he'd often find among the participants in the group. Several times, he said to me, "Sometimes I get so frustrated with the group because I feel like they're just using the idea of being relevant to rebel against the Church."

One day, he came upstairs in my house, journal in hand, and said, "I've got it! I think I know what bothers me about the whole concept of 'relevance.'" He read me some of his journal entry, and then summarized by saying, "So many people think that relevance is what kind of clothes you wear, what kind of music you listen to, or what kind of hairstyle you have, but now I see that what's truly relevant is *love*. You can have the dress, the lingo, and the act down, but without love, you are irrelevant with or without culture. Love is the most relevant thing in the world!"

It was a breakthrough word for Joe as the Holy Spirit guided him into grace. I believe it's a breakthrough word for all of us.

Love is the most relevant thing in the world.

BECOME LIKE THEM OR BECOME THEM?
Since grace brings us into liberty from living under law, I've seen some use grace as a license to make some unwise choices.

Culture isn't evil, but there is evil in culture, and there is danger in excess. How do we stay relevant *and holy*? I've found that when it comes to the areas of conscience, the answer usually lies not in abstinence or indulgence, but in *moderation*. Moderation allows you to enjoy permissible parts of culture without being mastered by addictive behavior. Moderation also gives you the opportunity to become streetwise and understand the times. Those who give into an excessive or obsessive indulgence of culture are in danger of being mastered by the spirit of the age.

We had a young man intern with us a few years ago who cited the verse "become all things to all men" as the motive for all his choices. He was obsessed with secular music, with fashion, and pop culture. Before I passed quick judgment and confronted him, I waited to see what the fruit of it was in his life. I wanted to see what else was in his heart. I never heard him talk about Jesus. He was consumed with temporary things, speaking constantly with others about his favorite shows, movies, and music, but never about Christ or the Word.

Soon, an addiction to pornography was exposed in his life, and I sat down with him and told him, "You know, I'm aware that the Bible teaches us to become all things to all men, but there is a difference between becoming *like* them and *becoming* them. After looking at the fruit of your life, I don't see any difference between you, and those you say you're trying to reach."

Not long after this, he left the ministry, and eventually the church. Last I heard, he was still addicted to porn and had added a drug habit to his resume.

Paul encourages us to be relevant for the sake of the gospel.

"For though I am free from all men, I have made myself a slave to all, so that I may win more. To the Jews I became as a Jew, so that I might win Jews; to those who are under the Law, as under the Law though not being myself under the Law, so that I might win those who are under the Law; to those who are without Law, as without Law, though not being without the Law of God but under the Law of Christ, so that I might win those who are without Law. To the weak I became weak, that I

might win the weak; I have become all things to all men, so that I may by all means save some. I do all things for the sake of the gospel, so that I may become a fellow partaker of it." (1 Corinthians 9:19-23, NASB)

This passage teaches us:

1. Do all things "to save some."

When we have "faith that works through love," the motive of our choices is purified and we make our choices not to be cool, to fit in, or gain man's approval—we already have the approval of the One who matters most!

Our choices are motivated by love. Our attempts to be relevant spring from a desire to see others receive salvation.

When Hudson Taylor went to China, he decided to adopt Chinese dress and culture in order to win the Chinese. He was ridiculed and scorned by other missionaries for this, but he won the hearts of many Chinese people by making this decision. He became all things to all men "to save some."

2. Do all things "for the sake of the gospel."

Remember that every one of us represent the gospel and create the gospel's reputation for a thousand souls. You're the only Bible some people may ever read. Beware of selfish ambition, a yearning for the praise of men, and a lust for reputation. When we make our choices, the true believer asks, "How will this affect the people around me and people's perception of God?"

I know of one pastor who decided to start drinking at the local bar, and the people in the town called him "the drunk reverend." His witness had failed because he felt he had the liberty to drink in a bar.

On the contrary, when I was in college, a few radical friends and I decided to start a ministry called *Operation G.I.N. (Gospel Infiltration Network).* Our goal was to take the gospel to environments where unbelievers were comfortable, and where Christians would not normally go. We'd go to bars, beer blasts, frat houses, and anywhere else unbelievers would gather, and we'd go "for the sake of the gospel." The point wasn't whether or not we were in a bar, but what the motive of our hearts was for being there.

3. Become "like them" — do not *become* them.

In recent days, there seems to be less and less of a distinction between believers and unbelievers. I do not wish to heap Law on anyone, but I do want to ask what is going on in our hearts that wouldn't cause us to want to live with passion for the glory of God? I believe that the less God's teachers teach grace, the less zeal and passion we will see for the kingdom of God. Christianity will become a compartment in people's lives, and not the whole. The world will barely see the difference between us and themselves.

> "*Therefore come out from them and be separate, says the Lord. Touch no unclean thing, and I will receive you*" (2 Corinthians 6:17, NIV).

How do we become like them to win them?

I was in a gas station, and I asked the cashier, "Hey man, has anyone told you today that Jesus loves you?"

"I'm not religious," he replied.

Become all things to all men.

"I'm not either," I said. "I hate religion."

Huh?

He did a double-take. He could not understand how someone who just told him that Jesus loved him could also say he hated religion.

"It was religious people who killed Jesus," I explained. "Why would I be interested in religion?"

By becoming like him, I was able to share Christ with him in a way he'd never heard.

I've seen others become like the bikers to win the bikers; like the rockers to win the rockers, like those in Hollywood to reach those in Hollywood. Every sector of society needs missionaries, and God will use us in all shapes and sizes as we walk in the Spirit.

RELEVANCE DOES NOT EQUAL LIBERALISM

I think we need to be careful to know that relevance does not equal liberalism. We can be completely relevant culturally, and completely healthy biblically.

With the rise of tolerance as the chief virtue in the western world, there is a great temptation to give in to compromise, almost apologizing for what we believe. I believe the absolute greatest fact in the universe is that Jesus Christ is Lord. This being our foundation, we bear with confidence and great joy any argument that undermines our faith.

I've heard it said that tolerance is the virtue of a man with no convictions. We cannot think that
We're gaining any ground if we surround ourselves with people who like us, or with big crowds that applaud our words. "Watch your life and doctrine closely" (1 Timothy 4:16, NIV).

Our generation believes "there are many ways to the top of the mountain." But grace teaches us that man was so depraved, hopeless, and helpless that only the Son of God's innocent blood could redeem us. That's why His grace is really amazing. Otherwise, if we could be saved another way, why did Jesus have to die?

But *universalism,* the idea that all religions are basically the same and all lead to God, is creeping into the Church. The moment we believe this is the moment we call God a liar and mock His grace.

When Jesus was in Gethsemane, Jesus prayed, "My Father, if it is possible, let this cup pass from Me" (Matthew 26:39, NASB). Jesus was looking at the suffering of the cross and saying, "Father, if there is another way to save the world; if there's another way to You, then let Me not have to go through all this."

A few moments later, He came back and said, "My Father, if it is not possible for this cup to be taken away unless I drink it, may your will be done" (Matthew 26:42, NIV).

301

If there was another way to the Father, Jesus would have seen it in that moment. His choice to go onward to the cross should convince us that there was no other way. Jesus is the Savior of the world.

If it is not possible…

It was not possible.

I'll never forget the days and weeks following the 9/11/01 terrorist attacks. I was heavily involved in taking ministry teams down to south Manhattan for six weeks following the disaster.

During that time, only a few days after the attack, Mayor Rudolph Guliani called a city-wide "interfaith prayer gathering" in Yankee stadium. I was heading out of the city on that day, and was listening on the radio as I drove along.

The stadium was packed with people from all over New York City. On the platform, one by one, representatives from nearly every religion in the city had a chance to step up to the microphone and pray. When the Muslim imam stepped to the podium, he shouted repeatedly, "Allah is God and Muhammed is his prophet! Allah is God and Muhammed is his prophet!"

There was nothing interfaith about the Muslim's prayers. To be honest, it was frightening, especially in light of what had happened a few miles south of Yankee Stadium only days before. At the same time, I respected the boldness he demonstrated in representing his religion with authenticity.

I looked forward to hearing the honored soul that would represent the Church. I longed to be refreshed by a person of biblical faith. I was driving by the stadium at the exact time the chosen pastor stepped up to the podium. He began with a Scripture passage in Romans 8, and read: "For I am convinced that neither death, nor life, nor angels, nor principalities, nor things present, nor things to come, nor powers, nor height, nor depth, nor any other created thing, will be able to separate us from the love of God."[303]

He closed his Bible.

---

[303] Romans 8:38-39a, NASB

"Keep reading!" I said out loud. "You left out the most important part!"

He began to pray a weak, religious prayer. This coward left out the end of the verse, which says, "...which is in Christ Jesus our Lord."

He was ashamed of the name of Jesus Christ. More and more, you see this kind of thing happening in the world today as America champions its virtue of tolerance. There is immense pressure to conform to culture's demands to count all beliefs as equal.

Now, we're biblically called to respect all beliefs, and an individual's right to believe, but it is *unbiblical* to suggest that all beliefs are *equal*. This mocks the cross and denies the resurrection.

We must be careful, in our quest to be relevant, to cling to the message of the cross and all the doctrines that make the cross the most important event in the history of the universe. We must be careful to not give into the temptation to fit in by making compromises and embracing clever lies that make the church more "open" to a lost world. The problem is, if we're not careful, we'll become just like the very people we're trying to reach—lost.

Why are we so afraid? When Christ's disciples were persecuted, they rejoiced! Sometimes, they shook the dust off their feet as Jesus commanded. [304] But what do we do? We say, "I was rejected. I must have presented it wrong." And we water down or alter the message. Many who long for man's acceptance have drifted from the faith entirely.

I was invited to lead worship at a regional conference for a certain denomination in Albany, NY. During one of our sets, as I was introducing the hymn "Blessed Assurance," I shared about my experiences in Islamic nations of the Middle East. I explained that Muslims believe that even if you obey every law in the Koran for your entire life, you are still not guaranteed a place in paradise. "But as believers in Jesus Christ," I explained, "we can know where we stand with God because of the blood of Jesus!" Then I

---

[304] Matthew 10:14

began to lead the crowd in singing, "Blessed Assurance, Jesus is mine..."

After the service, a female pastor confronted me and chided, "My leaders and I were very offended by your insensitive comments toward Muslims."

I tried to remember anything I said that might have been insensitive or controversial. I wasn't sure what she meant. "What did I say that offended you?" I asked.

"You suggested that Muslims are not going to heaven."

I was shocked. "You think the Muslims are going to heaven?"

"I don't wish to get in a theological discussion with you," she said. "I just want you to know that not everyone in this room believes what you believe."

"I don't believe you can embrace biblical Christianity and say what you just said," I told her.

She smiled arrogantly and said, "Yes, I know you believe that."

That night, as I led worship, I made sure that I quoted the Scripture, "Salvation is found in no one else, for there is no other name under heaven given among men by which we must be saved" (Acts 4:12).

Look for a moment into the lives of those who have carried the torch of the gospel through the ages and see the fires of conviction burning hot within them. They were so convinced that Christ was the sole solution to man's sin, they went to the ends of the earth, and even to their own death, to declare it.

THE EMERGING CHURCH MOVEMENT

As we look at some of the devil's schemes to undermine the purity of God's Word and grace, it's important to take a quick look at what is being called "The Emerging Church Movement."

The Emerging Church Movement is a broad and very influential movement that has been sweeping over the western world during the last twenty years. To try to understand it is to delve into a web of people, history, movements and spawned movements. For me to make a broad, sweeping, black and white statement about the movement, in light of its complex history, would be naïve and unfair, if not self-condemning. The movement certainly does have some good points to note. That said, the movement has created the grave potential for the dangerous pitfalls of heresy, license, universalism, and an obsession with imitating the world instead of Christ.

There are several different kinds of Emerging churches, all marked by an aggressive attempt to engage culture and find new ways of reaching people. The movement is also marked by the strange concoctions of hip modern culture, and yet a return to liturgy to capture a sense of God being surrounded by mystery. Other stripes of Emerging churches are those that embrace a strict business model with a robust marketing plan. With what seems to be an evangelistic fervor driving the whole movement, I'm sure we must walk on this path. At the same time, we must not be careless because there is a snake in the grass.

Let me make a distinction here between "Emerging" and "Emergent." The "Emerging" Church Movement is a broad movement that includes "innovative Christian leaders" from Australia, Europe, Canada, and the United States. These leaders have no real connection relationally except for their common interest in creating progressive ministries that are embracing culture and reaching youth. Mark Driscoll, a pastor who has long ties to the movement, wrote, "The Emerging church is a broad category that encompasses a wide variety of churches and Christians who are seeking to be effective missionaries wherever they live. This includes Europeans and Australians who are having the same conversation as their American counterparts."[305]

Christianity Today writer Scot McKnight, in an article titled "Five Streams of the Emerging Church" wrote, "Emerging catches into one term the global reshaping of how to 'do church' in postmodern culture. It has no central offices, and it is as varied as evangelicalism itself."[306]

---

[305] "A Pastoral Perspective on the Emerging Church" by Mark Driscoll: *Criswell Theological Review*, Spring 2006.
[306] "Five Streams of the Emerging Church: Key elements of the most controversial and misunderstood movement in the church today" by Scot McKnight: *Christianity Today* © 2007 posted 1/19/2007.

Emergent Village is a specific organization and movement that started in America in the early 1990s, and involves a network of leaders, gurus, thinkers, and innovators. [307] The Emerging Church Movement in the United States was really birthed by some of those who founded *Emergent*.

Mark Driscoll, who was a part of the original meetings that eventually became Emergent Village, left the group early on, and now says, "What started as a simple conversation nearly a decade ago by a handful of young pastors about how to do a hipper version of church has matured into a very serious conflict over what exactly it means to be a Christian."[308]

Dr. Ed Stetzer, a respected missiologist,[309] classifies the Emerging Church Movement into three distinct kinds of Christians: Relevants, Reconstructionists, and Revisionists.[310] Mark Driscoll describes the three groups this way:[311]

> *"Relevants are theologically conservative evangelicals who are not as interested in reshaping theology as much as updating such things as worship styles, preaching styles, and church leadership structures. Their goal is to be more relevant; thus, appealing to postmodern-minded people. Relevants commonly begin alternative worship services within evangelical churches to keep generally younger Christians from leaving their churches. They also plant new churches to reach emerging people. Relevant leaders look to people such as Dan Kimball, Donald Miller, and Rob Bell[312] as like-minded leaders. The common critique of Relevants is that they are doing little more*

---

[307] There is now an Emergent U.K. and is directed by Jason Clark.

[308] "A Pastoral Perspective on the Emerging Church" by Mark Driscoll: *Criswell Theological Review*, Spring 2006.

[309] A missiologist is someone that studies the activity and progress of the mission of the Christian Church, especially with respect to missionary activity throughout the world (partially drafted from the Merriam-Webster online Dictionary).

[310] "A Pastoral Perspective on the Emerging Church" by Mark Driscoll: *Criswell Theological Review*, Spring 2006.

[311] Ibid.

[312] At the *Convergent Conference* in 2007 at Southern Baptist Theological Seminary, Mark Driscoll publicly called Emergent leaders Rob Bell, Doug Pagitt and Brian McLaren heretics.

than conducting 'cool church' for hip young Christians and are not seeing significant conversion growth. Within the Relevants there is also a growing group of outreach-minded Reformed Relevants, which look to men like John Piper, Tim Keller, and D. A. Carson for theological direction.

"Reconstructionists are generally theologically evangelical and dissatisfied with the current forms of church (e.g. seeker, purpose, contemporary). They bolster their critique by noting that our nation is becoming less Christian and that those who profess faith are not living lives markedly different than non-Christians; thereby, proving that current church forms have failed to create life transformation. Subsequently, they propose more informal, incarnational, and organic church forms such as house churches.[313] Reconstructionists, who are more influenced by mainline Christian traditions, will also use terms like 'new monastic communities' and 'abbess.' Reconstructionist leaders look to such people as Neil Cole and Australians Michael Frost and Alan Hirsch. The common critique of Reconstructionists is that they are collecting disgruntled Christians who are overreacting to the megachurch trend but are not seeing significant conversion growth.

"Revisionists are theologically liberal and question key evangelical doctrines, critiquing their appropriateness for the emerging postmodern world. Reconstructionists look to such leaders as Brian McLaren and Doug Pagitt as well as other Emerging Christians. The common critique of Revisionists is that they are recycling the doctrinal debates of a previous generation and also not seeing significant conversion growth."

Basically, the relevants say, "The methods are bad."

The reconstructionists say, "The methods are bad and the structure is bad."

The revisionists say, "The methods are bad. The structure is bad. The *message* is bad."

---

[313] This pattern of restructuring the church is also known as the "postmodern" church.

In the desire to be relevant, some have completely walked off the edge, piercing themselves and their hearers with many griefs. Strangely, in an amazing demonstration of stupidity, those who teach "all roads leads to heaven," or other forms of liberalism, end up teaching the very things that people believe who don't go to church! In this, they guarantee small attendance at their pathetic gatherings.

We are *believers*, my brothers and sisters. That, in a word, means we *believe stuff*. Some who seek to be relevant have actually abandoned the thing that makes us believers — *believing stuff!*

I believe we find ourselves at one of those crucial times in history where we will either see one of the greatest moves of God the world has ever seen, or we will see massive numbers of Christians falling away, as deceived hordes unknowingly leave the faith.

The dark side of The Emerging Church Movement is part of the enemy's plan to pollute our understanding of God's grace, and to drive the saints away from the cross. These are dangerous times we live in, and the only way to navigate these waters is to stay close to Jesus and His Word. May God give all of us grace, and help us to be relevant and completely devoted to Christ and His commands.

CHAPTER 26
The Missionary Heart of God

"To win for the Lamb the reward of His suffering."
– The Mooravians

The more you understand grace, the more missions makes sense. Grace teaches us that God crossed every border, every ocean, every divide, and came as a foreigner from heaven to save the world on a cross. *A reflection of God, missionaries have crossed oceans and borders, and borne their own crosses to reach the lost.* Grace teaches us that God is most glorified in man's weakness. *Who is more helpless than the natural and spiritual orphans and widows of the nations?* Grace teaches us that God loved us when we were far away from Him. *Who is farther from God than the unreached of the nations?*

Over the last twenty years, there has been a fresh wind of worship that has blown through the Church that many have come to affectionately call "The Worship Movement." From small gatherings in homes, to local churches of all stripes, to thousands gathering at Christian conferences and festivals, followers of Jesus have experienced the presence of the Lord in a profound way. Songs and songwriters are emerging from every corner of the world, writing outstanding songs that enrich the saints and help the church to exalt Christ.

The buzzword in the worship movement has been "intimacy." The idea is that worship becomes an interactive experience, man to God and God to man, marked by honesty, sincerity, and passion.

As thankful as I am for charismatic, New Testament worship, our intimacy with God is never an end in itself. As we're sitting on Daddy's lap in His presence, we need to put our ears on Daddy's chest and hear His heartbeat. What we'll hear is the pounding sound of zeal and love saying, "That none should perish...That none should perish...That none should perish..."

God has a missionary heart.

I've heard it said that if you took missions out of the Bible, all you'd be left with is the cover. Truly, the story of the Scriptures is the story of God reaching out to man with His seeking heart. From the Garden of Eden, where He called out, "Adam, where are you?" to the Book of Revelation where He says, "'He who has an ear, let him hear what the Spirit says to the churches,"[314] God has been reaching out and calling a lost world unto Himself.

GOD OF THE FAR-OFF ONES

Ephesians 2:17 says, "He came and preached peace to you who were far away and peace to those who were near."[315]

...peace to you who were far away.

God is the God of the far-off ones. That's why you're reading this. That's why I'm writing this—because *He came and preached peace to you who were far away.*

When God's heart comes inside of ours, when we are infused with *zoe* and *dunamis,* we become like God. We become missionaries, seeking and saving the lost just like our Master.

That's how Paul the Apostle ended up in Asia.

That's how William Carey, and eventually Amy Carmichael, ended up in India.

That's how Hudson Taylor ended up in China.

That's how Adoniram Judson ended up in Burma.

That's how my wife ended up in a bar.

I remember a profound experience I had on the streets of Albany, New York, several years ago. I prayed with a young man named Chris to repent of his sins and receive Jesus as his own, and the moment we were done praying, he looked up, and immediately looked beyond me to a couple down the street. Then he grabbed my arm and yanked me over to the couple. "Tell them what you just told me!" he said.

The moment this young man was born again, his eyes looked *far-off.* He already had a missionary heart.

---

[314] Revelation 2:17, NASB
[315] NIV

AS THE WATERS COVER THE SEA

Habakkuk 2:14 says, "For the earth will be filled with the knowledge of the glory of the Lord, as the waters cover the sea."[316]

One day, my wife was reading this verse, and she said to me, "Derek, I think the Lord showed me something in this verse. The reason the knowledge of the glory of the Lord is going to cover the earth is because *we're going to cover the earth!*"

God's people are going to cover the earth, and His glory will shine in the nations through us.

> *"After these things I looked, and behold, a great multitude which no one could count, from every nation and all tribes and peoples and tongues, standing before the throne and before the Lamb, clothed in white robes, and palm branches were in their hands; and they cry out with a loud voice, saying, 'Salvation to our God who sits on the throne, and to the Lamb." (Revelation 7:9-10, NASB)*

This isn't just God's vision of heaven and what He hopes it might look like one day in the sweet by and by; it's something John *saw*. In the heart of God, it's already done. It's a prophetic vision of what will be, but has already occurred in God's realm, where He only lives in one tense: *I Am.*[317]

He was, is, and is to come. He does not live in the past or future; He is ever-present, all at once in the past, present, and future, *all at the same time.* Author Dr. Mike Brown of *Strong in the Lord Ministries* says, "God *am* in your past; He *am* in your present, and He *am* in your future!"[318] So when John saw this future event, it was already done by the Father.

Therefore, we already know that we will be successful in seeing the Great Commission become the Great Completion! But we must obey and do our part, knowing with full confidence that "it is God who is at work in you, both to will and to work for His

---

[316] NASB

[317] Exodus 3:14

[318] From a sermon Dr. Mike Brown delivered at Elim Gospel Church in Lima, NY, in June 2009.

good pleasure" (Philippians 2:13). Somehow, God's sovereign plan will be worked out as we obey Him.

A perfect example of this is when Paul the apostle went to preach the gospel in Corinth.

> *"One night the Lord spoke to Paul in a vision: 'Do not be afraid; keep on speaking, do not be silent. For I am with you, and no one is going to attack and harm you, because I have many people in this city.'" (Acts 18:9-10, NIV)*

The Lord spoke this to Paul long before the harvest had been reaped in that city. Only a few had come to Christ. Paul had faced much opposition, and the Lord encouraged him with this vision. It was an invitation for Paul to join God in sovereign election of the saints!

Please note that the knowledge that God had predestined some to come to saving faith did not cause Paul to say, "Oh, then I don't need to preach. God's got it covered." Instead, the knowledge that some were sovereignly chosen by the Lord energized Paul with holy boldness. Respected theologian Wayne Grudem says, "It's like telling a fisherman, 'I promise you're going to catch fish today!'"[319] What fisherman wouldn't want to fish under those conditions?

WHEN THE LORD COMES DOWN

As we see the encounter that Moses has with Jehovah God at the burning bush, we learn some amazing things about the way God thinks.

> *The Lord said, "I have surely seen the affliction of My people who are in Egypt, and have given heed to their cry because of their taskmasters, for I am aware of their sufferings. So I have come down to deliver them from the power of the Egyptians...Now, behold, the cry of the sons of Israel has come to Me; furthermore, I have seen the oppression with which the*

---

[319] Wayne Grudem, *Systematic Theology:* Zondervan Publishing (Grand Rapids, MI).

Egyptians are oppressing them. Therefore, come now, and I will send you to Pharaoh..." (Exodus 3:6-7a, 9-10a, NASB)

I have come down...I will send you.

When the Lord "comes down" to deliver someone, he sends you. What a profound look into the mysteries of God's ways and the union His people have with Him.

When China cries out, God comes down to deliver them and sends you.

When Africa cries out, God comes down and sends you.

When India bleeds, God comes down and sends you.

We will see this principle in a powerful way in the testimony of a Turkish friend of mine named Kamil. When I was in Turkey on an evangelistic music tour, he was our translator. He was a dear brother with a refreshing life-giving spirit. His smile seemed permanent. One night over dinner, I asked him how he came to Christ, and he shared his story with me.

He'd only become a Christian two years earlier. At the time, he was a successful translator who worked with European and American businessmen who would come to Turkey. One night, he was in the Mediterranean coastal city of Antalya; and when he had a break, he went swimming in the sea. As he came up out of the water, he looked at the beautiful night sky, and was taken in by its splendor. Creation testified to him that God was real, that He was looking down on Him, though Kamil did not know Him. Taken in with the moment, and dissatisfied with his experience within Islam, Kamil prayed to a God he did not know, "I know you are real, but I don't know who You are! Show me the way, and I will follow!"

Six months later, Kamil found himself in another city, translating for some American Christian businessmen. They invited Kamil to come to a local Christian service, and Kamil agreed to go if they would pay him for his translation services. At that meeting, Kamil was moved by the worship, and the sincerity of love for God that he saw in people's hearts. He was also shocked at the joy people seemed to have in a religious building. Then the small still voice of the Holy Spirit spoke to his heart, "Do you remember the prayer you prayed six months ago in the Mediterranean Sea? Today I am answering that prayer." Kamil received Jesus in that service.

As I reflected on Kamil's story in the days that followed, I wondered, "How many people are there like Kamil in Turkey?" How many are there like him in Asia? In Africa? In South America or Europe?

Listen to some quotes from lost souls among the unreached people groups of the 10/40 window:[320]

- "I desperately need a Bible; could you send me one?" (from a Muslim in the 10/40 Window)
- "I need your help, because I would like to know more about Jesus Christ, His life and His teaching." (from a Muslim in the 10/40 Window)
- "My one wish is to follow and learn more about Christianity!" (from Tariq, a Muslim Turkish Bible Correspondence student in Turkey)

Maybe God will use you to answer their prayers, just like God used men to answer Kamil's prayers. Missiologists believe that we can finish the Great Commission within one generation. To borrow the motto of the Student Missions Movement from the late 1800's, "We can do it, if we will."

---

[320] This is the longitudinal/latitudinal block inside which live over 3.2 billion unreached people.

Section 4

GRACE AND DISCIPLESHIP

CHAPTER 27
Teaching Grace

"What shall we say then? Are we to continue in sin so that grace may increase? May it never be! How shall we who died to sin still live in it?"
—Paul the Apostle (Romans 6:1-2, NASB)

Haddon Robinson once said, "The best preaching is one step away from heresy."

Paul preached grace so powerfully that he brought his hearers right to the doorstep of error, having to ask and answer the question in his own letter, *"What shall we say then? Are we to continue in sin so that grace may increase? May it never be! How shall we who died to sin still live in it?"* (Romans 6:1-2, NASB). And yet in some circles today, grace has become a dirty word.

There is a liberty that grace extends to every believer that I believe many preachers and teachers are afraid to offer their hearers because they either don't grasp grace themselves, or are afraid that it will be abused. But is this sufficient reason *not* to teach on the liberty of grace? People will abuse and distort any message that is preached, but this cannot keep us from telling the truth. The plain fact is, *a counterfeit cannot exist without the authentic.* In other words, there will always be those that will respond incorrectly to the correct teaching. Even Jesus had Judas, who heard Jesus preach for three and a half years! I suppose that we'll lessen the chance of seeing grace abused if we never preach grace, but we will also never see God's people walking in freedom.

It's a delusion to think we can protect our hearers from false teaching in the modern world, especially counterfeit grace. If we would be wise teachers, we must teach grace properly, and help our hearers to recognize the true from the false.

Objectors to the message of grace will always cite the abuses, and will ultimately accuse the grace teacher for introducing something that caused so much trouble, but this should not and cannot stop the grace teacher.

> *But if I say, "I will not mention him or speak any more in his name," his word is in my heart like a fire, a fire shut up in my bones. I am weary of holding it in; indeed, I cannot. (Jeremiah 20:9, NIV)*

I had one pastor request a meeting with me so that he could challenge my teaching, saying, "I'm concerned that young people will think you are giving them permission to sin. Is that what you believe?" Then he addressed a rumor he heard (which was completely untrue) about some of my understudies swearing and getting drunk.

No wonder so many young people fall away from the faith! In our great concern to be careful that they don't sin, we've ceased to teach them the source of power over sin, and our message has become nothing more than telling them to behave and pray.

I'd rather teach grace now and let them learn to apply it, occasionally coloring outside the lines, than force them into a robotic conformity to a rule-driven discipleship. That usually ends in rebellion and being disenchanted with the church.

Whenever someone discovers grace, there is a season when he may examine the borders of grace, but because the Holy Spirit abides in his heart, the Helper teaches his conscience where the lines are. Teachers of the Word, mentors, and disciplers all play a part in this, though we must be coaches and not drill sergeants. And we must refrain from playing Holy Spirit (we're not that good at it).

To disciple by grace, we must teach it the way the Word teaches it: with boldness, clarity, confidence, and love.

CHRIST-CENTERED GRACE

In teaching grace, be careful not to preach a man-centered grace. I would often hear teachings on God's grace, and still walk away feeling like something was lacking in the message. It wasn't until I was talking with my friend Mike Chorey that I realized what the problem is. Explaining his opinion on a certain teacher, he said, "The issue I had with his teaching was that he taught a man-centered grace, not a Christ-centered grace."

318

"That's it!" I told him. "You just cleared up a big question for me!" I could see what bothered me about some teachings I'd heard.

Man-centered grace puts man at the center of the message. It says that grace is for the believer, and that the believer may enjoy many good blessings and riches because of it. It says that God wants us all to live blessed and prosperous lives. Though much of this is true, the focus of the message is on man and not God.

Christ-centered grace puts Christ at the center of the message, that all is for Him, from Him, and to Him. It says that the heartbeat of grace is the glory of God. Man does not get the glory for his salvation or sanctification. God does! The exaltation of man is not the end of God's plans. His own glory is! Christ-centered grace makes the goal worship and not blessings. Are we blessed? Yes! But the blessings flow out of being Christ-centered, not seeing God as a rich uncle that gave us a blank check.

TEACHING THE MESSAGE OF THE CROSS

One of my earliest memories as a Christian after my conversion as a nine-year-old boy is hearing my pastor preach on Matthew 16:24, "Then Jesus said to His disciples, 'If anyone wishes to come after Me, he must deny himself, and take up his cross and follow Me.'"[321]

This Scripture became the theme of my life in my zealous teenage years, when I would preach the gospel in my high school, or gather believers to pray and pursue revival. When I had a grace conversion, however, I realized that I did not fully understand the cross.

Before my grace conversion, my understanding of the cross was that it was the ultimate example of self-denial—an example that we should imitate as we seek to be like Christ. Now, however, I see that the message of the cross is not *merely* self-denial, but is also the denial of self-*sufficiency*. Therefore, the true message of the cross is that it is an example of self-denial *and simultaneously* the source of our strength to deny ourselves. As a matter of fact, we

---

[321] NASB

cannot deny ourselves at all without first receiving grace from the cross to do it.

So when Jesus said to "deny yourself" in Matthew 16:24, He was not just telling us to refrain from giving in to our sinful appetites, but He was teaching us to "deny *self*" – deny trusting in ourselves, deny leaning on our own strength, deny dependence upon our own good works, flee from self-righteousness.

Therefore, when we teach "the message of the cross," we must be careful to teach "two crosses":[322] 1) Christ's cross as the object of our faith (the source of our strength and access to the Father), and 2) Our own cross as the joyful response to grace by denying ourselves and living for Him.

Most preaching I've heard on the cross focuses solely on #2. I am deeply moved, even to tears, when I hear my brothers or sisters preach and teach about the cross in this way, as I love the inspiring examples of dear saints who have denied themselves, not to mention Christ Himself. However, I often leave saddened that the teacher never pointed to the power source. As I outlined in the chapter "Grace Conversions," most men and women of God who have made a difference in this world have had grace conversions before their rise to effectiveness.

Recently, I heard a self-denial message that inspired me. I walked away encouraged to love God with all my heart, soul, mind, and strength. Everything I hear now comes through my grace filter, so I didn't believe that I would err in the application of the message. However, when one of the young guys I'm mentoring asked me, "So what did you think of the message?", I struggled to give him a straight answer. I was torn between the fact that I liked what I heard, but was also wondering where grace was, so I answered him as I often do, "It's not what they said. It's what they *didn't* say."

I often find myself with this evaluation. A lot of speakers have a lot of great stuff to share, but I continue to be concerned by what most of them *don't* say, because if we don't frame everything within grace, our hearers will be misled into self-sufficiency. The

---

[322] With thanks to dear friend Bob Santos, who developed a teaching on this concept, and has a rare and profound grasp on grace.

trumpet call must be clear that grace is the foundation of all Christian life.

How is this applied practically? Every teacher of God's word must always point back to the power source; the foundation; to the springhead of all Christian life. If we preach a word on personal holiness, we must always finish by telling our audience about the One who fulfilled the Law, became the perfect sacrifice, and made a way for us to become holy. If we preach on obedience, we must always tell them about the One who obeyed His Father in Gethsemane, accepting the tortures of the cross so that we could be clean and the Father could send the Holy Spirit to empower us to obedience. If we fail to point our hearers to the cross, and ultimately to grace, we're simply creating modern Pharisees.

PREACH THE WORD

The ordination certificate on my wall says, "Preach the Word." That sounds like it should be an obvious duty, but sometimes the most obvious things can be the most easily neglected. There are many in the pulpit today who entertain and do not preach the Word; many who inspire and do not preach the Word; many who present helpful advice, but do not preach the Word.

Only the Word of God can change the mind and transform the heart. Yet, there is much teaching today under the genre of *life application* that has little or nothing to do with the gospel. There is nothing inherently wrong with life application in itself, though as a preaching genre it has its weaknesses. This is basically a form of preaching that, instead of teaching passages of the Bible, focuses more on topics and then uses Scriptures to reinforce the points that are made. This can be dangerous because it's easy to fall into the temptation of getting the Scriptures to say whatever you want them to say. If done right, however, it can be extremely practical, though great discipline is required by the teacher to apply the passages with integrity.

Contrast that with *expository* preaching, which is studying a passage and then teaching the meaning directly from the passage. This is also called *exegesis*. Expository preaching lends itself more to discovering the actual meaning of the passage instead of randomly selecting miscellaneous verses and using them to bolster an idea. The weakness in this genre may be that the teacher fails to apply how the Bible affects every day life. Again, great discipline is required by the teacher to "keep the cookies on the low shelf" and to give the hearer something that is not too heady. It takes work and commitment for the teacher to make the text both practical and livable. It can also be work to avoid bogging down the audience in boring concepts. I personally believe that boring preaching is an enemy of evangelism and discipleship!

All that said, Haddon Robinson made the point, "More heresy is preached in application than in Bible exegesis."[323]

This is not to say that we cannot preach topically or preach life application. To do so would be self-incriminating, as there are topical chapters in this very book! What I am saying is that we must be disciplined to say what the Bible says, and careful not slip into merely giving good advice, half of the truth, or even worse, introducing heresy. When we teach the great passages of the Word, we agree with St. Augustine, who said, "What the Bible says, God says."

My encouragement here is to study the gospel and preach the Word to those in your hearing, whether it's one, ten, or a hundred. When grace is grasped by the hearer who can see it in God's Word, his life will never be the same. The assumption, of course, is that anyone who teaches would "study to shew thyself approved unto God, a workman that needeth not to be ashamed, rightly dividing the word of truth" (2 Timothy 2:15, KJV). This means we can't just get our theology from the latest books, famous radio or television preacher, or podcast. We must be students of God's Word ourselves.

If we will make developing a sincere faith in our hearers our goal, we must remember that "faith comes from hearing, and hearing by the word of Christ" (Romans 10:17, NASB).

---

[323] "The Heresy of Application" by Haddon Robinson on *ChristianityToday.com*.

CHAPTER 28
Strongholds: The Power of the Lie

*"So the great dragon was cast out, that serpent of old, called
the Devil and Satan, who deceives the whole world; he was cast to
the earth, and his angels were cast out with him."*
—John the Beloved (Revelation 12:9, NKJV)

A lot of Christian teachers and authors talk about spiritual
warfare, and get very mystical about it, speaking of angels and
demons, principalities and powers, and the like. Likewise, when
many believers speak of the devil attacking them, they speak of
sickness, financial woes, car trouble, bad weather, and relational
conflict. According to the verse above, however, Satan's schemes
are not that mystical, nor is he ultimately interested in our bodies,
cars, or bank accounts. If he is the one who deceives the world,
then what is he really interested in? Our *minds*. When he attacks
us, where does he attack us? Between the ears. He wants you and
me to *think incorrectly*.

Therefore, our war with the devil is a battle of truth versus
lies. This is why Jesus said in John 14:6, "I am the way, *the truth*,
and the life."[324] This is why He said in John 8:32, "You shall know
the truth and the truth shall make you free."[325] The Holy Spirit
"guides us into all truth."[326] This is also why the devil is called "the
Father of lies."[327] Consider this verse:

> *"The weapons we fight with are not the weapons of the world.
> On the contrary, they have divine power to demolish
> strongholds. We demolish arguments and every pretension that
> sets itself up against the knowledge of God, and we take captive
> every thought to make it obedient to Christ." (2 Corinthians
> 10:4-5, NIV)*

---

[324] NKJV, emphasis added
[325] NASB, emphasis added
[326] John 16:13
[327] John 8:44

According to this verse, a *stronghold* is not some mystical throne of power, but is an "argument," "knowledge" that undermines God's Word, or evil "thoughts." Again we see that the battlefield is the mind. Satan wants to set up strongholds in the minds of every believer—arguments, wicked knowledge, and thoughts.

Ed Silvoso once described a stronghold this way, "A stronghold is a way of thinking, impregnated with hopelessness, contrary to the Word of God."[328]

Second Corinthians 2:11 says, "...in order that no advantage be taken of us by Satan; for we are not ignorant of his schemes."[329] The Greek word here for *schemes* is the word *pnoema*. The actual meaning of the word is "thoughts." So, this verse could read, "...for we are not ignorant of the thoughts that Satan plants in our minds."

Jesus told His disciples in Matthew 28:18, "All authority in heaven and on earth has been given to me."[330] If Jesus has *all* authority, then how much does that leave for the devil? *None.*

If this is true, then why are so many Christians living defeated lives? It's because of *strongholds.* The devil has no power except the degree of the lie that you have believed.

For example, when I was a boy, my grandparents used to have two poodles. I couldn't stand them. They'd yap and bark at me like two beetles with bicycle horns. They scared me so much that I'd go running away from them. One day my father told me just to bark back, and so the next time they yapped at me, I barked back and they ran off in fear! So I want to ask you: What power did those dogs *actually* have over me? None except the belief that they did. It's the same with Satan's lies.

If we would disciple by grace, we must first allow God to tear down our own strongholds, and then arm ourselves to tear down the strongholds in the lives of others.

---

[328] Spoken in a message titled "Prayer Evangelism" at an ACM Leadership Conference in Orlando, Florida, 1998.
[329] NASB
[330] NIV

SATAN'S BEST SHOT

When Satan tempted Jesus in the wilderness, he came with his best shot. He could not come with a B-list temptation. It had to be A-prime. So here was his best punch:

> *"And the tempter came and said to Him, 'If You are the Son of God, command that these stones become bread.'" (Matthew 4:3, NASB)*

What makes this temptation so powerful? Let's break it down...

"If You are the Son of God"

Satan tried to get Jesus to question His *identity*. Satan tried to make Jesus doubt who He was as the Son of God, but Jesus knew who He was and did not need to prove it. One day, Jesus would do a similar miracle when He fed 5000 with five loaves and two fish, but He would not do it in the wilderness to prove who He was to Satan.

If Satan tried to do it to Jesus, do you think he might try to do this to you? Of course he will. He wants to set up a stronghold of doubt and insecurity in your mind until you walk in defeat, constantly performing to try to prove your identity or to earn God's love.

"Command that these stones become bread"

Satan is a master psychologist. Here he is trying to twist the motives for doing good works. As I've already written, Jesus would do this kind of miracle one day in obedience to the command of His Father, but He would not do it for Satan.

What is really happening here?

Satan is trying to get Jesus to do a *good work* for the *wrong reason*. He's trying to twist the good things of the faith into something dead by perverting the motive. *He's trying to trick Jesus into being a legalist.*

In the same way, if the deceiver can trick you and me into twisting the good things of the faith—Bible reading, prayer, fasting, serving the poor, evangelism, etc. — into performance and not love, he has won a great battle over our minds.

He's trying to set up *strongholds.*

But, just like our Savior overcame, so shall we overcome.

LABELS

If Jesus went to a psychiatrist after His experience in the wilderness, it might have gone something like this.

"So what happened out there?"

"Well," Jesus would say, "the devil talked to me."

"What did he tell you to do?"

"To turn stones into bread."

"Hmm," the psychiatrist would say, pondering this bizarre testimony, "and then what happened?"

"The devil took me up on the tallest point of the temple and told me to jump off."

This would surely concern the doctor. "No kidding! Wow..." He would think some more and then give his diagnosis. "I'm afraid you are a paranoid psychotic suicidal schizophrenic. I'll get you some meds."

What's my point here?

The point is that the world puts labels on us that can undermine who we really are. Jesus was *none* of those things, and yet that's exactly how He would be diagnosed by today's psychosomatic community! We live in a world that does not understand spiritual things, or even believe that there is a devil or supernatural realm, so it diagnoses and labels according to symptoms. The world has no idea where the symptoms come from or why they are there, but throw around terms to label and stigmatize people for their whole lives.

"You are schizophrenic."

"You are bipolar."

"You have an eating disorder."

"You have A.D.D."

"You have obsessive-compulsive disorder."

"You are an alcoholic."

326

And the list goes on and on. Some of these may be helpful in diagnosing the symptoms of a suffering person, but ultimately none of these represent the new man in Christ. If the devil can get us to buy into a label, we will live out who we believe that we are. We'll develop a victim-mentality that will paralyze us and put a ceiling on the potential of our lives.

The gospel breaks the power of these labels, which are really strongholds, and shows us who we really are in Christ!

The truth shall set you free.

My whole life I was told that because I was an alcoholic's son, I would have severe issues because of this. One man actually looked me right in the face and said, "You are the textbook example of an alcoholic's child."

"I refuse that label," I told him, even as a teen. "I know who I am in Christ."

I would not grow up as a victim.

On a side note, parents have to be careful how they speak to their children. There's a big difference between speaking to the sin and speaking to the person; speaking to the behavior versus speaking to someone's identity. As believers, we must always speak to the sin and strengthen the *new man* – the one that Christ is raising up. Isn't that what God did to Gideon when He said, "Arise, mighty man of valor"? Though Gideon was actually a terrified coward, hiding in the threshing floor, God spoke to the new man in Christ.

It's the devil's job to reinforce the *old man* – who we are without Christ. That's why I'm careful how I speak to my children. If my son is acting up, I don't say, "You little brat!" In Christ, he's not a little brat. He's a rising star in the kingdom of God! So instead, I say, "Son, you were acting like a brat. I know you're better than that. Repent of your bratness." (If that's not a word, it should be.)

Or to my daughter, I don't say, "You fat little toad! When will you stop eating desserts?"

Instead, you deal with the behavior, and don't make it part of their identity. "Sweetheart," I'll say, "do you know that the Bible teaches us not to overeat? It's called gluttony. As a young woman of God, this is not becoming to you."

How many parents damage their children because they speak out of anger or ignorance? Believe me, our words go deep into our children's hearts, whether for good or for bad.

"You're a little pig."

"I guess your sister got all the looks."

"You're a dummy just like everyone else in our family. College is not for us."

I had a young man who was part of the ministry for a while come in to my home and speak harshly to my children. He'd call them brats and whiners, and I had to speak to him about this. When I confronted him and explained these principles to him, I found out that he'd grown up being picked on and was told he was fat and stupid. The Lord had to set him free before he could see beyond the strongholds of others.

Paul the Apostle said, "It is no longer I, but sin which dwells in me." He understood the distinction between the old man and the new. "It's not the real me!" he's saying. "It's not the new man that Christ is raising up!"

When I was in India, I visited a village that had a thriving work, and found out that the people had once been traveling gypsies, going from village to village begging for food. One day, an evangelist came to them and preached, "You are not a beggar!" This word transformed their identity as a people, and caused them to settle down into a community, work hard and grow in faith. This evangelist destroyed their strongholds.

I'm writing this from JFK airport in New York City after a trip to Uganda, where I was brought to see the street orphans in downtown Kampala. It was disturbing, to say the least. When I was asked to share some words with them, I told them about their heavenly Father and preached, "You are not an orphan!"

The role of God's teachers, preachers, and disciplers, is to undo the strongholds of the one who deceives the nations.

DAVID'S STORY

I met David in Albany, NY, after a concert we performed there in a church. He came to me afterward with his wife and asked, "So basically, if I obey the Ten Commandments, I'll go to heaven, right?"

"No," I answered. "The Bible clearly teaches that, 'No one will be declared righteous by observing the Law, but rather through the Law we are made conscious of sin.'"[331]

"Oh," he said, "then how can I be saved?" (He came late to the concert and missed the message.)

I shared the gospel with him, and he prayed right there to repent of his sins and to receive Jesus. We talked more about this, when he said, "How does someone become demon-possessed?"

"Well, that's a tough one," I answered. "Some people are oppressed by spirits and some are possessed. But I think that the door can open through trauma, sexual experiences, drugs, the occult, and there are also reasons I don't know."

At this point, David turned to his wife and said, "See?"

"Why do you ask?" I pressed.

"Do you have time to talk?" he asked, looking very concerned.

We went into the pastor's office and he began telling me that he'd gotten deep into the occult "to show the devil that I was stronger than him" and was now in deep spiritual bondage. He told me that he could hear voices in his head every time he went near a graveyard. His friend, he added, didn't believe him, so he blindfolded David, and had him lie down in the backseat of his car. They drove through rural areas and David told him every time he heard voices. It was always when they were driving by a graveyard.

Then I gave him a piece of paper and instructed him to write down every occultic experience he had. He filled up the whole page with his demonic resume'. When he finished, I told him to take the list and to ask God to forgive him for every occultic practice he'd been involved in. David took the paper, scanned the

---

[331] Romans 3:20

enormity of it, looked up at me and said, "God won't forgive me for this."

"Why not?"

"It's too wicked," he insisted.

I opened my Bible to 1 John 1:9, which says, "If we confess our sins, He is faithful to forgive us our sins and cleanse us from all unrighteousness."[332] Then I took his lists of sins and put them next to my Bible in such a way that he could see both. Pointing at the word "all" in 1 John 1:9, I said, "Which of your sins is not included in the word *all?*"

He stared at it for a moment, and then looked up at me again, and said with tears forming in his eyes, "God will forgive me!"

The stronghold fell down.

He wept as he prayed for God's forgiveness.

After some time, he went home for the evening, and the next morning, I ministered in the local church service. David came back. His countenance, which the night before had looked distraught, exhausted, hardened, and old, was now shining with joy like the face of a little boy. He told me with excitement, "Last night, we drove by a graveyard on the way home and I could not hear voices! When we got home, I could not stop crying tears of joy! My wife made me a meal, and when I sat down to eat it, I fell on the kitchen floor weeping!"

God had brought a prodigal son home.

STAND IN TRUTH

If the battle is fought between lies and truth, our victory is in our faith, just as 1 John 5:4 says, "For whatever is born of God overcomes the world; and this is the victory that has overcome the world — our faith."[333]

I am convinced that the devil spends all his time trying to convince unbelievers that they are acceptable to God, and believers that they are *not*. We fight by believing in spite of how we feel or what our circumstances are.

---

[332] NASB
[333] NASB

> *"Submit therefore to God. Resist the devil and he will flee from you." (James 4:7, NASB)*

What does it mean to *submit to God?* It means to submit to what He says. It means to believe His Word. So when we are in the wilderness of temptation or suffering and the enemy is working overtime to trip us up, we believe God's Word and act on it—even if we don't feel like acting on it—because God's Word works just fine independent of our feelings. "Therefore put on the full armor of God, so that when the day of evil comes, you may be able to stand your ground, and after you have done everything, to stand" (Ephesians 6:13, NASB).

Soon you will find the enemy fleeing from you because you have put your trust in the Lord.

I've known several great saints who were great sinners before they came to a saving knowledge of Christ, and their past sins still come to haunt and bind. This is a stronghold of condemnation. Maybe you've known this agony of soul?

Submit therefore to God. Resist the devil.

Remember that God said that He has removed our sins "as far as the east is from the west."[334]

What an interesting picture this is! He did not say *as far as the north is from the south,* but east to west. I want you to think about that. You can go north and eventually begin to go south again, but you cannot go east and at any point begin to go west. How far is the east from the west? *It's infinite.*

Our dear sister Corrie Ten Boom once wrote, "When God throws our sins into the sea of forgetfulness and we go fishing there, God puts up a sign that says, 'No Fishing Allowed.'"

We must not believe the lies, my brothers and sisters. We must not be surprised when they come, because we know our enemy. We must stay close to Jesus and His Word, and then we will overcome temptation; we will overcome the world through faith.

---

[334] Psalm 103:12

CHAPTER 29
Discipleship is Relationship

"Discipleship is the grooming of friends who can be trusted."
— Keith Intrater[335]

I have a friend who was desperate to get into a discipleship relationship with a mentor, so he set up an appointment to discuss it with his pastor. "Pastor," he said, "I want you to disciple me."

"Explain what you mean by that," his pastor said.

My friend poured out his heart about how desperate he was to grow in God, and how the Bible says that "he who walks with the wise grows wise" (Proverbs 13:20, NIV).

After listening for a few minutes, his pastor said, "I think I know what you want. You may have access to my personal library of books any time you wish."

Not exactly what my friend was hoping for.

A few years ago, David, a young college student with a lot of zeal to grow in God, approached me. "Derek," he said, "I want you to disciple me."

"I'm always willing to invest in a hungry heart," I told him. Then I asked, "So, do you like football?" (I do.)

"Yes!" he answered. "Very much!"

"Good," I said, "then come over to my house an hour before Monday Night Football and we'll talk and then watch the game together."

For several months we met together and got to know each other, fellowshipping over a football game. Then one Monday night, he asked me, "So, Derek, when are you going to start discipling me?"

I laughed and said, "I'm doing it, brother!"

David's concept of discipleship was opening a Bible and studying together once a week or so. Now of course this can part

---

[335] Keith Intrater, *Covenant Relationships.* © 1989 Destiny Image Publishers: pg. 49

of discipleship, but what I was trying to show David is that *discipleship is relationship.*

Since the essence of our relationship with God is a loving relationship, do we think discipleship would be any different? Built into the gospel of grace is a love that burns strong for others. Consider this verse:

> *"One of them, an expert in the Law, tested him with this question: 'Teacher, which is the greatest commandment in the Law?' Jesus replied: 'Love the Lord your God with all your heart and with all your soul and with all your mind.' This is the first and greatest commandment. And the second is like it: 'Love your neighbor as yourself.' All the Law and the Prophets hang on these two commandments.'"* (Matthew 22:35-40, NIV)

The greatest two commandments have to do with relationship, vertical and horizontal. Jesus was the ultimate example of this with His own disciples. He spent about 1,275 days with His disciples. He had around 3,500 meals with His disciples. They laughed together. They rested together. They slept under the same trees. They had an intimate relationship with Jesus.

Ministries not driven by relationship ultimately must drift toward programs and rigid structures. Relationships shift a culture from programs toward trust. This is not to demonize programs as some have done, but to remind us that programs are only as powerful and anointed as the people and relationships within them.

As we're called to be imitators of Christ,[336] let's look at the pattern of discipleship in Jesus' life and ministry...

1. He grew up (Luke 2:40)
"The Child continued to grow and become strong, increasing in wisdom; and the grace of God was upon Him." (Luke 2:40, NASB)

---

[336] Ephesians 5:1

The most important stuff is what happens in secret. David didn't become great when he became king, but was great, therefore became king.

Like a root system is developed long before a tree grows strong and tall, so must we, and those we disciple, have the God stuff happening in the places of our lives where no one sees.

So many times, Christian young people obsess about what they are called to do, as if their lives hang in the balance if they don't go the right college, or choose the right career or major. But really, we don't know much about Jesus from the ages of 12 to 30. We know that He was in the temple and the carpenter's shop. I think the point wasn't specifically what He was doing, but that whatever He was doing *He did well*. Likewise, we need to encourage young people today to do all things with excellence, knowing that this will prepare them for whatever destiny God may have for them.

2. He was set apart (Matthew 3:17)

"And behold, a voice out of the heavens said, "This is My beloved Son, in whom I am well-pleased." (Matthew 3:17, NASB)

Like this verse demonstrates with Christ the Son, I believe that every one of us needs to hear the affirming, endorsing witness of the Spirit in our hearts, saying, "This is my child, whom I love, in whom I am well-pleased."

"God is pleased with me?" you might ask. Remember, He is pleased with *Christ,* and Christ is in you, and you have imputed righteousness, therefore there is nothing to keep you from His love.

Each disciple must have those "God moments" when he is transformed in God's presence, experiencing His grace and love, freely surrendering to the call on his life.

For Isaiah, it came after a revelation of His depravity when he said in Isaiah 6:

"'Woe to me!' I cried. 'I am ruined! For I am a man of unclean lips, and I live among a people of unclean lips, and my

eyes have seen the King, the Lord Almighty. Then one of the seraphs flew to me with a live coal in his hand, which he had taken with tongs from the altar. With it he touched my mouth and said, 'See, this has touched your lips; your guilt is taken away and your sin atoned for.'" (Isaiah 6:5-6, NIV)

Isaiah is in a broken state over his sin nature, and grace appears. This is all preparation for Isaiah to be set apart, which happens in the next few verses.

"Then I heard the voice of the Lord saying, 'Whom shall I send? And who will go for Us?' And I said, 'Here am I. Send me!' He said, 'Go and tell this people: Be ever hearing, but never understanding; be ever seeing, but never perceiving.'" (Isaiah 6:8-9, NIV)

As we relate to those we're discipling, do not think that their failures disqualify them, as these may be the preface to their God moments when they will finally see grace, and that their lives are owned by the Father.

3. He passed the test (Matthew 4:1)
"Then Jesus was led up by the Spirit into the wilderness to be tempted by the devil." (Matthew 4:1, NASB)

For each person God uses, He will allow his faith to be tested and purified.

There was once a young guy that I was mentoring, Justin, who really had a passion for God to use him. Riding in a car one day with me, he said, "I just want God to break me!"

I laughed out loud.

"What's so funny?" he asked.

"You don't realize what you just said!" I told him. "Do you mean that?"

"I think so," he said.

"Well, God heard that," I told him.

Within eighteen months, he was so depressed that he was considering walking away from the Lord, let alone ministry. Justin endured, and eventually, found himself serving as a youth pastor in a healthy local church with a strong testimony of grace. Today, he's married with three beautiful children, and still serving the Lord.

Paul Johansson, one-time president of Elim Bible Institute in Lima, NY, once told a story about when he and his brother, Robert, were young boys working in contruction in New York City. Their boss would holler down from fifty feet up, "Hey Robert, grab that plank right there and set it across those blocks!"

Robert would grab the plank and set it on the blocks.

"Now jump on it!" the boss would yell.

Robert would jump on the plank.

"Jump harder!" yelled the boss again.

Robert would jump harder.

If the plank wouldn't break, the boss would tell them to send it up, and he'd use it across 50-foot drops. Paul said, "How do you know if someone is ready for ministry? Before you test them fifty feet off the ground, test them at three!"

Please understand that I don't believe that Jesus was ever incapable of becoming the perfect model for all of us, so when I speak of testing, I don't mean that He had anything to prove. But when Jesus came to earth, He came to fulfill every jot and tittle of the Law on our behalf. Therefore, He was willing to model the process from discipleship to discipler so that we would all know the journey we must take.

4. He ministered alone (Matthew 4:17)
"From that time Jesus began to preach and say, 'Repent, for the kingdom of heaven is at hand.'" (Matthew 4:17, NASB)

The principle here is simple: Jesus *became* what He would eventually ask His disciples to become. He could not ask anyone to be what He was not willing to be. This should be an encouraging thought, because I believe that wherever we walk, we can expect others to follow. If you'll walk the miles, your sons and daughters will walk the miles.

I remember when I lived in Fort Worth, Texas, we used to go downtown to Sundance Square on outreaches. There was a certain brick wall in the middle of Sundance Square that surrounded a tree that adorned one of the streets. For weeks, I envisioned myself standing on that wall preaching the gospel. No one else would dare, so I knew it was me or no one.

Finally, one balmly Saturday night, I did it. A big crowd gathered on the street to hear me, and to make a long story short, one young homeless man named Greg received Christ and moved in with my wife and me for the next few months.

My outrageous act of obedience opened the door for others to follow. In the weeks that followed my debut preaching on that wall, *over twenty others from my church preached from that wall*, including a nine-year-old girl.

When we become the model of what we want our disciples to become, then they can walk where we walk, and even farther, just as Christ said, "Truly, truly, I say to you, he who believes in Me, the works that I do, he will do also; and greater works than these he will do; because I go to the Father" (John 14:12, NASB).

5. He chose His disciples (Matthew 4:18-22)

"Now as Jesus was walking by the Sea of Galilee, He saw two brothers, Simon who was called Peter, and Andrew his brother, casting a net into the sea; for they were fishermen. And He said to them, 'Follow Me, and I will make you fishers of men.'" (Matthew 4:18-19, NASB)

Now that Jesus had become the model of what He wanted His disciples to be, He chose His disciples. He begins to be *intentional* about who He was investing in and who He was not investing in.

So, now I have a question. At most conferences where I minister, hordes of believers will corporately assert that they are doing their best to fulfill the Great Commission. But remember that the Great Commission isn't simply to go and preach the gospel in an evangelistic sense. The Great Commission is to "Go

338

therefore and make disciples of all the nations" (Matthew 28:18a, NASB).

That said, here's my question is: *Who are your disciples?*

Jesus was able to name, number, and identify whom His disciples were. We must also be that intentional about investing in people.

6. He ministered with His disciples in the audience

Almost all of the miracles and teachings of Christ were done in view of His disciples. They were watching every move. Jesus simply modeled what He had already become. This was all part of their preparation and training for ministry.

7. He "withed" His disciples (Acts 4:13)

"Now as they observed the confidence of Peter and John and understood that they were uneducated and untrained men, they were amazed, and began to recognize them as having been with Jesus." (Acts 4:13, NASB)

This verse in Acts gives us a summary of Christ's discipleship program. He *withed* them. They spent time together. They walked together. They talked together. They stayed up late around the fire together. They ate together. As I've pointed out, Jesus had nearly 3,500 meals with His disciples. If a meal wasn't a good tool for discipleship, Jesus wouldn't have included it 3,500 times in His program!

8. He sent His disciples out to minister (Matthew 10:1)

"Jesus summoned His twelve disciples and gave them authority over unclean spirits, to cast them out, and to heal every kind of disease and every kind of sickness." (Matthew 10:1, NASB)

Jesus sent His disciples out to do what they had already been watching Him do. They preached, they healed the sick, they cast out demons, they blessed the poor.

They'd been with Jesus.

They hadn't read it in a book, they didn't watch a video series, they watched a living breathing person doing it for years, and they imitated Him.

9. He sent His disciples out to disciple (Matthew 28:19)

"Go therefore and make disciples of all the nations, baptizing them in the name of the Father and the Son and the Holy Spirit." (Matthew 28:19, NASB)

Now the pattern began to cycle as Jesus sent His disciples out to choose their own disciples. This they did, and the process began all over again.

Peter went through the wilderness, denying Christ and returning to fishing. Then Jesus set Him apart in John 21:

> "He said to him the third time, 'Simon, son of John, do you love Me?' Peter was grieved because He said to him the third time, 'Do you love Me?' And he said to Him, 'Lord, You know all things; You know that I love You.' Jesus said to him, 'Tend My sheep'" (John 21:17, NASB).

Peter preached on the Day of Pentecost, settled in Jerusalem as part of the pastoral team, and continued to perform signs and wonders in front of his own disciples, who led the church when he was martyred.

God is a friendly, fatherly God, who has chosen relationship as the means of impartation. As we seek to make disciples, "Be imitators of God, therefore, as dearly loved children and live a life of love, just as Christ loved us and gave himself up for us as a fragrant offering and sacrifice to God" (Ephesians 5:1-2, NIV).

CHAPTER 30
Servant Leadership

"Behold, I am going to send you Elijah the prophet before the coming of the great and terrible day of the LORD. 'He will restore the hearts of the fathers to their children and the hearts of the children to their fathers, so that I will not come and smite the land with a curse.'"
—The prophet Malachi (Malachi 4:6, NASB)

This verse is spoken of John the Baptist, who would precede the coming of Christ. It speaks of the days when God is preparing hearts to receive the gospel and the Messiah. Right in the middle of this prophetic fulfillment, we see these principles at work:

1. The older begin to serve the younger
"He will restore the hearts of the fathers to their children"

The whole of discipleship and evangelism is about carrying a father's heart toward the next generation of believers. Where God is moving, generations are thinking about the one after them. Where He is not moving, the older are self-serving and do not have a multi-generational vision.

In the days of great kings of ancient times, the wood used in building cathedrals would be taken from trees that took 100 years to grow into a useful condition. Therefore, kings would have to plant seedlings for their sons and grandsons 100 years beforehand, knowing that they would not be around to see their sons use the materials. Bible teacher Bob Mumford called this "cathedral thinking."[337] It's the idea that good men have a father's heart and can see beyond themselves to the next generation.

So that I will not come and smite the land with a curse.

God despises it when the father chooses himself over his own son. That is contrary to the nature of God.

---

[337] Bob Mumford is the founder and director of Lifechangers, Inc., a teaching ministry that has impacted the Body of Christ for over twenty years.

> *"Son of man, prophesy against the shepherds of Israel; prophesy and say to them: 'This is what the Sovereign Lord says: Woe to the shepherds of Israel who only take care of themselves! Should not shepherds take care of the flock?'"*
> (Ezekiel 34:2, NIV)

It is God's heart, and will be ours when we are in grace, to love our natural and spiritual children, finding within us a passion to love and disciple them.

2. The younger begin to admire and respect the older
"and the hearts of the children to their fathers"

Too often the older will demand respect and desire admiration from the younger generation, but too often there's nothing to respect and admire. We can't expect sincere respect, obedience, or esteem from those that are subordinate to us if we will not love them and serve them. Servant leadership is the only solution. Note that for the children to turn to the father, the father must first turn to the children.

Drew was a little boy with a wild temper in elementary school. He'd get angry and lose control and would throw whatever objects were near him across the room. No one was safe when Drew lost control. The teachers were baffled by his behavior, as only a few years before, it seemed he was a sweet little boy, but now he was a monster. Mom and Dad were furious, and "let him have it" when they'd get home from one of their many parent-teacher conferences. Drew's father Lou would yell and scream, and then "give him a good whipping."

"How dare you embarrass me!" he'd yell at his son. "You will behave and represent this family well!"

"Whatever," Drew responded coldly.

"I am your father and you will respect me!" Lou demanded.

Such a comment had become a mantra in Drew's house. *I am your father and you will respect me!*

What no one knew was that Lou had missed every Little League game that year because of his busy work schedule, and spent most of his time at home watching TV and drinking a couple of cool ones. Anytime Drew would ask for time, he would give an excuse or snap at him about how tired he was. Drew eventually just stopped asking. He got used to his father being home but not being home, all the while demanding the respect and admiration of his son.

Drew soon became the class bully, mistreating other children on the bus and at recess. By the time he was a teenager, he had a reputation for being a rebel and hell-raiser. Drew even had a short stint in jail for mouthing off to a police officer. "What's wrong with that kid?" people would ask. "He comes from a wealthy family. His parents seem like good people. I don't get it!" No one saw how bad his relationship was with his father.

When he was seventeen, Drew made the stupid decision to drive his car after another long night of partying with his friends. He lost control of his vehicle just after 4:00am, hit a tree and lost his life.

At his funeral, Lou wondered what went wrong and how this could have happened.

Contrast that story with the story of Rachel, whose father Brad made the choice early to love his daughter with all his heart. He prayed for her, and spent time with her as early as she could remember, making up games where she'd giggle and squeal with delight.

Rachel's father made it his life goal to make his daughter successful in every way. He'd go on dates with her, taking her to see movies, to get ice cream, or get her nails painted. He and his wife asked God for wisdom for how to direct her life. They encouraged her piano playing, her athletics, and her education. Brad made sure to tell his little girl how proud he was of her and how beautiful he thought she was as many times as he could. He was also sure to lovingly discipline her when he'd see her wander into sin.

When her first piano recital conflicted with a project at work, Brad chose to attend his daughter's recital, much to the dismay of his bosses. "They'll get over it," he told his wife. Rachel never forgot that.

Years later, on Rachel's graduation day, Rachel got to give the speech as the valedictorian of the class. During the speech, tears streamed down her face as she thanked her father and mother for all the sacrifices they made to make her life a success. Rachel told the story of her first piano recital.

Why do you think Drew failed in life and Lou failed in parenting? Why do you think Rachel succeeded in life and Brad succeeded in parenting? What's the difference between Lou and Brad? *Servant leadership.*

God never yelled at the world, "I am your Father and you will respect Me!" Instead, He demonstrated His love, power, and grace to us, and gave us *reasons* to admire and respect Him. He parted the Red Sea; He raised up Gideon and 300 men to defeat tens of thousands of enemies; He sent fire to Elijah's altar; He gave us His Word; He gave us His Son.

God is the ultimate servant leader.

The breakdown of servant leadership in our society has been the causal factor of much of the social and moral decline. I believe feminism exists because fathers and husbands failed at servant leadership. The gay-lesbian movement exists because fathers and mothers failed to properly love their sons and daughters. Hordes of people have left the organized church because pastors and priests have failed at servant leadership.

The only way to be a servant leader is to imitate the ultimate Servant Leader, Christ Himself. Only then can we expect those under our authority to respect us and to thrive in their destinies.

3. The kingdom is built on relationship

Once again, we also see in this Scripture the fact that the kingdom of God is built on relationship. God is a Father, and is a relational God. From the days in the Garden when God walked with Adam in the cool of the day to the days of Moses when "the LORD used to speak to Moses face to face, just as a man speaks to his friend" (Exodus 33:11, NASB) to the days when Jesus said, "No longer do I call you slaves...but I have called you friends" (John 15:15, NASB)—God has shown Himself to be more interested in our love than our coerced, robotic obedience.

God is a servant leader. Some thoughts about servant leaders:

1) Servant leaders extend grace to others as God extended it to them.
"Forgive as the Lord forgave you." (Colossians 3:13b, NASB)

If we are to be imitators of God, we must remember that God is an extender of grace. God is the source of grace. If we would be servant leaders, we must also be an extender of grace. We must be patient with others, edifying with our words, and extend the same grace to others that God extended to us. You did not become like Jesus overnight (I do not expect you would claim to have arrived yet), so do not have unrealistic expectations of where others should be in their journey with the Lord.

2) Servant leaders make everyone else around them successful.
"And He sat down, called the twelve, and said to them, 'If anyone desires to be first, he shall be last of all and servant of all.'" (Mark 9:35, NKJV)

A servant leader does not seek his own, but seeks to make others successful in the will of God for their lives. You and I won't be around here long. Any achievement or reputation you think you may have acquired will be quickly forgotten by the next generation. All that matters is the kingdom of God advancing on the earth through the next generation of believers.

Amy Carmichael's writings continue to touch thousands today though she hasn't been alive for over fifty years. As I understand it, near the end of her life, she tried to "disappear," throwing away her journals and different things she'd written so that people would not remember her. Thankfully, she was not entirely successful as some writings survived, but what a shining example of a woman who simply lived for the glory of God, seeking to make others successful and herself forgotten.

The worldly system of leadership puts the leader on top, the pinnacle of a pyramid, and everyone else beneath, serving and supporting the leader. Christ's model is flipped, where the pyramid is upside-down, the servant leader on the bottom, serving and supporting the rest.

Those who are not servant leaders feel threatened when strong believers rise up around them. They are satisfied being, in their minds, the one genius among a thousand dummies. Without servant leadership, this is what we have: One father and a thousand children who never grow up. But the servant leader longs for the success and maturity of those they lead!

3) Servant leaders sacrifice themselves for the good of those they serve.
"Just as the Son of Man did not come to be served, but to serve, and to give His life a ransom for many." (Matthew 20:28, NASB)

The servant leader sees that it is his duty to sacrifice himself for those he serves. Isn't this exactly what God did? God, the ultimate servant leader, laid Himself down so that we could live.

I think of the father who drowned while saving his son, or the husband who suffered terrible burns saving his wife from a fire — these are the images of a servant leader in action. But we can do this every day with the less dramatic decisions of how we spend our time, our money, and make our decisions.

4) Servant leaders have a vision worth serving
Ephesians 5:22 says, "Wives submit to your husbands as to the Lord."[338]

One of my spiritual fathers, Rick Sinclair, told a story about when he and his wife, Darlene were newly married. His wife came to him and said, "So what's our vision?"

"Well," Rick thought about it, "I'll work as a music teacher; we'll have some kids; and we'll grow a nice family."

Darlene stared blankly at him for a moment before she said, "That's it?"

Rick testifies that this was when he began to realize that as a husband, it wasn't enough for his wife to submit to him — *he had to*

---

[338] NIV

have a vision worth submitting to. Otherwise, he was making it difficult for his wife to walk out this Scripture.

A servant leader understands that the best thing he can do to serve those he's leading is to fulfill the vision God has given him. I learned this while interacting with Phil Neville, a friend who worked for me for seven years. When Phil came on staff, he was already an experienced young leader and a competent minister of the gospel in his own right. I wanted to see him fulfilled, and I wanted to make sure his gifts were being adequately used while he was with me. Not long after he joined me, I sat down with him in my office, and asked him, "You know my vision, Phil, but what do you want to do? What's your vision?"

He would say, "I'm here to serve you."

We would repeat this conversation several times in the months that followed. Phil would always answer the same way: "I'm here to serve you."

Finally, one day, I realized that the best thing I could do to help Phil fulfill the call of God on his life was for me to fulfill the call of God on mine. Eventually, as I followed my heart, I found that Phil found room within my vision to fulfill his. He ended up running a short-term missions program through the ministry that had a tremendous impact on young people that we sent out on domestic and international missions. Eventually, he left the ministry to launch and direct the missions program as its own ministry.[339]

This principle is exactly what God does with all of those who follow Him. He tell us things like, "I will build my church, and the gates of hell shall not prevail against it" (Matthew 16:18, KJV). We see a world that God envisions, and a thriving Church being perfected by grace, and we give our lives to this God-sized vision.

Again, servant leadership is all about imitating Christ, the One who modeled it for us in every way. Who would know that God has a humble heart?

---

[339] Phil and his wife Jill direct *Operation Acts* in Millersburgh, Ohio, a ministry with the two focuses of missions and adoption.

Discipleship by Grace

CHAPTER 31
Correct, Rebuke, and Encourage

"Preach the Word; be prepared in season and out of season; correct, rebuke and encourage — with great patience and careful instruction."
—Paul the Apostle to young Timothy (2 Timothy 4:2, NIV)

I remember when I was young in ministry, I decided that I would be "an encourager" and avoid confrontation as much as possible, primarily because I had not learned the leadership skills in my youth to confront in a loving way, and the idea of having to correct anyone made me uncomfortable.

Soon after, I began to have problems with younger team members in our ministry. That was when I read 2 Timothy 4:2: "...correct, rebuke and encourage — with great patience and careful instruction."[340]

The Holy Spirit spoke to my heart, "Derek, I've called you as a leader to correct, rebuke, *and* encourage. If all you want to do is encourage, you're missing two-thirds of what I've called you to do as a leader."

Grace doesn't coddle the sinful nature. It recognizes its existence, its propensity toward death and division, and is willing to call a brother or sister back to "living in a manner worthy of your calling."[341] Just as the old hymn says:

> *Prone to wander, Lord I feel it*
> *Prone to leave the God I love*
> *Here's my heart, oh take and seal it*
> *Seal it for Thy courts above*[342]

Here are some biblical reasons why we should correct:

---

[340] NIV
[341] Ephesians 4:1
[342] "Come Thou Fount of Every Blessing"

1. Because withholding correction is a sign of hatred and fear

The Bible is very clear on this. Withholding correction is the sign of an insecure leader. It's a sign of the fear of man, that the leader is more concerned about being disliked, or experiencing the discomfort of having to apply discipline, than to love the disciple enough to correct.

> *"He who withholds his rod hates his son, but he who loves him disciplines him diligently." (Proverbs 13:24, NASB)*

When the Scriptures say that the one who withholds the rod *hates* his own son, it means that the self-love of the father is stronger than the love he has for his son. His self-love makes him unwilling to endure the difficulties of correcting, rather choosing to stay comfortable.

My wife and I once had a young couple over, who explained to us that they don't spank their children because they love them. I told them, "I spank my children because I do."

> *"For the Lord disciplines the one he loves, and he punishes every son he accepts." (Hebrews 12:6, NIV)*

It's very simple: If we truly love those we lead, we'll be willing to endure whatever discomfort is necessary to correct them. We'll see this as necessary for them to see grace, as they will never understand grace unless they see their own weaknesses.

A good friend of mine, Garrett, who is now the senior pastor of a thriving church, was discipled by an excellent mentor named Christopher, who had a firm grasp on sin and grace. Garrett told me that Christopher loved him, and would not let him "get away" with playing the victim or coddling his own sinful nature. He understood that helping Garrett see his own weaknesses would be prerequisite to Garrett understanding grace.

Garrett told me that once, he went in to talk with Christopher, and began explaining to him a situation that hurt his feelings. "When Rosa told me they didn't choose me, I was offended and decided that I'd—"

Christopher stopped him mid-sentence. "Let me help you to explain this."

"Okay," said Garrett.

"Say...'I was worshiping my own reputation and preferring myself over others, and decided that I'd...' Okay, Garrett, please use those words, and continue."

Garrett used the words Christopher gave him, and discovered as he continued that the real problem wasn't Rosa, but his own sin nature. His mentor loved him enough to correct his attitude.

2. Because correction strengthens a believer

One word of loving correction can alter the course of a disciple's life.

I remember when I was in college, I used to lead worship at the college meetings. At the time, I did not understand grace, and was obsessed with repentance and revival. My basic approach to worship services was to start by asking the question, "What's wrong with us today?" I thought it my duty to create an environment where we could "invite the presence of God" and people could examine themselves and repent of their current sins. This went on week after week.

On one particular night, the other students weren't tracking with me. Once again, I saw myself as Keith Green, challenging and rebuking the half-hearted. As I sang "Create in Me a Clean Heart," the others just stared at me, including Rick, who almost seemed to pity me. The next day, Rick asked me, "Can I share some things to strengthen your worship ministry?"

I knew it was about the previous night. "Sure," I said.

"It seems like you have a 'commitment and repentance' button that you push if you have no other direction to go. It's almost like a 'default' button. I think last night you pushed that button," he explained. Then he asked rhetorically, "Isn't there a time to come in to a service, and say, 'Hey! God has chosen us! Christ is in us the hope of glory—let's praise Him with all our heart!"

This correction had a profound impact on me as a worship leader, and it was one of the first times my eyes were opened to the fact that I had some struggles with legalism.

I've never regretted submitting myself to correction from a loving leader. It's been one of the greatest tools God has used to strengthen me in grace. Here are some great verses on this concept:

"He who neglects discipline despises himself, but he who listens to reproof acquires understanding." (Proverbs 15:32, NASB)

"Whoever loves discipline loves knowledge, but he who hates reproof is stupid." (Proverbs 12:1, NASB)

"He who walks with wise men will be wise, but the companion of fools will suffer harm." (Proverbs 13:20, NAS)

I had a young guy in our band a few years back that really took to the truths of grace. He became a real comrade in being a zealous herald of the message of grace. At one point during his time with me, however, he began to drift from the joy of the Lord. He was rude to others, making some poor moral choices in his life, and generally a miserable person to be around. During this time, he'd still speak about grace with vigor whether it was in a ministry setting or with friends. Finally, I sat down with him and said, "You have the theology of grace, but not the spirit of it."

"You're right," he said, and within days, "pulled out" of the nosedive as he went back to the Vine.

A few years ago, my wife and I noticed one of our daughters restraining herself in worship because some friends were around, and she feared what they would think. "Sweetheart," I asked her after the service, "what was I seeing during worship tonight?"

"I don't know," she answered.

"Is what your friends think more important than what God thinks?" I asked.

She broke down and wept, her heart tender and humble before the Lord. "I'm sorry, Daddy!" she said. "I'll never do that again!"

And to this day, she never has.

3. Because correction saves souls

Proverbs 15:10 says, "Correction is grievous unto him that forsaketh the way and he that hateth reproof shall die."[343]

On May 9, 1980, part of the Sunshine Skyway Bridge in Tampa, Florida collapsed because the freighter *M/V Summit Venture* collided with a pier during a storm. This caused a 1400 foot section of the bridge to collapse, sending massive sections plummeting into Tampa Bay. The collapse caused six automobiles and a Greyhound bus to fall 165 feet into the waters below, killing 35 people. Some of the cars drove right over the edge because they could not see that the pieces were missing. It wasn't until Richard Hornbuckle slammed on his brakes and slid to within fourteen inches of the severed edge that anyone was available to stand in the road and wave down the other vehicles to keep them from plummeting to their deaths.

What would you think of Richard Hornbuckle if he saw cars driving toward the precipice, and didn't stop them because he felt awkward and didn't want to offend them? You would think him an accomplice to a crime, wouldn't you? How much more should we give the word of correction to our brothers and sisters when we see them spiritually driving toward the edge?

It is love and concern that speaks up, not judgment and criticism.

HOW?

It is established then, that leaders must correct as well as encourage, but it is not enough just to correct. The spirit in which it is done must be a spirit of love and grace. Paul puts it this way: "...correct, rebuke and encourage—with great patience and

---

[343] KJV

careful instruction" (2 Timothy 4:2b, NIV). Let's look at what Paul is teaching:

Great patience

This means we should not be soul-driven, reactive leaders, but we should speak carefully and lovingly, knowing that our words will build or destroy, also knowing that the *spirit* of our words can build or destroy. It's amazing how a leader can say all the right words, but if those words are spoken in a spirit of anger, the person that the leader hopes to help will not hear them. The only thing the person will hear is the anger. Every future attempt to appeal to the person will be met with, "Yeah, but you got mad at me." The anger will eclipse the message.

The Scriptures have much to say about not speaking hastily:

> *"Do you see a man who is hasty in his words? There is more hope for a fool than for him." (Proverbs 29:20, NASB)*

> *"Do not go out hastily to argue your case; Otherwise, what will you do in the end, When your neighbor humiliates you?" (Proverbs 25:8, NASB)*

A good principle that I abide by as a discipler is that "events need grace, patterns need discipline." In other words, if I see a person doing something once (I'm not speaking of gross public sin), I don't necessarily feel the need to correct him. I'll just assume that it is an uncharacteristic mistake. But if it becomes a pattern, I need to bring correction. This principle keeps me from being a nitpicker, and from playing Holy Spirit.

Another good guiding principle, which we looked at in discussing evangelism, is "law to the proud and grace to the humble."[344] If I see the disciple responding with a proud and defensive spirit, then I will give them Law to bring their haughtiness down, but if I see humility, I will give them grace. This is a good principle for evangelism and discipleship.

---

[344] Ray Comfort

Careful instruction

Choose your words carefully when speaking to a disciple who needs correction. One of the things that Rick Sinclair taught me was that it takes effort and prayer to use words that will construct, edify, and build. Anyone can lash out, and "speak his mind," but if you really want to build the person and impart grace, the words must come with more reverence. You will either build up or tear down one of Christ's own disciples. .

There's a difference between *renovation* and *restoration.*

Think about *renovating* an old house. The construction worker will grab a hammer and start smashing things. Contrast this with a person *restoring* an old house. That person will *carefully* remove the molding or casing, *carefully* strip the walls, and *carefully* protect the molding, etc. The person is careful.

Phil McNeil, a pastor friend of mine, said, "If you sow grace, you reap grace." That's a pretty good rule to live by. When correcting someone, we need to have an attitude of restoration and not renovation. Then we can truly strengthen the person in his faith and his walk with the Lord.

COMMON EXCUSES

There are common excuses you'll hear when you correct people, and I thought it would be helpful to discuss them.

"You're judging me."

This is perhaps the most overused argument in the church today.

Jesus actually encourages us to "make a righteous judgment" in John 7:24. The kind of judgment He told us to avoid was condemnation, and that's not what we're doing when we correct in love. We're trying to build up but condemnation tears down. Bible teacher Bob Cornell said, "Judgment is conclusion without a cure."[345] This is the kind of judging that Jesus condemned.

---

[345] Bob Cornell said this in a seminar at *Niagara 2008* in Niagara Falls, NY, a conference hosted by Joshua Revolution.

"You don't know me."

Do you really have to know someone to know if his deeds are evil? Jesus told us that we would recognize what is false by its fruit. An apple tree will grow apples. A poison sumac tree will grow poison sumac. I don't need to "know someone's heart" to analyze his deeds any more than I need to know the heart of a sumac tree. That said, it is the wise leader that earns the right through relationship and trust to speak into someone's life.

"It's Jonny's fault not mine."

This has been happening since the Garden of Eden when Adam told God, "It was the woman you gave me!"[346] This can manifest in many ways:

"It was the way my parents treated me!"

"I was hurt by a pastor."

"I've had a hard life."

"My whole family is like that."

"I was betrayed by a friend."

Et cetera.

The point is, the person will want to blame some outside person or situation for his sin.

What my wife and I teach our own children is that "your part is to own your own sin and to give up trying to look good. Then let God deal with the other person." That's a pretty good rule of thumb with any of us. That's the only way to truly resolve relational conflicts, let alone the conflicts in our own soul.

God's perspective is that correction equals love. It reveals the depravity of our hearts, and illuminates the need for grace. If we would disciple by grace, we must be willing to correct in love.

---

[346] Genesis 3:12

CHAPTER 32
Appealing to Conscience

"It is neither right nor safe to go against my conscience."
— Martin Luther

"Everything is permissible" — but not everything is beneficial. "Everything is permissible" — but not everything is constructive. Nobody should seek his own good, but the good of others.

Eat anything sold in the meat market without raising questions of conscience, for, "The earth is the Lord's, and everything in it."

If some unbeliever invites you to a meal and you want to go, eat whatever is put before you without raising questions of conscience. But if anyone says to you, "This has been offered in sacrifice," then do not eat it, both for the sake of the man who told you and for conscience' sake — the other man's conscience, I mean, not yours. For why should my freedom be judged by another's conscience? If I take part in the meal with thankfulness, why am I denounced because of something I thank God for?

So whether you eat or drink or whatever you do, do it all for the glory of God. Do not cause anyone to stumble, whether Jews, Greeks or the church of God — even as I try to please everybody in every way. For I am not seeking my own good but the good of many, so that they may be saved. (1 Corinthians 10:23-33, NASB)

If we want to disciple by grace, we must not turn conscience issues into laws, and must be willing to extend the liberty of grace that the New Covenant offers. Otherwise, we may inadvertently introduce leaven though we had hoped to disciple by grace. That said, we may appeal to the conscience of our disciples, to whom we must trust that the Holy Spirit is speaking. We must see

357

ourselves as partners with the Holy Spirit and remember that the Holy Spirit guides into all truth.[347] Therefore, when we appeal to the conscience of a believer, we should find conviction.

How do we make an appeal to conscience?

1. Discover the motive of the heart

As I've previously stated, God is more interested in the motive of the heart than the action itself. For example, when it comes to prayer, Jesus weighed the motive of a Pharisee versus the motive of a true believer:

> *"And when you pray, do not be like the hypocrites, for they love to pray standing in the synagogues and on the street corners to be seen by men. I tell you the truth, they have received their reward in full. But when you pray, go into your room, close the door and pray to your Father, who is unseen. Then your Father, who sees what is done in secret, will reward you." (Matthew 7:5-6, NIV)*

Both the Pharisee and the true believer are *praying,* but one is condemned and one is commended. Why? One is *self-righteous* and one is truly *righteous.* One seeks the praise of men, and one seeks the praise of God.

As we disciple by grace, we must go after the motive of the heart. *Why are you praying at 5am every day? Why are you watching R-rated movies? Why are you giving money to that televangelist? Why did you get your lip pierced?*

You never know what you may find if you knock on that door. We may find rebellion or we may find love. We may find a desire to fit in or we may find a passion for evangelism. We may find bitterness toward a parent or we may find a desire in them to be authentic. We may find giving out of guilt or we may find giving motivated by faith and love. The bottom line is, these are the real issues, not the act that provoked the questions.

---

[347] John 16:13

> *"But he who doubts is condemned if he eats, because his eating is not from faith; and whatever is not from faith is sin."* (Romans 14:23, NASB)

Whatever is not from faith is sin.

There's the truth of the matter. If we find anything other than *faith*, then we've discovered sin in the person's life. The hope is that the appeal to conscience will help the person to see that.

I had a young staff member once who went out and had a few beers with a friend. He didn't get drunk, but another young adult from the church saw him, and was offended. Not only that, but the offended observer told some other young adults in our church.

"Shane," I asked him, "did I hear that you went out and had a few beers last night with Frank?"

He turned red with embarrassment. "Yes," he said.

"First of all," I continued, "that's your choice to do that, but I want to ask you some questions."

"Okay," he said, and he seemed legitimately teachable.

I asked him, "Did you hear the Holy Spirit speak to your heart at any point that this was something He didn't want you to do?"

"Yes," he explained, "I did feel uneasy."

"Then why did you do it anyway?"

"In hind's sight," he said, "I shouldn't have."

"You also drank in front of Jimmy, and he seemed pretty upset about it. Do you think that was wise?"

"No," he answered, "it wasn't."

"I would agree," I told him, "because the Bible teaches that it's your duty not to cause your brother to stumble.[348] What do you think you should do?"

"I'll repent to the Lord and apologize to those I offended. I'm sorry, Derek. It won't happen again."

I did not go after the behavior, because the behavior was a gray area of the Scriptures. Instead, I went after the motive of his heart, and found that the Holy Spirit had already been speaking to him.

---

[348] Romans 14:13-23

2. Discern if it is wise

Since the Bible teaches us to "live in a manner worthy of our calling," what might be okay for some may not be okay for others. To make an appeal to conscience, remind your brother of his high calling and compare his behavior with the calling. Do they harmonize?

> *"Therefore, since we are surrounded by such a great cloud of witnesses, let us throw off everything that hinders and the sin that so easily entangles, and let us run with perseverance the race marked out for us." (Hebrews 12:1, NIV)*

This is an interesting Scripture because it makes a distinction between "things that hinder" and "sin that entangles." There are things that hinder in our lives that may not be sinful. For example, the Bible doesn't say that it's sin to stay up until 4am watching old Disney movies, but if you want to get up early to pray and get to work on time, *is it wise to stay up until 4am watching old Disney movies?*

Things that hinder.

Amy was a young woman with an amazing passion to go to the nations. She was accepted by a missions agency, and began making preparations to go to Uganda. That's when Oliver came along. Oliver was a good guy, but not of Amy's caliber. Amy fell for him. Candice, the pastor's wife told Amy, "You have a high call on your life, Amy. We are all excited for what God wants to do with your life."

"Thanks," Amy said, shifting nervously.

"Do you think it is wise to be in a relationship right now, right before you're planning to go to Uganda?"

"Oliver and I can make it work," she said.

"Picture yourself about the work of the Lord in Uganda, having a divided heart when you could be having a single focus. I'm just concerned that it's a distraction from the great things God has planned for you," Candice ventured. "Isn't God already speaking that to your heart?"

Amy knew she was right. Tears began to well up in her eyes.

"I have one question," Candice continued, "are you *sure* this is the will of God for you?"

Amy hung her head, and quietly said, "No."

Reminding Amy of her high calling pricked her conscience, helping her to see that she was acting unwisely.

3. Make certain the person isn't "condemning himself" with what he approves

Romans 14:22 says, "The faith which you have, have as your own conviction before God. Happy is he who does not condemn himself in what he approves."[349]

Help your understudy to look at the fruit of the behavior in his heart. There may not yet be any positive or negative fruit externally, but there is always something happening internally. If you look inside with your disciple, and find condemnation, you've saved him from a lot of suffering.

Julie had not been in a romantic relationship for a long time, though she was obsessed with the topic in her life. She would often request prayer about it with her small group leader, Tara, and would find herself in frequent conversations about it with Christian friends.

She wondered how someone that wasn't tied up in a relationship with the opposite sex could be so tied up in her heart with the opposite sex.

Julie would frequently have friends over to watch "chick flicks" or spend her time alone watching those kinds of films. One morning, Tara was spending time praying for Julie, and thought of her movie-watching habit. She called her on the phone that night.

"Julie," she said, "there's something I want to talk to you about."

"What's up?" she asked.

"I was praying for you this morning, and sensed the Lord might be telling me something about what might be feeding your obsession with romance."

---

[349] NASB

Julie laughed nervously. "Okay..."

"Though I know the Bible doesn't say, 'Thou shalt not watch chick flicks,' do you think it's possible that these may be contributing to your problem?" Tara asked.

"Hmm...I never thought about it that way."

"Have you ever felt the Lord speaking to you about this?"

"I have wondered if I watch too many," Julie offered.

"Let me ask you this," Tara continued. "What's the fruit of it in your life? Is it perpetuating a fleshly yearning for a boyfriend?"

"Hmm..."

"When you put your head on your pillow at night, what's going on in your heart?"

Julie knew the answer. "It makes me fantasize about romance."

"Do you think that pleases the Lord?" Tara asked.

She heard Julie sniffling. Finally, Julie quietly answered, "No."

Julie had been condemning herself with what she approved, and didn't even realize it until Tara helped prick her conscience. The Holy Spirit had already been speaking with a small still voice, and finally, Julie could see (and hear) clearly.

4. Determine if the person is causing another to stumble

It is a sin to use your liberty to cause someone else to stumble. We must be wise and careful in how we use our liberty, as flaunting it may lead someone else into sin or offense. The plain fact is, as I've already discussed, *what might not be sin for one may be for another*, and when you act in a way that someone else considers sinful, you are committing a crime against your brother by causing him to "stumble."

> "*I know and am convinced in the Lord Jesus that nothing is unclean in itself; but to him who thinks anything to be unclean, to him it is unclean. For if because of food your brother is hurt, you are no longer walking according to love. Do not destroy with your food him for whom Christ died.*" *(Romans 14:14-15, NASB)*

"Let us therefore make every effort to do what leads to peace and to mutual edification. Do not destroy the work of God for the sake of food. All food is clean, but it is wrong for a man to eat anything that causes someone else to stumble. It is better not to eat meat or drink wine or to do anything else that will cause your brother to fall." (Romans 14:19-21, NIV)

I was ministering at a youth conference, sitting backstage before the session began, watching one of the big video screens that flanked the stage. Thousands of youth were in the room while the camera showed kids around the room goofing around and dancing to the Christian rock music that was playing. One of the cameras focused on the front part of the stage, where a group of teenage girls were dancing. I was already a bit uneasy with the sight, as the girls were bordering on being provocative, when one of the girls took her outer shirt off, leaving nothing on but a small tight mid-drift undershirt that bordered on looking like a bra.

That was it. I stepped out of my seat from backstage, and made my way to the front of the stage, where I found her, dancing for her camera audience.

"Excuse me!" I called to her over the music.

She came over, looking confused.

"Could you please put your shirt back on?" I asked.

She was immediately defensive. "What? Why?"

"It's too provocative," I told her. "You have a responsibility to not cause your brothers to stumble."

Her face contorted with anger. "If they want to lust after me, that's their problem!" she snapped.

"No," I said, "that's yours."

She stormed off to her seat.

I returned to the backstage area, where my drummer found me and asked, "What were you doing out there? I could see you on the screen!"

I told him what happened, and he said, "You did that? You're nuts!"

I received a letter from the girl's friends a week later, thanking me for confronting her, explaining that this had been an ongoing problem.

I have another friend that used a swear word in a blog and then received a seething email from another Christian about what a terrible example he was being to other believers. My friend was furious, believing the one who wrote the email to be legalistic. I explained to him that he really should be careful about his choice of words, as it could cause others to stumble (as it already had), even if he used this word in private.

When a follower of Christ is acting in *love*, he will choose to sacrifice his liberty so that he will not offend his brother or sister in Christ. Love for the saints is the fruit of grace at work in the heart.

Appealing to the conscience of a believer is the mark of a servant leader that is discipling by grace. May God give disciple-makers, parents, and mentors wisdom in applying these principles.

CHAPTER 33
The Grace of Ministry

"According to the grace of God which was given to me, like a wise master builder I laid a foundation, and another is building on it. But each man must be careful how he builds on it." — Paul the Apostle (1 Corinthians 3:10, NASB)

"I became a servant of this gospel by the gift of God's grace given me through the working of his power. Although I am less than the least of all God's people, this grace was given me: to preach to the Gentiles the unsearchable riches of Christ." — Paul the Apostle (Ephesians 3:7-8, NIV)

There are stages of grace. The first is a revelation of sin; then comes a revelation of grace; then comes a revelation of the Father's heart; then comes the knowledge of who we are in Christ; then comes the knowledge of who we are *in ministry*.

God wants to bring all of His children into their destinies. This is the journey of grace.

As we see in the Scriptures above, Paul constantly refers to his ministry as "a grace." As I've previously mentioned, we should encourage believers to insert the phrase "power beyond my ability" wherever we see the word grace appear, especially as pertains to ministry. So the verses might be read:

"According to the [power beyond my ability] which was given to me, like a wise master builder I laid a foundation, and another is building on it. But each man must be careful how he builds on it." (1 Corinthians 3:10, NASB)

"I became a servant of this gospel by the gift of [power beyond my ability] given me through the working of his power. Although I am less than the least of all God's people, this [power beyond my ability] was given me: to preach to the Gentiles the unsearchable riches of Christ." (Ephesians 3:7-8, NIV)

Power beyond my ability.

When we understand this, two significant things happen: 1) We gain confidence in what God has gifted us to do, and 2) We gain peace with what we are not called to do or be. If we don't have the power to do it, why do it? The disciple and discipler both will benefit from understanding these facets of grace. Let's take a look at each of these points.

1. We gain confidence in what God has gifted us to do

Seeing the grace given him, Paul knew exactly what his assignment was. Therefore, he moved in confidence, knowing that there was no reason to be proud since it was all grace, and also that there was no reason to be sheepish, seeing that he was charged through grace with a calling.

No longer would Paul need the approval of men, or to seek man's empty praise. All would be done for love and God's glory. The one moving in grace knows that since it's all grace, God alone will bring the empowerment and success in the work.

I remember being at a large conference, looking out into the crowd just before I stepped out to minister on stage, and I saw several famous people in the crowd who I might like to impress. I began to get nervous, hoping that they would like me, and wondering what opportunities I might miss if they didn't. The Lord gently rebuked my soul, and reminded me that the only One I needed to please was Him, and then He said to my heart, "No one that you will ever minister in front of holds your destiny in their hands."

What a liberating word this was!

The alpha to omega of my calling would by Christ; by Christ, through Christ, and for Christ.

Looking at our assignments through the eyes of grace, we see what was impossible as *possible,* and walk toward the vision with joy and confident strides. My close friend and pastor, Josh Finley, once said, "It is more important for us to remain focused on the source of our strength than the size of our task."

As we do so, grace takes over, and we find wings to take flight into our destiny in God.

2. We gain peace with what we are not called to do or be.

As I've already said, when we are settled in grace, we are at peace with what we are not called to do as well as what we are called to do. This can be a liberating revelation.

As we understand that we can only be what God has created and gifted us to be, all our other pursuits are understood to be unnecessary and of the flesh. The immature Christian covets another man's gifting, but the one settled in grace says, "I am what I am by the grace of God, and I am not what I am not by the grace of God!"

I know this can be a journey (and sometimes a long journey) to arrive at this place of peace with ourselves, but as the Holy Spirit guides us into all truth, this is part of the "all truth" He guides us into. We must simply do the revealed will of God for our lives, and allow God to perfect our faith during the journey. God will purify our motives as we walk out our godly ambitions. Our selfish ambitions will fade away in the shadow of the cross and in the mercy of God's refining work within us.

I used to think myself disqualified when I would see how many selfish ambitions I had within. I would see others succeeding in the grace God had given them, and I would covet, and compete, and sink into jealousy and self-love. My conclusion would often be that I was not fit for ministry, as the devil would ravage my heart with condemnation. Then I read this passage:

> "*An argument started among them as to which of them might be the greatest. But Jesus, knowing what they were thinking in their heart, took a child and stood him by His side, and said to them, 'Whoever receives this child in My name receives Me, and whoever receives Me receives Him who sent Me; for the one who is least among all of you, this is the one who is great.'*" (Luke 9:46-48, NASB)

What encouraged me so much about this passage is what Jesus *didn't* do. He didn't say, "What are you guys arguing about? Who's the greatest? How could you be so selfish? Forget about Me ever using you now. Just go back home!"

Though their selfish ambitions were on display in plain view, He didn't disqualify them. He was merciful to them, knowing their weaknesses, and pointed the way to a better path.

Likewise, the devil will try to kick you off the team because you will find your motives so *unlike* Jesus, but Jesus will not disqualify you, my brother, my sister. He will lead you on a journey that will purify your heart, perfect your faith, and make you like Him.

In the year 2000, I was invited to a church in Williamsburg, Virginia, to do a joint concert with a Christian artist that was having an impact on the east coast, Jason Upton. The youth pastor friend of mine that put the event together told me, "You'll love this guy! You two are cut from the same cloth!"

The concert was powerful. I went first, and the worship environment was electrified as an awareness of God's presence filled our hearts. When Jason took over, his impact on the people was profound. My band and I were moved by his music and heart for God.

During the whole night I found Jason to be a refreshing brother, and it was one of the few times that I sensed I was meeting someone with a similar heart for music ministry. We were both content not pursuing the fame and glories of Nashville, and were both having an impact on our respective regions of the country (me in the northeast and Jason on the east coast). I went home and told my wife, "You've got to hear this guy's music! He's one of the most stirring writers I've ever heard." No one I knew had heard of him in the northeast.

Later that year, Jason ministered at *The Call D.C.*, a gathering of over 400,000 young people in Washington D.C. for the purpose of prayer, worship, and fasting. His impact was astonishing at this event, and overnight, Jason Upton became an underground international phenomenon. Everywhere I went, people started to tell me about him, asking if I'd ever heard his music.

Jealousy began to rise in my heart.

Not long after that, I was asked to lead worship and speak at a youth conference, and the conference host told me, "Well, I gotta be honest with you, we asked Jason Upton to do this conference first, but he couldn't come." Then he laughed and added, "How does that feel to be *Jason Upton's* replacement!"

He didn't realize how much the comment hurt me (my flesh, that is) and added to my already brewing jealousy.

Around that time, I was also ministering at another youth conference, where a lot of tables and booths were set up in the foyer area. One table was hawking a lot of Jason Upton material, and another was advertising having him come and minister at their music festival. I noticed on an ad for the festival that they'd published some information about Jason. Among the text, it quoted Lou Engle, who said something to the effect of, "I believe this young man bears the mantle of Keith Green." The ad also mentioned that Melody Green (Keith Green's wife) had said something similar.

Now, you may not know who Keith Green is, but he was a prophet-musician that shook a generation of believers back in the late 1970s and early 1980s. He died in a plane crash in 1982.

I grew up listening to Keith Green's music. In many ways, he discipled me through his music though I never met him. When I went into music ministry, I so much wanted to emulate him, and asked God to help me to impact others as he impacted me. Many people had actually noted over the years that I reminded them of Keith Green, and for me, this was a huge compliment. Several others had actually prophesied that I was carrying the mantle of Keith Green.

When I read that Jason was the chosen one, my jealousy peaked.

Please understand: Jason did nothing wrong at any point. My conflict existed only because of my selfishness. I repented many times, fought discouragement, and asked God to change my heart, but I couldn't escape my own flesh. When all seemed hopeless, the Holy Spirit reminded me of what John the Baptist said: "He must increase, but I must decrease" (John 3:30, NASB).

"What does this have to do with me?" I wondered. "John said that about Jesus."

"Yes, but who is the *Body of Christ?*"

"God's people," I answered.

"Isn't Jason in the Body of Christ?" the Holy Spirit whispered.

"Yes."

"If Christ must increase and you must decrease, shouldn't the same be true of *His Body?* Shouldn't His Body increase while you decrease?"

I'd never thought about it that way. "Yes, Lord," I answered.

"Then pray for Jason to increase and for you to decrease."

Ouch. That one hit the right spot.

For the next year or so, that's exactly how I prayed.

Slowly, like a deep wound healing, my jealousy lifted. I began to truly love and appreciate this brother in a profound way. This trial of soul also coincided with my journey into the wilderness of depression and spiritual burnout, and was one of the many things God would use to teach me His grace. Jason's music actually ministered to my wife and me in a profound way during my season of darkness.

God finally brought me to this revelation: "I don't want to be Keith Green. I don't want to be Jason Upton. I want to be Derek Joseph Levendusky!"

When grace appeared, I was finally content with who I am in Christ and *with who I am not.* The roots of jealousy, covetousness, and competition were violently ripped out of my soul, and as painful as it was, I am so thankful today for the transforming work of grace.

We must be content with who God has made us to be, and teach our disciples who God has made them to be. You do your assignment; they will do theirs; I will do mine. Together we will see the glory of God shine among all nations; together we will see the message of grace go to the ends of the earth; together we will disciple by grace.